First edition published 1998
Second edition published 2002
Third edition published 2006

3 5 7 9 10 8 6 4

ISBN-13: 978-1-57660-193-8

The Library of Congress has cataloged the earlier printing as follows:

Block, Ralph L.
    Investing in REITs : real estate investment trusts / Ralph L. Block. -- 3rd ed.
        p. cm.
    Includes index.
    ISBN 1-57660-193-5 (alk. paper)
  1. Real estate investment trusts. I. Title: REITs. II. Title: Real estate investment trusts. III. Title.

HG5095.B553 2006

332.63'247–dc22   2005025538

Edited by Tracy Tait

INVESTING IN
REITs

**REAL
ESTATE
INVESTMENT
TRUSTS**
THIRD
EDITION

RALPH L. BLOCK

BLOOMBERG PRESS
NEW YORK

Also available from
BLOOMBERG PRESS

The Money-Making Guide to Bonds
Hildy Richelson and Stan Richelson

Investing in Hedge Funds
Joseph G. Nicholas

Hedge Fund of Funds Investing:
An Investor's Guide
Joseph G. Nicholas

New Insights on Covered Call Writing:
The Powerful Technique That Enhances Return
and Lowers Risk in Stock Investing
Richard Lehman and Lawrence G. McMillan

Cracking Your Retirement Nest Egg
Without Scrambling Your Finances
Margaret A. Malaspina

The Trader's Guide to Key Economic Indicators
Richard Yamarone

———————

A complete list of our titles is available at
www.bloomberg.com/books

INVESTING IN
REITs

"Ralph Block has made the world of REITs accessible to all. **THIS IS A SUPERB BOOK FOR EVERY INVESTOR.**"
> Tom Gardner
> Cofounder, The Motley Fool

"*Finally,* a book that **DEMYSTIFIES REITS FOR BOTH ARMCHAIR INVESTORS AND SEASONED PROFESSIONALS.** *Investing in REITs* by Ralph Block is a balanced, clearly written guide that fills a major void in today's investment literature."
> Jonathan Litt
> Senior Real Estate Analyst
> Salomon Smith Barney

"Whether you're an individual or institutional investor, **YOU WON'T FIND A BETTER PRIMER ON REIT INVESTING.** Ralph Block takes the complex issues that must be addressed to produce above-average results when investing in REITland, and makes them simple and easy to understand. **A MUST FOR EVERY SERIOUS REIT INVESTOR'S LIBRARY, AND A FUN READ, TO BOOT.**"
> Geoffrey Dohrmann
> Publisher and Editor in Chief
> *Institutional Real Estate Securities*

"*Investing in REITs* is a must-read for *anyone* wishing to gain a better understanding of this thriving sector of the capital markets. Given the continued transformation of private real estate to the public markets, **THIS BOOK IS AN ESSENTIAL RESOURCE FOR STUDENTS, INDIVIDUAL AND INSTITUTIONAL INVESTORS, AND ANYONE ELSE INTERESTED IN UNDERSTANDING THE REIT MARKET.**"
> David J. Hartzell
> Distinguished Professor of Finance and Real Estate
> Director of the Real Estate Program
> The Kenan-Flager Business School
> The University of North Carolina at Chapel Hill

To my father, Jack,
who has always been the original "REIT man"
and without whom this book,
in more ways than one,
would never have been possible.
My only regret is that he was not
able to witness its birth and popularity.

ACKNOWLEDGMENTS

The investor's chief problem—
and even his worst enemy—
is likely to be himself.
—BENJAMIN GRAHAM

Much to my surprise and delight, *Investing in REITs* has been popular enough to justify this third edition. I cannot, of course, claim all, or even most, of the credit for the book's success. REITs' transition from the sleepy backwaters of the world of equities to a mainstream investment choice has been key to the interest in *Investing in REITs*. Even more important, many kind, perceptive, and dedicated professionals have been instrumental in the creation of the original edition of the book and its subsequent revisions. I would be remiss if I didn't mention a few of these outstanding individuals.

Bill Schaff and Gary Pollock, founders of Bay Isle Financial, provided the essential encouragement and support for the book's predecessor, and Alan Fass, Jared Kieling, John Crutcher, and many other outstanding professionals at Bloomberg Press got the book into its present form and exposed it to the marketplace—to sink or swim. Thanks, too, to Veronica J. McDavid, Kathleen Peterson, and Jim Douglas, whose editing skills were very helpful to me in the first and second editions. And, of course, as a computer semi-literate, I owe much gratitude to Steve Block for helping me with the graphs and charts, particularly for this current edition. Steve isn't an exact chip off the ol' Block—he's better-looking and a lot smarter than me.

I'd also like to express my appreciation to Jon Fosheim, Mike Kirby, and their all-star analysts at that quintessential research firm, Green Street Advisors, for their outstanding research and analysis on REITs over the years. Jon has left to pursue REIT portfolio management, but his inquiring spirit has made its mark. Thanks, also, to the many REIT and real estate enthusiasts I've had the pleasure of meeting and corresponding with over the years, all of whom have helped me to sharpen my understanding of the world of real estate and REITs. I wish I could name them all. I would particularly like to thank Waynor Rogers for looking over my shoulder and providing valuable suggestions for the second edition.

I owe much to Milton Cooper, a giant of the REIT world and a gentleman in every respect, who provided me with the necessary moral support to undertake my first book on REIT investing, which led ultimately to *Investing in REITs,* and to the folks at NAREIT, including Steve Wechsler and Michael Grupe, who have always been available with the requested REIT statistics and information. Limited space prevents me from noting specifically the many other individuals whose support and assistance I gratefully acknowledge and to whom I'm very much indebted.

Finally, allow me to express my gratitude to my lovely wife, Paula, who has put up with a great deal of "benign neglect" during the time it's taken me to complete this book, and its subsequent revised editions, for Bloomberg Press.

INTRODUCTION

ALL OF US THINK we know real estate, and we have all been involved with it in one way or another since our arrival in the hospital delivery room. That building, our earliest impression of the world, is real estate; the residence we were taken home to, whether a single-family house or an apartment, is real estate; the malls and neighborhood centers where we shop, the factories and office buildings where we work, the hotels and resorts where we vacation, even the acres of undeveloped land we have trod—all are real estate. Real estate surrounds us. But do we really understand it?

For many years we have had a schizophrenic relationship with real estate. We love our homes and fully expect that they will appreciate in value. We admire real estate tycoons, past and present, such as Joseph Kennedy, Conrad Hilton, and the Rockefellers; we even find Donald Trump and Leona Helmsley fascinating. Yet we believe real estate to be a risky investment and marvel at how major Japanese companies and other sophisticated institutional investors spent hundreds of millions of dollars on U.S. hotels, golf courses, major office buildings, and other "trophy" properties during the 1980s, only to see their values plummet in the real estate recession of the late 1980s and early 1990s. During the last ten years, real estate values have climbed substantially, but we've experienced gut-wrenching changes in occupancies and rental rates, particularly with respect to office properties.

Is real estate a good investment? Real estate investment trusts, or "REITs," own, and sometimes provide loans for, commercial real estate and have delivered excellent returns to their investors—but will this continue? Can we still make money in REITs regardless of the ups and downs of real estate cycles?

This book answers those questions and more. It not only makes a convincing case for investing in REITs, but also provides the details, background, and guidance investors should have before delving into these highly rewarding investments. Here's what's in store:

Part I: Meet the REIT serves as an introduction to REITs. The first order of business is to explain why REITs are excellent investments that belong in every well-diversified portfolio. From there, we'll explore the "nature of the beast," and obtain a good working familiarity with REITs and their characteristics. We will follow with a description of the types of properties REITs own and the investment characteristics of each. And, finally, this section compares REITs with other traditional investments and also describes the structure and evolution of REITs.

Upon reaching **Part II: History and Mythology**, readers should find REITs such an intriguing investment that they'll wonder why these solid and profitable companies have been neglected for much of their history. This section answers this question and dispels some old myths about REITs. We'll take a look back to study the forty-two-year history of the REIT world since its inception in 1962, and trace REITs' progress up to today, when they have finally come of age.

Part III: Choosing REITs and Watching Them Grow provides the basic tools investors need to understand the dynamics of REITs' revenue and earnings growth, distinguish the blue-chip REITs from their more ordinary relatives, and consider ways to value the shares of a particular REIT. It will also get into the nitty-gritty of building REIT portfolios with adequate diversification.

Finally, **Part IV: Risks and Future Prospects** presents a necessary discussion of the risks investors face as they become more familiar with the REIT world. And, at last, we'll do some speculating as to the future growth of the REIT industry and how we might profit from future trends.

By the time you finish this book, you will have a firm understanding and appreciation of one of the most rewarding investments on Wall Street. Even more important, you will be able to build your own portfolio of outstanding real estate companies that should provide you with attractive current dividend yields and the prospects of significant capital appreciation in the years ahead. By investing in investment-quality REITs, investors large and small have been able to earn total returns averaging 12 percent annually, with steady income, low market-price volatility, and investment safety.

REIT investors today have a much wider choice of investment properties than ever before and can choose from some of the most experienced and capable managements that have ever invested in and operated real estate in the United States. As you read on, you'll see why REITs should be an essential part of every investor's portfolio; REIT investors with a long-term time horizon have benefited mightily since the first REIT was organized more than forty years ago, and REIT investing remains alive and well!

MEET THE
REIT

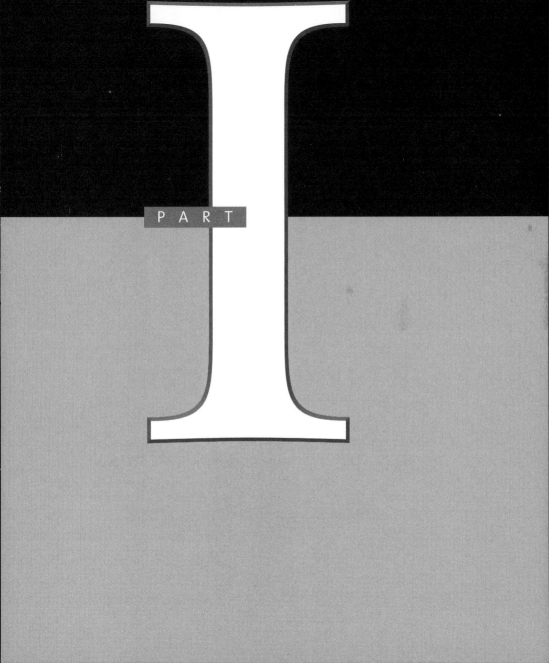

PART

I

CHAPTER

REITs:
What They Are
AND HOW THEY
WORK

WHAT'S YOUR IDEA of the perfect investment? How about one that promises not to double overnight or make you an instant millionaire, but instead will pay you a consistent 4, 5, or 6 percent in quarterly dividends and can rise another 4, 5, or 6 percent annually as surely and steadily as if they were, say, rental payments? How about real estate?

Sure, you say, but only if there were a hassle-free way to buy and own real estate, as if an experienced professional dealt with the business of owning and managing it and just gave you the profits. And only if you could sell your real estate—if you wanted to—easily, as easily as you can sell a common stock like General Electric or Intel. Well, read on. This is all possible with real estate investment trusts, or REITs (pronounced "reets"), as they are commonly called.

REITs have provided individual investors all over the country with a way to buy skyscrapers and shopping malls and hotels and apartment buildings—in fact, just about any kind of commercial real property you can think of. REITs give you the steady and predictable cash flow that real estate leases provide, but with the benefit of a common stock's liquidity. Equally important, REITs usually have access to capital and can therefore acquire and build additional properties as part of their ongoing real estate business.

Besides that, REITs can add stability to your investment portfolio, because real estate as an asset class has long been perceived as an inflation hedge and has enjoyed low correlation with other asset classes.

REITs have been around for more than forty years, but it's only been in the past dozen years that most people have really started buying into these higher-yielding investments. From the end of 1992 through the end of 2004, the size of the REIT industry has increased by almost twenty times, from $16 billion to $308 billion. But, according to many experts, the REIT industry, having so far captured only about 10 percent of the $4 trillion commercial real estate market, still has plenty of room left for growth.

Stan Ross, former managing partner of Ernst & Young's Real Estate Group, defined REITs by saying, "They are real operating companies that lease, renovate, manage, tear down, rebuild, and develop from scratch." That helps define a REIT, but you need to know not only what a REIT is, but also what it can be to you and what you can expect from it in terms of investment behavior.

REITS ARE A LIQUID ASSET

A LIQUID ASSET or investment is one that has a generally accepted value and a market where it can be sold easily and quickly at little or no discount to that value. Direct investment in real estate, whether it be a golf course in California or a skyscraper in Manhattan, is not liquid. A qualified buyer must be found, and even then, the value is not clearly established. Most publicly traded stocks *are* liquid. REITs are real estate–related investments that enjoy the benefit of a common stock's liquidity.

REITs provide substantial dividend yields, which during most market cycles average between 4 and 7 percent, making them an ideal investment for an IRA or other tax-deferred portfolio. But unlike most high-yielding investments, REIT shares have a strong likelihood of increasing in value over time as the REIT's properties generate higher cash flows and additional properties are added to the portfolio.

REITs own real estate, but, when you buy a REIT, you're not just buying real estate, you're also buying a business.

When you buy stock in Gillette, for example, you're buying more than razor blades. And with REITs, you own more than its real estate. REITs are corporate real estate entities overseen by financially sophisticated, skilled management teams who have the ability to grow the REIT's cash flows by 4–6 percent annually—and sometimes much more. Adding a 5 percent dividend yield to capital appreciation of 4–6 percent, resulting from 4–6 percent annual increases in operating cash flow, provides for total return prospects of 9–11 percent.

A successful REIT's management team will accept risk only where the odds of success are very strong. This is because, generally, they are investing their money right alongside yours and don't want to risk loss of capital any more than you do. REITs run the properties in such a way that they generate steady income; but they also have an eye to the future and are interested in growth of the property portfolio and its cash flows, and in taking advantage of new opportunities.

TYPES OF REITS

There are two basic categories of REITs: equity REITs and mortgage REITs.

An equity REIT is a publicly traded company that, as its principal business, buys, manages, renovates, maintains, and occasionally sells real properties. Many are also able to develop new properties when the economics are favorable. It is tax advantaged in that it is not taxed on the corporate level, and, by law, must pay out at least 90 percent of its net income as dividends to its investors.

A mortgage REIT is a REIT that makes and holds loans and other bond-like obligations that are secured by real estate collateral.

The focus of this book is equity REITs rather than mortgage or hybrid REITs (REITs that own both properties and mortgages). Although mortgage REITs can, at times, deliver spectacular investment returns, equity REITs are less vulnerable to changes in interest rates and have historically provided better long-term total returns, more stable market-price performance, lower risk, and greater liquidity. In addition to that, equity REITs allow the investor to determine not only the type of property he or she invests in, but also the geographic location of the properties.

GENERAL INVESTMENT CHARACTERISTICS

PERFORMANCE AND RETURNS

During the twenty-year period ending December 2004, equity REITs have delivered an average annual total return to their investors of 12.7 percent. Compared to the performance of the stock market during that period, those returns aren't bad, are they? Look at the chart shown below. According to the REIT trade association, the National Association of Real Estate Investment Trusts, or NAREIT, equity REITs have, over long time periods, provided their investors with compounded annual total returns very close to that of the S&P 500 index.

However, if REITs' performance was merely comparable to the S&P 500, you wouldn't be reading a book about them. The per-

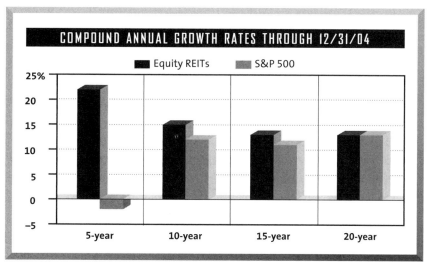

formance of many high-risk stocks has substantially exceeded the returns provided by the broad market. Here's the difference: REITs have nearly matched the S&P's total return in spite of having benefits not usually enjoyed by stocks that keep pace with the market, namely low correlation with other asset classes, low market-price volatility, limited investment risk, and high current returns.

LOW CORRELATIONS

Correlations measure how much predictive power the price behavior of one asset class has on another to which it's compared. In other words, if we want to predict what effect a 1 percent rise (or fall) in the S&P 500 will have upon REIT stocks, small caps, or bonds for any particular time period, we look at their relative correlations. For example, if the correlation of an S&P 500 index fund with the S&P 500 index is complete, that is, 1.0, then a 2 percent move in the S&P 500 index would predict that the move in the index fund for the same period would also be 2 percent. Correlations range from a perfect +1.0, in which case the movements of two investments will be perfectly matched, to a (1.0), in which case their movements will be completely opposite. Correlations in the investment world are important, as they allow financial planners, investment advisers, and individual or institutional investors to structure broadly diversified investment portfolios with the objective of having the ups and downs of each asset class cancel each other out. This, ideally, results

LOW VOLATILITY

A stock's "volatility" refers to the extent to which its price tends to bounce around from day to day, or even hour to hour. My observations of the REIT market over the last thirty years have led me to the conclusion that REIT stocks are simply less volatile, on a daily basis, than other equities. Although REITs' increased popularity over the last few years has brought in new investors with different agendas and thus created more volatility, REIT stocks still remain less volatile than their non-REIT brethren.

REITs' higher current yields often act as a shock absorber against daily market fluctuations.

Equally important, there is a predictability and steadiness to most REITs' operating and financial performance from quarter to quarter and from year to year, and there is simply less concern about major negative surprises that can stoke volatility.

Why is this important? Our biggest investment mistakes are emotional ones. When our stocks are going up, we tend to throw caution to the wind in our pursuit of ever greater profits. Likewise, when our stocks are dropping, we tend to panic and dump otherwise sound investments, because we're afraid of ever greater losses. When is the "right" time to sell or buy? Prudent investors have learned through experience to temper their emotional reactions, but low volatility in a stock can make patient and disciplined investors of us all.

Sometimes our financial decisions are not based on prudent market strategy but on what's going on in our personal life. Let's say the market is having a bad week. You know this is not the time to sell, but your daughter's tuition is due. Not to worry. If your shares are in a REIT instead of a tech stock, chances are you can sell them at very close to the price at which they were trading last month or even last year—and they've been paying all those fat dividends in the meantime.

LOW RISK

There's just no way to avoid risk completely. Simple preservation of capital carries its own risk—inflation. Since inflation came along, there's no such thing as "no risk." Real estate ownership and management, like any other business or commercial endeavor, is subject to all sorts of risks. Mall REITs are subject to the changing tastes and lifestyles of consumers; apartment REITs are subject to the rising popularity of single-family dwellings and declining job growth in their properties' geographical areas; and health care REITs are subject to the politics of government cuts in health care reimbursement, to cite just a few examples. In general, all REITs are subject to increased supply of rental properties and demand-weakening recessions.

Yet, despite this, those who own commercial real estate can limit risk, including the risk of tenant bankruptcies—if they are diversified in sector, geographic location, and tenant roster. For example, if one tenant is doing badly, there are usually other tenants who are doing fine. This kind of thing happened repeatedly in the history of the retail industry, and the retail REITs have continued to do well; they continually find new tenants to replace the losers. Beware, however, of real property designed for a single use, where the departure of the one and only tenant could present a real problem for the property owner.

Holders of most common stocks must contend with yet another type of risk, related not to the fundamentals of a company's business but to the fickle nature of the financial markets. Let's say you own shares in a company whose business is doing well. The earnings report comes out and the news is that earnings are up 15 percent over last year. But because analysts expected a 20 percent increase, the price of the stock drops precipitously. This has been a common phenomenon in the stock market in recent years, but REIT investors have rarely suffered from this syndrome.

Analysts who follow REITs are normally able to accurately forecast quarterly results, within one or two cents, quarter after quarter.

This is because of the stability and predictability of REITs' rental revenues, occupancy rates, and real estate operating costs. True, compared to tech stocks, REITs are not very exciting, but think of what you'll save on aspirin and Maalox.

When you look at the riskiness of equity REITs, you see that very few have gotten into serious financial trouble over the years. Those

◆ REITs provide diversification to your portfolio because their price movements are not highly correlated with the rest of the market.

◆ REITs' higher current yields frequently act as a shock absorber against daily market fluctuations.

◆ Analysts who follow REITs are normally able to forecast quarterly results within one or two cents, quarter after quarter, year after year, thus minimizing the chances for "negative surprises."

◆ REITs' higher yields raise the overall yield of the portfolio, thus minimizing volatility and providing stable cash flows even in major bear markets.

◆ REITs are the easiest way for individuals to own commercial real estate and allow for the greatest possible real estate diversification.

◆ REIT stocks are equities and are subject to the prevailing winds blowing across the investment world.

CHAPTER

REITs

VERSUS COMPETITIVE
INVESTMENTS

GROWTH PROSPECTS

Utility stocks' long-term total returns, as measured by the S&P Utility Index, have been competitive with those of REITs. However, that index can be misleading, as it includes the performance of many telephone and gas companies whose dividend yields have become very small as those companies have sought more rapid growth. Further, the averages mask wide differences in performance even among electric utility companies. Conversely, there has been more consistency of performance among REITs when categorized by size.

The deregulation of the utility industry is indeed a work in process, but it's taking a lot more time to unfold than previously expected—most likely because our elected politicians are trying to take the time to "do it right." Few are talking today about re-regulation. The new industry trend is that the old power companies are splitting off their generating units, which have more growth potential, from their transmission business—or simply organizing new "merchant" generating companies.

These new companies have much greater growth potential, but their prospects are less certain (they hinge on prevailing forces in the new electricity markets) and more volatile; and they will be stingy with their dividends while they plow all available funds into growth opportunities.

The best transmission companies, conversely, may be able to grow earnings at a pace of 3–4 percent, with similar increases in dividends. They are, however, very much subject to state regulation and may charge customers only what state regulators will allow. Also, each is still pretty much locked into a few geographical areas. Expansion internationally has been beneficial for a few utility companies, but it's risky; furthermore, going this route doesn't seem to be high on the agendas of most power companies.

The flip side of greater growth prospects for some utility companies is that risk is increasing. Not only are the generating companies increasingly subject to shifting market forces in supply and demand, but they have been levering up their balance sheets with substantial additional debt, and average coverage of interest costs has declined.

GROWTH PROSPECTS

Utility stocks' long-term total returns, as measured by the S&P Utility Index, have been competitive with those of REITs. However, that index can be misleading, as it includes the performance of many telephone and gas companies whose dividend yields have become very small as those companies have sought more rapid growth. Further, the averages mask wide differences in performance even among electric utility companies. Conversely, there has been more consistency of performance among REITs when categorized by size.

The deregulation of the utility industry is indeed a work in process, but it's taking a lot more time to unfold than previously expected—most likely because our elected politicians are trying to take the time to "do it right." Few are talking today about re-regulation. The new industry trend is that the old power companies are splitting off their generating units, which have more growth potential, from their transmission business—or simply organizing new "merchant" generating companies.

These new companies have much greater growth potential, but their prospects are less certain (they hinge on prevailing forces in the new electricity markets) and more volatile; and they will be stingy with their dividends while they plow all available funds into growth opportunities.

The best transmission companies, conversely, may be able to grow earnings at a pace of 3–4 percent, with similar increases in dividends. They are, however, very much subject to state regulation and may charge customers only what state regulators will allow. Also, each is still pretty much locked into a few geographical areas. Expansion internationally has been beneficial for a few utility companies, but it's risky; furthermore, going this route doesn't seem to be high on the agendas of most power companies.

The flip side of greater growth prospects for some utility companies is that risk is increasing. Not only are the generating companies increasingly subject to shifting market forces in supply and demand, but they have been levering up their balance sheets with substantial additional debt, and average coverage of interest costs has declined.

REITS VERSUS ELECTRIC UTILITIES

Way back in 1994 I did an informal study of REITs' popularity in relation to utility stocks. According to a *Barron*'s mutual fund section in April 1994, seventy-one mutual funds had been specifically designed to invest in utilities, compared with only eleven specializing in real estate securities. The aggregate asset value of these utility funds was $25.3 billion versus only $1.27 billion for the REIT funds. Five utility funds each had assets greater than all eleven of the REIT funds combined. So, historically, utilities have been much more popular higher-yielding investments than REITs—but this situation has been changing rapidly in recent years.

A few years ago Robert McConnaughey, of Prudential Real Estate Securities at the time, stated that "there are tremendous unanswered questions facing [the electric utility] industry in the face of deregulation. What are the electric companies really worth," he asks, "if the market evolves in the Enron model and power is openly traded at the lowest cost of generation?" Using Enron was a poor choice, with hindsight, but some utility stocks spiked in 2000 on the prospects for the sale of unregulated power at high prices. Yet history has shown that the power business has become much more volatile and uncertain. Just ask the shareholders of PG&E and Edison International, California's largest electric companies, or of Enron!

There is a strong case to be made that REITs are clearly superior investments to utilities and that smart investors who have a large segment of their portfolios in electric utilities should be reallocating those funds to REITs.

Milton Cooper, founding CEO of Kimco Realty Corporation and former chairman of the National Association of Real Estate Investment Trusts (NAREIT), observed in January 1997 that "income-oriented investors, who dropped their utility stocks last year when lower inflation depressed stock yields and the threat of deregulation increased the risk of holding a utility, found a safe harbor in REITs." The price action in REIT stocks from 2000 through 2004 has shown that this trend continues.

BEFORE DECIDING if REITs are an appropriate investment for you, it's important to measure their merits, point by point, against those of other investments. That comparison becomes more meaningful, of course, if the comparison is made with investments that are truly similar. This point brings us to a concept known as *relevant market.*

In antitrust law, relevant market is very significant. Suppose, for example, that Nestlé wanted to acquire Hershey Foods. In order to determine whether this might create an antitrust problem arising from a company's acquisition of a competitor, lawyers and justice departments must figure out what the relevant market is. Is the market simply chocolate bars, is it a wider market such as candy, or is it a still wider market such as snack foods? There might or might not be an antitrust problem, depending upon which market is perceived as being the relevant market.

A similar issue arises when we compare the merits of REITs to those of other investments. Is it appropriate to compare REITs with *all* common stocks, or does it make more sense to compare them with the more narrow market of high-yield investments? Up to this point we've been comparing them to the broad spectrum of common stocks, which, technically, they are. Many investors, however, see them as somehow different from stocks of such companies as Pfizer, Ford, Disney, or Intel, because of their higher dividend yields and lower capital appreciation prospects. Indeed, REITs are, arguably, a separate asset class.

Thus, while it is always interesting to compare REITs to growth stocks, REITs might be more meaningfully compared to securities investments with similar characteristics: utility stocks, preferred stocks, bonds, and convertibles. These are the investments of choice for those who normally invest in higher-yielding securities that offer lower volatility, modest capital appreciation prospects, and less investment risk.

A common comparison is to electric utility stocks, since, with their high yields, moderate dividend growth, and modest capital appreciation prospects, they are closer to REITs than most other securitized investments. And, although they are not as close in nature, we'll also make the comparison to nonconvertible bonds and preferred stocks, and with convertibles and other real estate investments.

REITs

VERSUS COMPETITIVE
INVESTMENTS

REITs are not threatened by the twin specters of deregulation and new competition; utilities are.

MANAGEMENT

While there are certainly some REITs being run by "caretaker" managements that do not seek to use imagination and their available resources to grow the business, the good ones are run by extremely capable individuals who have had many years of experience in the successful ownership and management of real properties. They are energetic, entrepreneurial, and quick to seize new opportunities.

It is very important to note that many REITs are managed by people who have most of their own net worth invested in the shares.

Although the managements of some of the utilities may be very capable, most are not entrepreneurial types known for their vision and innovation. Further, they are not as heavily invested in their own companies as are most REIT managements.

REGULATION

For electric utilities, regulation is the ultimate obstacle to growth. For the regulatory commissions of most states, rate regulation is a "heads-we-win, tails-you-lose" proposition. A number of years ago many utilities built nuclear power plants in response to the public need for more electricity. While there were some issues of inept decision-making by the utilities' management, the difficulty of building these plants within construction budgets could not have been predicted. Result? The shareholders of the utilities, not the taxpayers or consumers, ate most of these unexpected costs. The uncertainties of regulation remain a problem for the utilities and their shareholders.

Who pays for mistakes? It's not hard to figure out. When it comes to counting votes, there are more people using utilities than investing in them. Regulators, having been appointed by elected officials, will simply pass on the costs to shareholders. Deregulation may provide opportunities for utility management and their shareholders but, so far, the results are mixed at best.

REITs, on the other hand, are not subject to significant regulatory supervision.

COMPETITION

Electric utilities today are facing something they have never had to deal with: competition. Until recently, the power companies had a Faustian bargain with regulators: "You tell us what we can charge our customers and how much we can keep, and we get a monopoly on supplying all the power in our area." But that bargain has begun to crumble as former monopolies are being opened up to new competition.

These new competitors, whether upstart cogeneration companies or major power generation companies, threaten to siphon off large commercial electricity users, causing the local companies to seek significant rate increases from the consumer to make up for lost revenue. Power company managements are not used to the street fighting of competition, and may even seek legislation to restrict competition.

REIT managements, on the other hand, have been competing with real estate companies, merchant builders, and knowledgeable private investors since they first got into the business. They know their way around the block, and they have a very good idea of what they will earn on any new real estate investment.

INVESTMENT TRENDS

The investment merits of utility stocks are already widely known. It's unlikely that there will be a major surge of new investors who suddenly discover their virtues. REITs, on the other hand, have been largely ignored by investors since their arrival on the scene more than forty years ago. Although their popularity has increased substantially in recent years, they are not yet heavily represented in most investment portfolios. The point here is that there are hundreds of thousands of potential REIT investors out there, both individual and institutional, looking for excellent yields with reasonably good growth prospects, who are not yet invested in REITs. Will they all become REIT enthusiasts? Probably not, but REITs began a new surge of popularity in 1996, and again in 2000. The prospect of a substantial increase in the amount of new investment funds flowing

SOURCES: NAREIT, CITIGROUP, SMITH BARNEY

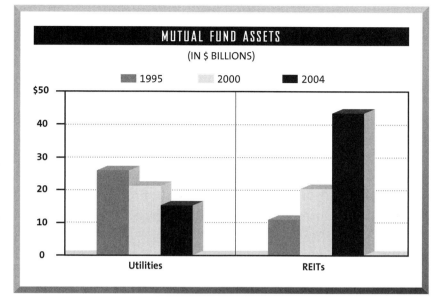

MUTUAL FUND ASSETS
(IN $ BILLIONS)

■ 1995 ■ 2000 ■ 2004

into REITs instead of into utility stocks is very enticing. REIT representation in popular 401(k) plans has only just begun.

REITS VERSUS BONDS

While REITs do compete directly with utilities for the investment funds of yield-oriented investors, they are not *quite* so analogous with bonds. Although bonds generally provide somewhat higher yields than the average REIT stock, the investor gets only the interest coupon, but no growth potential. Bonds do offer something that REITs cannot provide: a promise of repayment of principal at maturity so that, in the absence of bankruptcy or other default, investors will always get back their investments. It is this feature that makes the comparison between REITs and bonds (or REITs and preferred stocks) flawed. For that reason, if absolute safety of capital is paramount regardless of what it costs you in terms of total return, REITs may not be the ideal investment for you. But let's look at the returns each can yield.

With bonds, what you see is what you get: pure yield and very little else. Let's assume that you invest $10,000 in a bond that yields 6 percent and matures in ten years. At the end of ten years, you will have your $10,000 in cash, plus the cumulative amount of the interest you received (10 × $600), or a total of $16,000, less taxes on the interest.

If, however, you invest the same amount of money in a typical REIT, the total return would probably calculate something like this: Assume the purchase of 1,000 shares of a REIT trading at $10 per share, providing a 5 percent yield (or $.50 per share). Let's also assume that the REIT increases its adjusted funds from operations (adjusted funds from operations, or AFFO, is essentially free cash flow) by 5 percent annually and increases the dividend by 5 percent annually. Finally, let's assume that the shares will rise proportionately with increased AFFO and dividend payments. Ten years later, the REIT will be paying $.776 in dividends, and your total investment will be worth $22,579 ($6,290 in cumulative dividends received plus $16,289 in share value at that time). That's $22,579 from the REIT, versus only $17,000 from the 10-year bond, or a difference of $5,579. Taxes, of course, will have to be paid on both the bond interest and the dividend payments (see the chart below). Of course, conventional wisdom says that REITs *should* provide a higher total return, because they are riskier than bonds. However, that's not necessarily true if you consider inflation.

REITS' HIGHER TOTAL RETURN

REITS' 5 PERCENT annual dividend, compounded at 5 percent annual growth rate

END YEAR	STOCK PRICE	DIVIDENDS
1	$10.50	$0.500
2	$11.02	$0.525
3	$11.58	$0.551
4	$12.16	$0.579
5	$12.76	$0.608
6	$13.40	$0.638
7	$14.07	$0.670
8	$14.77	$0.704
9	$15.51	$0.739
10	$16.29	$0.776
		$6.290
x 1,000 shares	$16,289	$6,290
TOTAL INVESTMENT VALUE		$22,579

It is true that, unlike bonds, REIT shares offer no specific maturity date, and there is no guarantee of the price you'll get when you sell them. However, with bonds you get no inflation protection, and so you are at a substantial risk of the declining purchasing power of the dollar. It's all a question of how one measures risk.

If history is any guide, REITs, unlike bonds, will appreciate in value as the value of their underlying real estate appreciates and the rents from their tenants increase over time.

And if we measure risk in terms of price volatility, we also need to consider the appropriate time horizon. A longer time horizon minimizes risk. The chart below shows the path of the FFOs (funds from operations) and the stock price of Kimco Realty, a well-known and widely respected retail REIT, since shortly after it went public. As you can see, there are no roller coaster rides here; there are only the normal price fluctuations you might see with bonds as well.

In fact, the risks are stacked against the bond investor, since, if inflation rises, so generally will interest rates, which reduces the market value of the bond while it's being held and results in an actual loss of capital if the bond is sold prior to maturity. On the other hand, if interest rates decline, perhaps due to lower inflation,

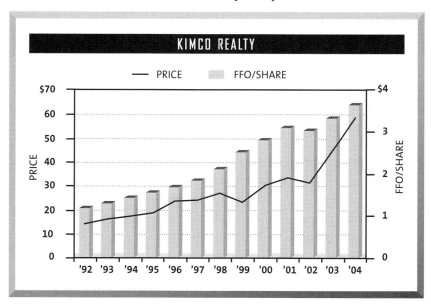

SOURCES: KIMCO, COMPUSTAT

many bonds are called before their maturity dates. This deprives investors of what, with hindsight, was a very attractive yield and forces them to find other investment vehicles, but ones that will pay a lower rate of interest. (Of course, a REIT's stock price may decline in response to higher interest rates, but higher interest rates often come with fast-growing economic conditions, which help to grow REIT cash flows over time.)

U.S. Treasury bonds are not callable prior to maturity and entail no repayment risk, but their yields are lower than those of corporate bonds and also fluctuate with interest rates. Bonds are certainly suitable investments for most investors; however, for the reasons stated above, they should not be regarded as good substitutes for REIT stocks in a broadly diversified portfolio.

REITS VERSUS PREFERRED STOCKS

Now let's take a look at how well REITs stack up against preferred stocks. Unlike bonds, preferred stocks do not represent the promise of the issuer to repay a specific amount at a specified date in the future, and in the legal pecking order their claims against the corporation are below those of every other creditor. Unless the terms of the preferred stock provide for the right of the holder to demand redemption, preferred shares have certain disadvantages: They do not have a fixed maturity date, nor are their holders considered creditors. And they have little or no capital appreciation prospects. They do, however, provide relatively high yields during most market environments, many offering as much as 7 percent.

REITs are not as interest-rate sensitive as bonds, preferred stocks, or utilities.

The problem here is, as with bonds, what you see is what you get: pure yield and very little else. While the high dividends are enticing, preferred stocks, unlike REITs and common stocks, offer little in the way of price-appreciation potential or hedge against inflation. And their prices, like bonds', are very interest-rate sensitive.

REITS VERSUS CONVERTIBLES

When we compare REITs to *convertible* bonds and *convertible* preferred stocks, we finally come to investments that do, in fact, provide direct competition for REITs. These securities offer yields comparable to those of many REITs *as well as* appreciation potential—if the common stock into which the convertible bonds or preferred stock may be converted rises substantially. In the case of convertible bonds, there is the security of a fixed maturity date in case the underlying common stock fails to appreciate in value. Convertibles can be a relatively attractive investment concept.

The problem with good convertibles is that most companies don't issue them. The yield-hungry investor just has to keep an eye out for these hybrids, and, from time to time, there is a small window of opportunity to purchase them. Then, if the underlying common stock appears to be a good investment, the convertible may also be a good investment. Some REITs have occasionally issued convertible securities, primarily convertible preferred stock. The investor should consider whether the extra safety and slightly higher yields on these convertibles outweigh the conversion premium and their relative lack of liquidity.

REITS VERSUS OTHER REAL ESTATE INVESTMENT VEHICLES

As an asset class, real estate has normally been a very good investment. A well-situated, well-maintained investment property may grow in value over the years, and its rental revenues may grow with it. While buildings may depreciate over time and neighborhoods change, only a finite amount of land exists upon which an apartment, store, or building can be built. If you own such a property in the right area, it can be, if not a gold mine, a cash cow whose value is likely to increase over the years. New, competitive buildings will not be built unless either rents or property values are high enough to justify the development costs. In either such event, owners of existing properties will be wealthier.

However, contrary to popular wisdom, there is no automatic correlation between inflation and the value of real estate. Real estate observer Pablo Galarza has concluded that, based upon a study of real estate performance data between 1978 and 1993, the net operating income of the properties studied did not even come close to keeping up with inflation in that period (*Financial World,* January 2, 1996). Of course, that was a period of unusually high inflation and substantial overbuilding, and history has shown that well-maintained properties in economically healthy areas, particularly if they are protected against competing properties because of land scarcity or entitlement restrictions, are likely to rise in value over time. However, the point remains that real estate owners do not always benefit from inflation, at least over the short term.

REIT ownership addresses all the problems raised by every other real estate investment vehicle: REITs offer diversification, liquidity, management, and, in most cases, very limited conflicts of interest between management and investors.

Accepting that well-located and well-maintained commercial property is likely to remain a good long-term investment, how does real estate as an asset class fit within a well-diversified portfolio? Since it has historically behaved differently from other assets—stocks (both foreign and domestic), bonds, cash, or possibly gold or art—it adds another dimension and therefore helps to diversify one's asset base. There are a number of ways, however, in which you can choose to hold real estate.

DIRECT OWNERSHIP
Direct ownership means that you're in the real estate business. Do you have the time to manage property, or do you already have a full-time career? Do you know the best time to buy, sell, or hold? Sometimes buying real estate at cheap prices, then selling it, is more profitable than holding and managing it, depending on the market climate. Would you recognize when it's smarter to sell the property than to hold onto it? For most individual investors, having a real estate professional make this decision is far wiser than being in real estate directly. Effective and efficient property management is also crucial; the importance of competent, experienced management cannot be overstated, and individuals often lack the resources—time, money, or expertise—to accomplish this.

Direct ownership may sometimes offer higher profits than investing in REITs, but most individuals don't have the time or experience to be in the real estate business.

Although it is sometimes more profitable not to have to share returns from a great real estate investment with other investors, it is also clearly riskier. The investment value of real estate is quite often determined by the local economy; at any given time, apartment buildings may be doing well, say, in Los Angeles, but poorly in Atlanta. Most individuals simply do not have the financial resources to buy enough properties to be safely diversified, either by property type or by geography.

Then there is the problem of liquidity: Selling a single piece of real property may be very time-consuming and costly. Furthermore, it may not happen when you want it to, although selling may sometimes be your only way to cash out.

Finally, even if you are willing to accept all the inconveniences and disadvantages of inexperience, limited diversification, and illiquidity, would you want to be the one who gets the call that there's been a break-in, or the air conditioning is on the fritz, or the elevator's stuck? And if you use an outside management company, your profits will be significantly reduced.

Some investors claim that they don't need REIT investments, as they own their own home—which, of course, is real estate. However, the dynamics of home price movements are very different from those of commercial real estate; further, there is no diversification if the only real estate an investor owns is a home. Another key point is that capturing the appreciated value in a single-family residence requires its sale, and most individuals would be reluctant to sell their beloved home and move into an apartment building or find another home in a different state. Of course, equity can be pulled out of one's home through a refinancing, but this will require substantially higher monthly mortgage payments.

C CORPORATIONS

As we have said, REIT investing offers wide diversification in real estate ownership, liquidity, and professional management. The REIT is also the most tax-efficient way for individuals to own real estate in public (or securitized) form, since the REIT pays no taxes on its net income if the REIT distributes that income to shareholders in the form of dividends (by law, at least 90 percent of net income must be so distributed). However, there is another publicly traded security that can own real estate. It is the C corporation. A C corporation is not a REIT, and thus it pays taxes on its net income, whether or not it distributes any income to its shareholders. One example of a C corporation that owns real estate is Brookfield Properties, which owns office buildings in major cities.

Since a C corporation is not required to distribute any income to shareholders, it may thus have more capital available for growth and expansion. This can be a major advantage for the investor seeking maximum capital appreciation. However, the dividend yields of C corporations are puny compared to REIT yields, and most investors who choose to own real estate prefer substantial dividends. And not having a high dividend to support the stock price can often mean greater volatility. The bottom line is that aggressive real estate investors who are more interested in capital appreciation than income might want to take a look at the C corporations that own and manage real estate; however, the substantial dividends provided by REITs make them more appealing to most investors.

PRIVATE PARTNERSHIP

Ownership through a private partnership—whether with two, ten, or twenty partners—is yet another option for real estate ownership. Here, the investor gets to delegate, either to a general partner or to an outside company, the tasks of property leasing and management—at a price, of course. Usually, however, most private partnerships of this type own only one or very few properties, and those properties are rarely diversified in terms of property type or location.

In a private partnership, liquidity may depend on the financial solvency of the investor's partners. Although it might be theoretically possible for one partner to sell his or her interest to another partner without the underlying property being sold, it often just doesn't happen that way. Also, in private partnerships, conflicts of interest often abound between the general partner and the limited partners, perhaps with regard either to compensation or to the decision to sell or refinance the partnership property. Finally, there is the question of the personal liability of the individual partners if the partnership gets into financial trouble, a situation not uncommon a number of years ago.

PUBLICLY TRADED LIMITED PARTNERSHIP

Publicly traded real estate limited partnerships were very popular with investors for a period of time up until 1990. There is a world of difference between REITs and real estate limited partnerships, and these differences cost the investors in the latter dearly. The limited-partnership sponsors of the 1980s plucked billions of dollars from investors who were seeking the benefits of real estate ownership combined with tax breaks. Unsuspecting investors during that time did *so* poorly that they were lucky to recover ten or twenty cents on the dollar.

There were several reasons for their failure: Sometimes it was that fees were so high that there were no profits for the ultimate owner, the investor. Sometimes it was that the partnerships bought too late in the real estate cycle. After they grossly overpaid for the properties, they hired mediocre managers, failing to recognize that, particularly in the 1990s, real estate was—and still is—a very management-intensive business. Other times, these limited partnerships had conflicts of interest with the general partners, to the detriment of the investors. The major differences between real estate limited partnerships and REITs will be discussed in a later chapter.

THE PRIVATE REIT PHENOMENON

Beginning in 2000, another real estate alternative to public REITs burst on the scene—"private REITs." These entities are organizations that comply with the U.S. REIT laws, but their shares do not trade in public markets. Sponsored by various real estate organizations, for example, Inland Real Estate or Wells Real Estate, they are usually sold to small investors by financial planners. A private REIT will own a number of commercial properties, usually in different locations, and the income from the properties is distributed to the private REIT's shareholders as dividends. The yields to investors are normally higher than available from an investment in public REITs.

However, there are some drawbacks to private REITs that investors should be aware of. Perhaps most important, they are not liquid investments. Although some private REITs promise to offer to repurchase a number of shares at certain times and under certain conditions, shares cannot be quickly sold by calling one's broker. Furthermore, private REIT shares are normally sold with large commissions going to the seller (sometimes exceeding 12 percent), so fewer investment dollars are available for real estate investment; and, quite often, the sponsor earns significant additional revenues via property acquisitions and management fees. Accordingly, prospective investors in private REITs should be aware of potential conflicts of interest that may result from a desire of some sponsors to grow the size of the REIT merely in order to generate increasing revenues for itself.

Investors therefore should be careful to balance the promised benefits of private REITs against their inherent disadvantages, and should carefully analyze their organizational structure, acquisition criteria, operating costs and fee payments, prospective cash flows and balance sheet, dividend coverage, and potential conflicts of interest.

SUMMARY

◆ There is a strong case to be made that REITs are superior investments to utilities and that smart investors who have a large segment of their portfolios in electric utilities should be reallocating at least some portion of those funds to REITs.

◆ REITs are not threatened by the twin specters of deregulation and competition—utilities are.

◆ Many REITs are managed by people who have most of their own net worth invested in the REIT's shares.

◆ If history is any guide, REITs, unlike bonds, will appreciate in value as the value of their underlying real estate appreciates and the rents from their tenants increase over time.

◆ REITs are not as interest-rate sensitive as bonds, preferred stocks, or utilities.

◆ Bonds and preferred stocks have no potential for dividend income growth, and utilities have very modest growth potential—but REITs have substantial dividend yields and growth prospects in the mid-single digits.

◆ REIT ownership addresses all the issues raised by every other real estate investment vehicle: REITs offer diversification, liquidity, management, and, in most cases, very limited conflicts of interest between management and investors.

◆ Direct real estate ownership may sometimes deliver higher profits than investing in a REIT, but most individuals don't have the time or experience to be in the real estate business full time.

CHAPTER

Today's
REITs

NOW THAT YOU HAVE a general sense of what REITs are and how they compare to other investments, let's take a closer look at the structure of REITs and how they've adapted to changing conditions over the years.

THE FIRST REIT

The REIT was defined and authorized by the U.S. Congress, in the Real Estate Investment Trust Act of 1960, and the first REIT was actually formed in 1963. The legislation was meant to provide individual investors with the opportunity to participate in the benefits, already available to large institutional investors, of owning and/or financing a diversified portfolio of commercial real estate.

The avoidance of "double taxation" is one of the key advantages to the REIT structure.

A key hallmark of the REIT structure is that the REIT can deduct from its taxable income all dividends paid to its shareholders—thus the REIT pays no corporate taxes if it distributes to shareholders all otherwise taxable income. By law, however, it must pay out at least 90 percent of its net income to its shareholders. The shareholders, of course, must pay income taxes on the dividends, unless the REIT shares are held in an IRA, 401(k), or other tax-deferred account. Often, however, a portion of a REIT's dividend is not immediately taxable, as we'll see later.

THE TAX REFORM ACT OF 1986

The tax reform act of 1986 was a significant milestone in the REIT industry, as it relaxed some of the restrictions historically limiting REIT activities. Originally, management was legally obliged to hire outside companies to provide property leasing and management services, but a REIT is now allowed to perform these essential services within its own organization. This change was highly significant because imaginative and efficient leasing and property management are key elements in being a successful and profitable property owner.

Most of today's REITs are fully integrated operating companies that can handle all aspects of real estate operations internally:

UNIQUE LEGAL CHARACTERISTICS OF A REIT

1 The REIT must distribute at least 90 percent of its annual taxable income, excluding capital gains, as dividends to its shareholders.

2 The REIT must have at least 75 percent of its assets invested in real estate, mortgage loans, shares in other REITs, cash, or government securities.

3 The REIT must derive at least 75 percent of its gross income from rents, mortgage interest, or gains from the sale of real property. And at least 95 percent must come from these sources, together with dividends, interest, and gains from securities sales.

4 The REIT must have at least 100 shareholders and must have less than 50 percent of the outstanding shares concentrated in the hands of five or fewer shareholders.

◆ Acquisitions and sales of properties
◆ Property management and leasing
◆ Property rehabilitation and repositioning
◆ Property development

UPREIT AND DOWNREIT

In studying different REITs, you might come across the terms "UPREIT" and "DownREIT." These are terms used to describe differences in the corporate structure of REITs. The UPREIT concept was first implemented in 1992 by creative investment bankers. Its purpose was to enable long-established real estate operating companies to bring properties they already own under the umbrella of a REIT structure, without actually having to sell the properties to the REIT, since by such a sale the existing owners would incur significant capital gains taxes.

UPREIT just means "Umbrella Partnership REIT." Generally, it works like this: The REIT itself might not own any properties directly; what it does own is a controlling interest in a limited partnership that, in turn, owns the real estate. The other limited partners often include management and private investors who had indirectly owned the organization's properties prior to its having become a REIT. The owners of the limited-partnership units have the right to convert them into shares of the REIT, to vote as if they were REIT shareholders, and to receive the same dividends as if they held publicly traded REIT shares. In short, they enjoy virtually the same attributes of ownership as the REIT shareholders.

DownREITs are structured similarly but are usually formed after the REIT becomes a public company, and generally do not include members of management among the limited partners in the controlled partnership.

REITs structured as UPREITs or DownREITs can exchange operating partnership (OP) units for interests in other real estate partnerships that own properties the REIT wants to acquire. Such an exchange can defer capital gains taxes for the seller. By receiving OP units in a "like-kind" exchange, the sellers can then not only defer the payment of taxes but also gain the advantage of having a more diversified form of investment, that is, an indirect interest in many properties. This gives the UPREIT or DownREIT a competitive edge over a regular REIT when it comes to making a deal with tax-sensitive property sellers. Home Properties, among others, has made very effective use of this tool.

Originally conceived as a tax-deferral device, the UPREIT structure has also become an attractive acquisition tool for the REIT.

One negative aspect of the UPREIT structure, however, is that it creates an opportunity for conflicts of interest. Management often owns units in the UPREIT's partnership rather than, or in addition to, shares in the REIT, and their OP units will usually have a low cost basis. Since the sale of a property could trigger taxable income to the holders of the UPREIT's units but not to the shareholders of the REIT, management might be reluctant to sell a property, or even the REIT itself—even if, for instance, the property is a disappointment or the third-party offer is a generous one. Investors should watch how management handles the conflict issues. There is less concern, of course, in a DownREIT structure where management owns no OP units.

UPREITs and DownREITs simply allow existing property owners to "REITize" their existing property without incurring immediate capital gains taxes.

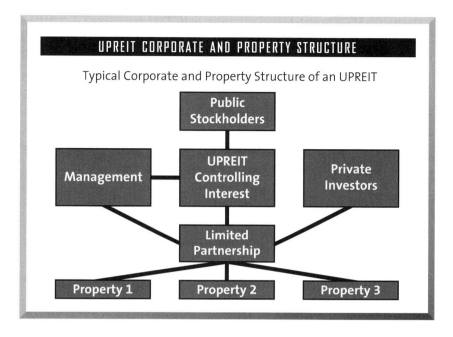

UPREIT CORPORATE AND PROPERTY STRUCTURE

Typical Corporate and Property Structure of an UPREIT

REIT MODERNIZATION ACT

In December 1999, President Clinton signed into law the REIT Modernization Act (RMA). The most important feature of this new legislation enables every REIT organization to form and own a "taxable REIT subsidiary" (TRS). The legislation enables a REIT, through ownership of up to 100 percent of a TRS, to provide substantial services to its tenants, as well as others, without jeopardizing the REIT's legal standing; this had been a major issue in the past. The new law also greatly expands the nature and extent of services that a REIT may offer or engage in, which may now include such activities as concierge services to apartment tenants, "merchant" development, offering discount buying of supplies and services to office tenants, and engaging in a variety of real estate–related businesses; the TRS may also engage in joint ventures with other parties to provide additional services. Furthermore, even noncustomary services may now be offered by a REIT without having to use a third-party independent contractor.

However, certain limitations do apply. For example, the TRS cannot exceed certain size limitations (no more than 20 percent of a REIT's gross assets may consist of securities of a TRS). Loan and rental transactions between a REIT and its TRS are limited, and a substantial excise tax is imposed on transactions not conducted on an arm's-length basis. Furthermore, while restrictions upon hotel and health care REITs have been relaxed, such REITs may not operate or manage hotels or health care facilities (but a hotel TRS may lease lodging facilities from its related REIT if operated independently).

The National Association of Real Estate Investment Trusts (NAREIT) has suggested several potential benefits to REIT organizations arising from the RMA. These include the ability to provide new services to tenants (thus remaining competitive with non-REIT property owners), better quality control over the services offered (which may now be delivered directly by the REIT's controlled subsidiary), and the prospects of earning substantial nonrental revenues for the REIT and its shareholders. However, there is still substantial disagreement over the extent to which the RMA (and the TRS) will generate significant additional revenues for the REIT and its shareholders, and whether the added risks will offset the extra rewards.

Milton Cooper, the widely respected founding CEO of Kimco Realty, has referred to the RMA as "The REIT Liberation Act," while industry leader Sam Zell has stated that the opportunities provided by the TRS could eventually produce up to 50 percent of total revenues for his REITs in future years (though this presumably includes higher rent levels resulting from additional services provided to tenants under the RMA). On the other hand, such well-known and highly successful REIT executives as Boston Properties' Ed Linde and Vornado Realty's Steve Roth have been much less sanguine about the significance of future revenue contributions via the TRS.

The bottom line for REIT investors is that it's too soon to know whether the TRS vehicle will lead to major benefits for REIT shareholders in the years ahead. Many early TRS ventures, particularly with respect to technology and Internet investments, have been failures. However, more recently a significant number of REITs have successfully implemented TRS strategies that will generate substantial additional revenue and allow these companies to compete very favorably with their peers. Some, of course, will be more successful than others. The net result of the RMA is that it is clearly a very positive development for the REIT industry, but the extent of its importance will not be known for a number of years.

THE INFAMOUS LIMITED PARTNERSHIPS OF YESTERYEAR

We cannot talk about the REIT structure without also discussing real estate limited partnerships. The real estate limited partnerships so popular in the 1980s were designed for the purpose of buying and owning commercial properties and generating positive cash flows for their limited partner investors; however, in many cases, the properties did not live up to expectations. What investors really bought was the tax shelter these properties offered, along with the hope of capital appreciation. In a rapidly rising real estate market, simply holding the property for six months or a year, even if it was operating at a loss, would mean that investors could enjoy a nice capital gain. When, however, the tax laws were changed in 1986, followed by a cooling off in the real estate markets, the arrangement no longer worked. Investors were unwilling to continue suffering losses for any length of time when upside was limited and the loss was no longer a good tax shelter. Excessive debt made the problems worse, and there was an epidemic of bankruptcies.

Today's REITs are an entirely different animal from the notorious real estate limited partnerships of the late 1980s.

Let's compare the two different real estate investment vehicles point by point:

Limited partnerships were marketed mostly as tax shelters, rather than investments that generated substantial cash flow. When investors were buying a tax shelter, many of the partnerships, even though operationally unprofitable, made sense. But once the properties were rendered useless as a tax shelter, the bottom line suddenly became significant. As a tax shelter, the partnership investment could afford high management fees and high interest payments but not when the tax shelter benefits vanished.

Today's REITs are not tax shelters. What they focus on is strong total returns, consisting of both current income and capital appreciation. The REIT's success is measured by its ability to increase its free cash flow and its dividend payments to its shareholders.

The limited partnership had a built-in recipe for trouble: the management's fee system. Usually, outside advisers were hired and paid on the basis of the volume of the properties owned. This gave them a strong incentive to add properties that would generate increased fees, but these properties were not always well-located or did not offer rent growth potential, and excessive prices were often paid for them. Often only caretaker managers were hired who had no incentives to manage the properties efficiently.

Today's REITs are allowed to manage their properties internally, and the management of well-regarded REITs is comprised of experienced executives who generally have a significant stake in the company, which often comprises most of their net worth.

With the limited-partnership structure, the only chance for growth was through increasing rental revenues and thereby increasing the properties' values, since property prices are generally determined on the basis of multiples of revenues or operating income. However, for tax-shelter investors, operating cash flow growth was not the primary goal.

Today's well-run REIT is a dynamic business. It achieves growth by increasing the operating income on the properties it owns and by raising capital for acquisitions and new property development. Good REIT managements are frequently able to raise such capital and find attractive opportunities.

Limited partnerships were not liquid investments. Since most of the limited partnerships were creatures of syndicators, the partnership interests could not be easily traded in public markets. If you wanted out of the investment, you were out of luck. Narrow trading markets eventually were created, but the bid/ask spreads were large enough to make a pawnbroker blush.

Today's REIT shares, on the other hand, can be bought or sold quickly, several thousand shares at a time, in organized markets such as the New York Stock Exchange.

Limited partnerships were promoted by brokers as having high yields, and many did pay 9 or 10 percent with, they claimed, "appreciation potential." This rate sounds good now, but remember, in 1989, the prime rate was as high as 11.5 percent. A 10 percent yield wasn't extraordinary in that interest-rate climate, and, as far as the potential for income growth went, it was quite often only that—potential.

Today's REITs offer very good yields in today's lower-interest-rate climate, and, what is more, they deliver on dividend growth rates, many of them growing in the vicinity of 3–4 percent or more a year.

Limited partnerships, when it came to capital appreciation, presented two very different pictures. Those who came early to the party, when real estate inflation was still spiraling upward, enjoyed reasonably good capital appreciation, but the late arrivals were lucky to get out with their shirts on their backs.

Most of today's REITs have been able to generate steadily increasing cash flows, which, coupled with their high dividends, provide double-digit total return potential, yet in a low-risk investment.

REITS AND THE traditional real estate limited partnerships have almost nothing in common except the nature of their underlying assets, but, until the last few years, REITs have suffered from an undeserved guilt by association.

LENDING REITS VERSUS OWNERSHIP REITS

We discussed earlier what the statutory requirements were for a REIT. According to those requirements, there is nothing in the legislation requiring a REIT to *own* real properties. It is within the boundaries of the legal definition for the REIT merely to lend funds on the strength of the collateral value of real estate by originating, acquiring, and holding real estate mortgages and related loans. These mortgages might be secured by residential or commercial properties. As of the end of 2004, there were thirty-three mortgage REITs. Hybrid REITs both own properties and hold mortgages on properties. They were popular some years ago, but, except for certain health care REITs, are not widely prevalent in today's REIT industry.

In the late 1960s and early 1970s, lending REITs were the most popular type of REIT, as many large regional and "money-center"

banks and mortgage brokers formed their own REITs. Almost sixty
new REITs were formed back then, all lending funds to property
developers at high interest rates. However, in 1973, interest rates
rose substantially, new developments couldn't be sold or leased,
nonperforming loans spiraled way out of control, and most of these
REITs crashed and burned, leaving investors holding the bag. A
decade later, a number of REITs sprang up to invest in collateralized mortgage obligations (CMOs), and they didn't fare much
better. More recently, however, the quality of mortgage REITs has
improved substantially, and their shares have performed a lot better
than they had in the past.

Mortgage REITs present several challenges for the REIT investor. First, they tend to be more highly levered with debt than the
"equity" REITs that own real estate, and this increased leverage can
make earning streams and dividend payments much more volatile. Second, mortgage REITs tend to be more sensitive to interest
rates than equity REITs, and a general increase in interest rates (or
even a significant change in the spread between short-term and
long-term interest rates) can impact earnings substantially. Finally,
as they do not own real estate whose values can be estimated, the
shares of mortgage REITs can be very difficult to value.

Thus, mortgage REITs are best viewed as trading vehicles, and their
business strategies, balance sheets, and sensitivity to interest rates must
be constantly and carefully monitored. They can be good investments
but they do occupy a specialty niche in REIT world. Accordingly, most
conservative investors will prefer to own equity REITs.

**The vast majority of today's REITs own real property rather than
make real estate loans.**

Throughout the rest of this book, then, the term *REIT* will refer
to REITs that *own* real estate in one sector or another.

EXPANSION OF REIT
PROPERTY SECTOR OFFERINGS

In Chapter 1, we briefly mentioned some of the different sectors
in which today's REITs own properties. This, too, is a story that has
evolved over time. In the beginning and until 1993, REITs owned

properties in a limited number of sectors: neighborhood (or "strip") shopping centers, apartments, health care facilities, and, to a very limited extent, office buildings. If you wanted to invest in another sector, such as a major shopping mall, you were out of luck.

By the end of 1994, as a result of a huge increase in the quantity and dollar amount of initial and secondary public offerings, the REIT industry had mushroomed. According to NAREIT statistics, the total dollar amount of offerings in those two years was $18.3 billion and $14.7 billion, respectively—about 117 percent and 46 percent of the total REIT market capitalization at the time. This trend continued in subsequent years, and by the end of 2004, equity REITs' total equity market capitalization had grown to more than $275 billion, including 153 publicly traded equity REITs. The importance of this wide array of investment choices cannot be over-emphasized.

The 1993–94 REIT-IPO boom changed the REIT industry forever. Today's investor has a choice of many well-managed REITs in many different sectors.

Each property sector, which we'll discuss in the next chapter, has its own set of investment characteristics, including its individual economic cycles and particular risk factors, competition threats, and growth potential. Each sector might be in a different phase of the broad real estate cycle. Wise REIT investors will be well diversified among the different property sectors, perhaps sometimes seeking to avoid those whose market cycles create an unfavorable risk/ reward ratio. But for the long-term investor, investing in REITs with management that is knowledgeable, creative, and experienced in real estate should provide outstanding total returns over the years.

SUMMARY

◆ Most REITs are operating companies that own and manage real property as a business and must comply with certain technical rules that generally do not affect them as investments.

◆ The avoidance of double taxation is one of the key advantages to the REIT structure.

◆ Originally conceived as a tax-deferral device, UPREIT and DownREIT structures have also become attractive acquisition tools for the REIT.

◆ The REIT Modernization Act allows today's REITs to form taxable subsidiaries that enable them to engage in various real estate–related businesses.

◆ The vast majority of today's REITs are in the business of owning, managing, and even developing real property rather than making real estate loans.

◆ Mortgage REITs can, at times, provide good returns to the careful investor, but must be closely monitored, particularly with respect to interest-rate movements.

◆ The 1993–94 REIT-IPO boom changed the REIT industry forever. Today's investor has a choice of many well-managed REITs in many different property sectors.

CHAPTER

4

Property
Sectors
AND THEIR CYCLES

ERTAIN THINGS are true of all commercial properties: Their value and profitability depend on property-specific issues such as location, lease revenues and expenses, occupancy rates, prevailing market rental rates and tenant quality; real estate issues such as "cap rates" and market supply/demand conditions; threats from competing properties; demographic issues; and such "macro" forces as the economy, interest rates, and inflation.

That said, properties can be quite dissimilar. The owner of a large, luxury apartment complex, for example, has financial concerns very different from the owner of a neighborhood strip mall or a skyscraper office building. And those are just three of the more common property types.

You can invest your money in nearly any kind of real estate imaginable: apartment buildings, manufactured-home communities, malls, neighborhood shopping centers, outlet centers, offices, industrial properties, hotels, self-storage facilities, nursing homes and hospitals— even timberland, movie theaters, and prisons.

The chart below, based upon data compiled by NAREIT, provides a glimpse of the diversity within the world of REITs.

The point is, the choices are as numerous as the differences

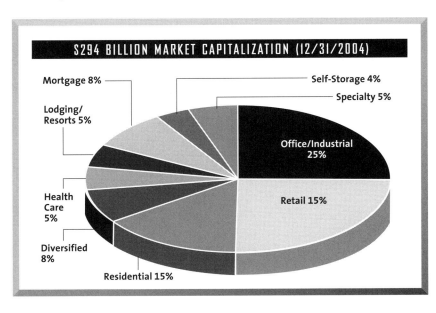

$294 BILLION MARKET CAPITALIZATION (12/31/2004)

Mortgage 8%
Self-Storage 4%
Specialty 5%
Lodging/Resorts 5%
Office/Industrial 25%
Health Care 5%
Retail 15%
Diversified 8%
Residential 15%

SOURCE: NAREIT

among various property sectors. Before selecting a particular REIT, it's necessary to understand the specific investment characteristics that set each kind of property apart. While REIT investors need not be experts on apartments, malls, or any other specific sector, they need to know some of the basics.

UPS AND DOWNS

Before we examine the individual sectors of REIT properties, let's first look at the general nature of real estate. Real estate prices and profits move in cycles, usually predictable in type but not in length or severity. And there are two kinds of cycles: one is the "space market" cycle, which deals with supply of, and demand for, real estate space, and the other is the "capital markets" cycle, which relates to capital flows and investments in commercial real estate. If you're a long-term, conservative REIT investor, you might choose to buy and hold your REITs even as their properties and stock prices move through their inevitable ups and downs. Nevertheless, you should understand and be aware of these cycles, since they can dramatically affect a REIT's cash flow and dividend growth, as well as its stock price, from time to time. If you consider yourself more of a short-term market timer, you may want to plan your REIT investments either in accordance with a real estate cycle, a capital markets cycle, or even the cycle of an individual property sector.

The phases of the real estate cycle are depression, recovery, boom, and overbuilding and downturn.

THE REAL ESTATE CYCLES

The following phases refer to the space market cycle, as opposed to the capital market cycle.

◆ **Phase 1: The Depression.** Vacancies are high, rents are low. Concessions to tenants are prevalent and substantial. Many properties, particularly those financed with excessive debt, may be in foreclosure. There is little or no new construction.

◆ **Phase 2: The Gradual Recovery.** Occupancy rates rise, rents stabilize and gradually increase, and bargaining power between owners and tenants reaches equilibrium. There is often little or no new building, but developers begin to seek new entitlements from planning commissions.

◆ **Phase 3: The Boom.** After a while, the most desirable vacant space has been absorbed, allowing property owners to boost rents rapidly. With high occupancy and rising rents, landlords are getting excellent returns. New construction is feasible, and developers start flexing their muscles. Investors and lenders are confident, and provide ample financing. During this phase, the media may write admiring stories about real estate moguls.

◆ **Phase 4: Overbuilding and Downturn.** After rents have been rising rapidly, overbuilding frequently follows as everyone tries to capitalize on the high profits being earned by real estate owners. Vacancy rates therefore increase, and rents moderate in response to the new supply. Eventually there will be an economic recession, perhaps brought about by high interest rates. As the return on real estate investment declines, bullish investors pull in their horns. Eventually, this downturn phase may turn into a depression phase, depending upon the severity of overbuilding or the economic recession. Now the cycle is complete and begins anew.

Sometimes the capital and space markets are in synch, and property prices and property cash flows rise and fall together. However, there are other times, as we saw from 2000 to 2004, when real estate profitability is almost irrelevant to real estate prices. Ultimately, however, real estate market conditions and asset pricing tend to converge.

Why do these cycles occur? Commercial real estate is tied closely not only to the national economy, but also to local economies. Years ago, for example, when the steel mills in Pittsburgh or the rubber companies in Akron laid off workers, the local economy, from retail to real estate, became depressed. The part of the country known as "Smokestack America" very quickly became "Rust Belt America." Families doubled up, with grown children moving in with parents or leaving for greener pastures elsewhere. As the number of households declined, apartment vacancy rates rose and office and industrial space went begging.

Conversely, when the Olympic Committee decided to hold the summer games in Atlanta, or when Michelin Tires decided to build a plant in Greenville, South Carolina, the entire local economy picked up. Business improved for all the local residents, from dentists to dry cleaners, and job growth expanded.

Recessions can be local or national in scope, but they all affect real estate. As economies are cyclical, so is real estate.

Sometimes cycles become even more extreme than is justified by economic conditions, however, and the boom phase becomes truly manic. Periods of substantial overbuilding will negatively affect real estate owners, in some markets more than others. Of course, it's not just real estate that's cyclical. You've seen manic cycles in the stock market. During bull market conditions, investors often throw caution to the wind. New York City's shoe-shine operators and taxi drivers hand out stock tips, and cocktail party chatter and Internet discussion groups are replete with details of the latest killing on Wall Street—that is, until the music stops.

When real estate is booming, there is—shall we say—"irrational exuberance," but the exuberance isn't limited to investors. When real estate prices, rents, and operating income are rising rapidly, developers, syndicators, venture-fund managers, and even lenders want a piece of the action. The traditional use of debt to leverage real estate investments only exacerbates the situation. This was the scenario that commenced in the mid-1980s. Investors were buying up apartments at furious rates—individually, through syndications, and through limited partnerships. Developers were building everywhere. The banks and savings and loans were only too eager to provide the necessary liquidity to drive the boom ever higher. Even Congress got into the act, passing legislation to encourage real estate investment by allowing property owners to shelter other income with depreciation expenses and allow faster depreciation write-offs.

Eventually, and not surprisingly, apartments, office buildings, shopping centers, and other property types all over the nation became overbuilt, and property owners had to contend with depression-like conditions for several years thereafter.

While there is evidence that greater discipline and more accessible information is helping to moderate these cycles, as we'll discuss later, the bottom line is that some cyclicity is inevitable. In such times, investors must repeat to themselves, "This, too, shall pass." The value in a quality building in a good location will never disappear.

THE PROPERTY SECTORS

There's such a wide assortment of "REITized" properties that it's hard to know where to begin. There are apartment buildings, shopping centers, office buildings, industrial parks, factory outlet centers, health care facilities, and—you name it, it's out there. All these properties are owned by REITs and all have specific advantages, risks, idiosyncrasies, and cycles that set them apart from the others. The difficulty for the investor is deciding how much weight to give to each factor when trying to evaluate them. The pie chart at the beginning of this chapter shows the percentages of the REITs' aggregate market value represented by the different sectors of REIT properties as of December 31, 2004. As you'll see, there's a veritable feast of offerings.

APARTMENTS

The past 10–15 years have been witness to a virtual explosion in the number of publicly traded apartment REITs. Before the 1993–94 binge of new REIT public offerings, there were only four major apartment REITs: United Dominion, Merry Land, Property Trust of America, and South West Property Trust. By late 1996, that number had grown to at least thirty residential equity REITs, each with a market cap of more than $100 million; many of these have continued to grow in size, while others have been merged with other REITs. These REITs own and manage apartment communities in various geographical areas throughout the United States. Some have properties located only in very specific areas, while others own

WHAT IS A "CAP RATE"?

CAP RATE (capitalization rate) refers to the unleveraged return expected by a buyer of a commercial real estate property, expressed as the anticipated cash flow return (before depreciation) as a percentage of the purchase price. For example, paying $1 million for a 7 percent cap rate property should produce an initial unleveraged return on the investment of $70,000 per year, before capital expenditures needed to keep the property competitive and attractive.

units in markets across the country. Archstone-Smith is even exploring the possibility of acquiring rental units in Europe. Some managements have specialized development skills that enable them to
build new properties in healthy markets where rents and occupancy
rates are rising quickly or where profitable niche markets exist.

Well-run apartments have, over the years, been able to generate
5–10 percent initial yields for their owners, and many such investments offer the prospects of substantial property value appreciation. Today, most "cap rates" range from 5–7 percent, depending
upon location, property quality, age, condition, condo conversion
potential, and supply/demand factors.

Apartment owners do well when the economy is expanding
because of the resulting new jobs normally created and the rise
in the formation of new households. Relatively high interest rates
on home mortgages tend to help apartment owners, as this makes
single-family dwellings less affordable. Another very important factor for apartment owners is the rate of construction of new units
in the local area. Such competing properties, if built when demand
for apartment space is slowing, can force the owners of existing
units to reduce rents or to offer concessions, and often result in
lower occupancy rates.

Inflation also determines an apartment owner's economic fortunes, since inflation can cause higher operating expenses for
everything from maintenance to insurance to loan interest, which
cannot normally be passed along to the tenant. But inflation is a
double-edged sword. It can hurt on the way up, as expenses escalate.
However, owners of newly constructed apartment communities will
need to charge higher rents because of inflated construction costs,
and owners of existing units can then, as the new buildings become
fully occupied, raise their own rents. Eventually, as land costs and
inflation increase further, new construction may no longer even be
profitable. At some point, however, the economy will slow, and the
cycle will have run its course.

Condominium ownership has always been a competitive issue
for apartment owners, especially as mortgage interest, but not rent,
is deductible from taxable income. The "condo threat" varies in
scope from time to time, but is more pronounced during periods
of low mortgage rates. "Condomania" hurt apartment owners from

2003 through 2005, but rental growth had again commenced by early 2005.

Apartment REIT investors need to be mindful of certain risks. Even if the national economy is doing fine, the regional or local economy can drop into a recession, or worse, causing occupancy rates to decline and rents to flatten or even fall. This will be more of an issue for apartment REITs that focus on narrow geographical areas. Overbuilding can occur, especially where land is cheap and available to developers and the entitlement process is easy. Poor property management, including a failure to respond quickly to changing market forces, can also result in a general deterioration of the value or profitability of apartment assets.

Fortunately, these adverse developments rarely occur overnight, and vigilant apartment REIT owners will usually be able to spot negative trends early enough to react to them without significant financial damage. The trick, of course, is to be able to distinguish a temporary blip from a long secular decline.

As an additional safety measure, the well-diversified REIT owner will normally own several apartment REITs in order to spread the risk over many geographical areas and management teams.

During the late 1980s and early 1990s, earning reasonable returns from apartment ownership was difficult. The loan largesse of the banks and S&Ls and the real estate limited partnerships and other syndicators had sharply accentuated the boom phase. Hapless investors put large amounts of capital into new construction, only to have many buildings fall into the hands of the Resolution Trust Corporation (RTC). Rents fell, and free rent was offered to attract tenants. Occupancies declined, and market values diminished.

Eventually, beginning in 1993–94, the supply-demand imbalance began to right itself as the economy strengthened, and very few new units were built. By 1995, rents were rising once more, and, by the end of the following year, occupancy levels were back over 90 percent. Occupancy rates remained firm and market rents rose steadily throughout the rest of the decade, but softened beginning in 2001 due to the national recession. Weak job growth and competition from single-family housing, spurred by low mortgage rates, negatively impacted the profitability of apartment REITs until the cycle bottomed in late 2004.

Assuming a reasonably healthy economy and steady job growth, apartment ownership looks as though it will continue to be rewarding for investors, with occasional blips in local markets and subject to recurring real estate cycles. New construction has generally not been exceeding demand, and remains below the peak levels of the 1980s; demand for single-family homes and condos may, by siphoning off tenants, be more of a threat than excessive supply. However, unlike owners of other property types, apartment owners will tend to benefit from moderately rising interest rates, which reduce demand for single-family housing. Apartment owners in most areas should be able to get, over time, average annual rent increases of 2–3 percent, while expenses generally rise with inflation. If management is capable, apartment ownership and operation will continue to be a good, steady business.

RETAIL

The various retail-sector REITs behave somewhat differently from one another, and each retail sector should be considered on its own merits.

◆ **Neighborhood shopping centers.** For many years, before the advent of major regional shopping malls, shoppers bought everything locally at the small stores on Main Street or in downtown shopping areas. That was then; this is now. Over the last thirty years, major malls have sprung up from Maine to California, equipped with piped-in music, elevators, food courts, and enclosures to ward off the elements. These malls offer apparel, shoes, cameras, CDs, and software—just about anything a shopper might wish for. In an even more recent trend, discount megastores, such as Wal-Mart, Target, Home Depot, and Costco, started spreading across the country. Although the neighborhood shopping center has lost a lot of business to these megacompetitors, Americans still love their conveniences, and proximity is a great time-saver. For certain run-in-and-run-out errands, such as grocery shopping, picking up drug prescriptions, dry cleaning, and shoe repair, most people don't want to be bothered with a mall or a mega-store.

A desirable neighborhood shopping center is usually anchored by one or two major stores—most often a supermarket and a drug-store—and contains a number of additional stores that offer other basic services and necessities. As a result, these centers tend to be almost recession-proof and not significantly affected by national or regional slowdowns. The property owner charges a minimum rent to the tenants, and the lease is often structured to contain fixed "rent bumps" that increase the rental obligation each year. In addi-tion, or in lieu of fixed rent bumps, the lease may contain "over-age" rental provisions, which result in increased rent if annual sales exceed certain minimum levels. Often "triple-net" leases are signed, which make expenses like real estate taxes and assessments, repairs, maintenance, and insurance the responsibility of the tenant.

Some question whether retail properties have been overbuilt. According to data compiled by Bear Stearns, there were 20.2 square feet of retail real estate for every man, woman, and child in the U.S., up from 18.1 in 1990 and 13.1 in 1980. According to Marc Halperin, of Federated Investors in New York, "The U.S. market is massive-ly over-stored." Despite a growing economy and rising consumer spending in the U.S., a significant number of major retailers either filed bankruptcy proceedings or otherwise closed stores in recent years. Yet, despite the very competitive retail landscape, occupancy and rental rates have held up well, even during the 2000–2002 reces-sion—and retailers continue to demand quality space.

Retail real estate owners, of course, face a number of recurring challenges. The retail environment remains very competitive, and the prospect of more retailer failures, store closings, and consolida-tions remains a concern. And the continual in-roads being made by Wal-Mart and other powerful discounters upon supermarkets and other traditional stores, as well as the threat from Internet retailers, is always a worry. If more trouble lies ahead for retail real estate owners, should investors shun the sector? Not at all. We have seen that the resilient American consumer is very diverse in his or her shopping tastes, and likes to patronize a number of different stores and partake of many divergent product offerings. A key element for the investor, however, is location. A well-located shopping center, offering an interesting array of vendors, products, and services, will continue to thrive. If one or a few stores underperform (or just cannot make it), the owner of an attractive and well-located center will be able to find new replacement tenants that can attract shoppers.

Furthermore, if I may digress a bit, the cyclical nature of real estate—whether retail, residential, or otherwise—demonstrates an important irony of REIT investing:

Throughout many—if not most—periods in REITs' history, very strong property markets have proved difficult for growth-oriented REITs while poor markets have proven a boon.

Strong markets often eventually lead to overbuilding—which heightens competitive conditions and can depress operating income for up to several years into the future. Weak and troubled markets, conversely, offer unusual external growth opportunities. Because financially solid REITs frequently have far better access to reasonably priced capital during weak markets than do other prospective buyers, they may have the ability to buy properties with good long-term prospects at bargain-basement prices. Of course, the extent of the opportunities presented during major market downturns must be weighed against prospective declines in a REIT's cash flows from its *existing* properties. The quality of a REIT's management and its access to capital, while always important, are particularly critical during times of overbuilt markets or depressed economic conditions. Difficult times create the most opportunities for those who can take advantage of them.

◆ **Regional malls.** If neighborhood shopping centers provide the basics, large regional malls provide greater choice and luxury. From candles to chocolates, the mall has almost anything you can imagine. The concept of going to the mall is that shopping is not necessarily related to need; it is a *recreational* activity.

The economics of malls are very different from those of neighborhood shopping centers. Rent payable by the tenant is higher, but so are the dollar volumes of sales per square foot. Despite higher rent, a retailer can do very well in a mall because of the high traffic and larger sales potential per store. Because of higher overhead, however, stores that can't generate strong sales can quickly run into trouble, and so there is a premium on the mall owner's finding and signing leases with the most successful retailers. Some mall REITs own nationally renowned supermalls, containing more than 1 million square feet, where rental rates are high (more than $40 per square foot) and sales per square foot can reach well in excess of $500. Other owners have found success in smaller malls, which are usually located in less densely populated cities, where rental rates are close to $20 per square foot and sales per square foot don't get much above $250–$300. In spite of the entertainment-related activities they now offer, malls are truly in the retail business. Their success depends upon keeping their malls attractive and exciting for shoppers, leasing to successful retailers who can attract the fickle and demanding customer, and upon the overall strength of the national, regional, and local retail economies.

 **Mall REITs are relatively new, and were unavailable to REIT investors until 1992.**

Before 1992, malls were owned only by large, private real estate organizations and by institutional investors; there was no way a REIT investor could own a piece of the great "trophy" shopping properties of America. However, between 1992 and 1994, the large shopping-mall developers such as Martin and Matthew Bucksbaum, Herbert and Melvin Simon, and Alfred Taubman "REITized" their empires by going public as REITs. There are now nine REITs that own and operate regional and super-regional shopping malls.

Are malls and the REITs that own them good investments? Before we tackle this question, let's first take a quick look at some mall history. The 1980s were the golden years for the regional mall. Women were launching their careers in record numbers, and they had to buy clothes for the workplace. Baby boomers were spending their double incomes like giddy teenagers. Tenant sales rose briskly, the major retailers *had* to have space in all the malls, and mall owners could increase rental rates easily. Malls were truly attractive investments, and most large property-investing institutions wanted to own them.

By the early 1990s, however, this great era of consumerism stalled, thanks to the same recession that knocked President George Bush (the elder) out of office and created waves of corporate restructuring. Wage gains were hard to come by, fears of layoffs were rampant, and consumer confidence declined. "Deep discount" became the American consumer's rallying cry. Further, on a longer-term basis, the baby boomers suddenly began to consider the prospect of their own retirements and decided that investing in mutual funds was at least as important as buying Armani suits.

These developments took their toll on mall owners and their tenants until the mid-1990s. But, sales again rose briskly in the latter part of the last decade, driven by full employment, good wage gains, and a buoyant stock market, only to slow again in 2001 with the onslaught of another recession. However, low interest rates and some well-timed tax cuts soon restored consumer confidence, and mall sales and occupancy rates were trending higher again. Malls have thus proven to be quite resilient, notwithstanding their continual dependency upon the health of the American consumer.

Another issue for mall REITs has been the extent of their external growth opportunities. REITs can generate "external" profit growth (in addition to increased revenues from owned properties) by developing or acquiring additional properties. However, there are few opportunities through development, as most of the best locations for malls have already been exploited. Mall REITs have been buying independently owned malls (and even other mall REITs) over the last several years, but these opportunities appear to be waning as REITs become the dominant owners of this property type. So, must REITs rely primarily upon internal growth, that is, revenue improvements within each mall through increases in tenants' rents, increasing occupancy rates, and "specialty retailing" via kiosks at the malls, in order to create substantial increases in cash flows? And, if so, does this make mall REITs the slowest growers in the REIT industry? Should REIT investors forget mall REITs altogether and look for better prospects elsewhere?

No. Reports of the malls' demise (or, perhaps, their obsolescence) have been greatly exaggerated, and they have more lives than the proverbial cat. Since the cost of building a new mall will easily reach $100 million or more, overbuilding within a given geographical area has rarely been a major concern. This reduces risk and provides for very reliable and predictable cash flows.

Another advantage of mall ownership is that many major retailers continue to rely on malls for most of their total sales. It's significant that, despite the widely heralded problems of many retailers over the last decade, malls' occupancy rates have been holding steady and recently have even been increasing. Although the large department stores' performance has been disappointing in recent years, which has created a wave of industry mergers and consolidations, most profits of mall owners come from smaller "in-line" specialty stores that have generally performed much better. And while there are always retailers who disappoint, capable mall owners historically have been able to reconfigure retail space and bring in new tenants to meet changing consumer demands.

Simon Property Group and other mall owners have been adding entertainment venues to their malls, attracting such new tenants as theaters, restaurants, family entertainment, and other special attractions. "Specialty leasing" via in-store kiosks is another good revenue source. Mills has been developing new forms of shopping malls that emphasize food and entertainment. The mega-mall near Minneapolis–St. Paul, known as The Mall of America, announced plans to double in size, but with more than 50 percent of the new space being devoted to entertainment providers. Many shoppers now come as much for the entertainment as for the wide variety of specialty shops.

Since mall owners have taken their companies public as REITs in the early 1990s, investors have learned that the mall is a very stable and predictable property type. Malls have had to deal with numerous challenges, including the increased numbers of working spouses who no longer spend their days shopping, periodic retailer bankruptcies, the ups and downs of the apparel industry, problems of the major department store chains, inroads being made by the big-box discounters, and the advent of e-commerce. A more recent challenge is the "lifestyle" center, which is usually smaller, open-air, more easily accessible, and entertainment oriented (some mall owners have even been developing these properties themselves). But the best mall owners are nothing if not imaginative, and they have been able to keep their malls attractive to both important retailers and the shopping public. Occupancy rates have been very stable, rents continue to rise, and underperforming tenants are replaced with better-performing retailers and new retailing concepts.

A recent trend in retail real estate is that a significant number of retailers are diversifying away from the traditional retail formats they have long used, and are experimenting with others. Thus, Barnes & Noble, Sak's, and other traditional mall tenants are experimenting with lifestyle centers, and well-known discounters such as Wal-Mart and Target are considering (and accepting) invitations to become mall tenants. Simon has been looking for ways to encourage outlet center retailers to take space in their malls, and for mall tenants to lease space in the Chelsea outlet centers which Simon acquired in 2004. This new trend is due to changing consumer preferences, increasing competition among developers, and the needs and preferences of both retailers and retail real estate owners, all of which have been influenced by the waning popularity of the traditional department store.

A related trend is that the lines between different types of retail formats are becoming less clear and defined. "No longer can you look at a tenant and say, 'That's someone that goes into a mall,'" says Gwen MacKenzie, vice president of retail investment for Sperry Van Ness, commercial real estate advisors. "All retailers and landlords are playing. There's a lot of blurring going on." Indeed, some believe that the traditional concept of a mall as an enclosed space containing several department store "anchors" and many smaller shops, with a handful of restaurants, is a relic of the past. According to Friedman, Billings, Ramsey REIT analyst Paul Morgan, just three of the thirty-seven major mall projects opening in 2004 and 2005 were traditional, enclosed regional malls. The rest were lifestyle, hybrid, or mixed-use projects. Mall REIT management teams are very much aware of this trend, and are seeking to turn it to their advantage.

The better-managed mall REITs, aided by selective acquisitions and developments and the use of debt leverage, should be able to deliver, on a long-term basis, 4–6 percent FFO growth—at or slightly above the long-term FFO growth prospects of the entire REIT industry. Despite the occasional bumps in the road, mall REITs should be solid performers in the years ahead.

◆ **Factory outlet centers.** If neighborhood shopping centers provide the necessities, and malls provide luxuries and lifestyle, what's left?

Factory outlet centers have been around for many years, but began a wave of new popularity in the early 1990s. These centers' primary tenants are major manufacturers, such as Liz Claiborne, Polo Ralph Lauren, Brooks Brothers, Crate & Barrel, Williams-Sonoma, and Donna Karan. The centers are normally located some distance from densely populated areas, primarily because the manufacturers don't want to compete with their own customers, such as the mall retailers.

While most outlet centers' tenants are manufacturers who normally sell to the major retailers, the outlet center allows them to also sell directly to the public at cut-rate prices. The theory is that they sell overstocked goods, odd sizes, irregulars, or fashion ideas that just didn't click. The goods, priced at 25–35 percent below retail, often move quickly.

Although the industry expanded rapidly throughout much of the 1990s (GLA, or gross leasable area, increased from 18.3 million feet in December 1988 to 55.4 million feet by December 1997, according to *Value Retail News*), growth has flattened considerably since then. GLA was 55.3 million feet at the end of 2001, representing just 3 percent of U.S. general merchandise sales. Shoppers, it seems, are most interested only in outlet centers that offer popular brand-name merchandise at very attractive prices, and in good locations. They can afford to be more demanding due to the proliferation of discounters such as Wal-Mart, Target, and Ross. As a result, only two outlet center REITs developed successful track records (several others fell by the wayside), and one of them, Chelsea Property Group, was acquired by Simon Property Group in late 2004; this leaves only Tanger Factory Outlet Centers to occupy this small niche. Nevertheless, outlet centers remain a viable property type, and tenants are still attracted to them due to their low occupancy costs (which are generally 8–9 percent of tenant sales compared with approximately 12 percent for the typical mall), the prospects of selling excess inventory to price-sensitive consumers in an efficient manner, and as a way of expanding brand-name recognition.

One other retail format should be mentioned. In recent years, the American shopper has seen the rise of the powerful discounter, perhaps typified by Wal-Mart, Target, and Home Depot, which utilize "big-box" formats of very large size, for example, 100,000–200,000 square feet of space per store. These tend to be stand-alone properties, although they are sometimes clustered in a group as "power centers," and often specialize in one type of product, such as consumer electronics (e.g., Circuit City or Fry's). Each property is occupied by a single tenant.

REITs traditionally have not specialized in this property type, perhaps because many of these large discounters have traditionally owned their own stores; for example, at the end of 2003, only 7 percent of Target's 1,125 stores were leased. A few REITs, however, have been successful in this niche, including Developers Diversified Realty, whose four largest tenants include Wal-Mart, Target, Lowe's Home Improvement, and Home Depot. These properties are characterized by long-term leases, which generate stable and predictable cash flows for the property owners, but often lack significant opportunities for increased rents.

REIT investors who like this sector of retail real estate should look for REIT management teams with substantial experience in this property type, and with the ability to develop new properties for typical big-box tenants. Also, as institutional investors tend to like this property type for its consistent and stable cash flows, REITs that have the ability to form joint ventures with such investors can create additional value for shareholders through the receipt of fee income.

OFFICES AND INDUSTRIAL PROPERTIES

Office buildings and industrial properties are often grouped together in REIT discussions. While many of their economic characteristics are very different, they are the primary types of properties leased to businesses that do not cater to individual consumers. In that respect they are very different from apartments, retail stores, self-storage facilities, manufactured-home communities, or even health care institutions. In addition, some of the REITs in this sector own both office buildings and industrial properties.

◆ **Office buildings.** Office buildings are normally a very stable property group; after all, millions of employees who provide service to customers and clients must have an office somewhere. But due to the long lag time between beginning construction of a major office building and its completion, overbuilding in this sector can be a real problem for investors. As much as overbuilding was a problem for apartments in the late 1980s, it was far worse for office properties, with vacancy rates rising to more than 20 percent in some major markets. Vacancy rates rose to these high levels again more recently, due to a significant contraction in office space required by tenants. This sector takes longer to turn around than apartments, due in part to the long lease terms. If all that weren't enough bad news, there is also the fact that office leases normally have fixed rental rates, with perhaps a small annual rental step-up, tied to an inflation index such as the Consumer Price Index. As these leases run for much longer terms than do apartment leases, declining market rental rates resulting from overbuilding or a lack of demand for space can affect owners' cash flows for longer periods as rents are "rolled down" to the new lower rent levels upon lease expiration. Increased tenant concessions exacerbate the problems encountered during weak economic periods.

Through the mid-1990s, as older, higher-rate leases expired, many building owners saw their cash flows diminished by the newer and lower lease rates, even apart from losses due to higher vacancy rates. This happened again in almost all office markets from 2001 through 2005, as many leases were signed in 1999–2000 at very high rental rates. Thus, periodic bouts of overbuilding and sudden but unforeseeable reductions in demand for office space have made the office property sector deeply cyclical.

As noted above, a problem unique to the office sector is the long lag time between obtaining building permits and final completion. Once the development process has begun, even if the builder or lender realizes that there is no longer sufficient demand for that new spiffy office building, it is often too late to stop the process.

An important question mark for owners of office buildings, as well as REIT investors, is where businesses will choose to locate. Until fairly recently we witnessed a drift to the suburbs, rural areas, and even to states not known for their central business districts. Tenants were lost to such hot areas as Oregon, Utah, Arizona, North Carolina, Tennessee, Florida, and some parts of Texas—not only to improve the executives' and employees' quality of life, but also to take advantage of lower taxes, lower operating costs, and cheaper labor. More recently, however, we've seen a migration to the nation's "twenty-four–hour cities" such as New York, Boston, Washington, D.C., and San Francisco. But will the terrorist attacks of September 11, and the fear of further acts of terrorism, cause businesses to want to relocate, again, away from skyscrapers in the big cities? Thus far we have seen no evidence of this, but the crystal ball remains cloudy.

Rental space and the prices that can be charged for it are, like most things, governed by the laws of supply and demand. During the 1990–91 economic slump when office jobs declined, net office space absorption nationwide was still positive, indicating an over-supply of space, not a lack of demand. Investors and lenders shut off the capital spigots, and there was very little development of new office buildings until office rents and occupancy rates firmed up in the mid-1990s. The moderate increase in supply of new buildings was readily absorbed by increasing demand, and the office markets were in equilibrium through the end of the decade. In a few hot markets, such as the San Francisco Bay Area, rents spiked in 1999 and 2000, stimulated in part by a flood of technology-driven new capital. However, absorption turned negative in 2001, for the first time, due to large job losses and the recession—the culprit this time was insufficient demand for office space, while existing lessees returned unwanted space back to the market in the form of sub-lease space. These adverse conditions remained in effect until 2005, when they began to stabilize; the poor supply-demand conditions required virtually all office owners to spend large sums for leasing commissions and to fund capital improvements in order to attract tenants.

There has been much debate over the issue of whether it's more profitable, on a long-term basis, to own low-rise suburban office buildings in rapidly growing cities such as Dallas, Atlanta, Phoenix, and Denver, or whether the office owner will do better with large high-rise (or even trophy) properties in major cities such as New York or Boston. The costs of construction and opera-tion are much lower for the first type, and capital expenditures for tenant improvements upon signing a new lease will also be lower. And, with a steady influx of new businesses and increasing job growth, it's often not been terribly difficult to replace vacating tenants. Rents, of course, will be lower, but so will the investment and maintenance costs, and obsolescence is likely to be less of a risk.

Proponents of major central business district (CBD) office buildings in America's most important cities claim that the high land and construction costs and difficulty of obtaining building entitlements in these crowded urban areas make it less likely that such assets will suffer the bane of real estate owners: overbuilding. They argue that this advantage, together with the preference of many companies for a presence in prestigious locations in "high-barrier-to-entry" markets, will ensure that rental rates and cash flows will grow at an above-average rate over time. These proponents had the upper hand in this argument during much of the 1990s, due to rental spikes in several major metropolitan markets, but rents began falling sharply in many of them in 2001, as well as in suburban markets, as demand dropped suddenly. The one thing that seems clear is that rental rates can be volatile in *any* office market, and owners' prospects will depend upon new supply, the level of demand for space, macroeconomic issues, and other factors.

Office REITs comprise a significant portion of the REIT universe, and they belong in every diversified REIT investor's portfolio. Although the sector can be volatile, as noted earlier, as well as being subject to deep and prolonged real estate cycles, a good quality building located in a healthy business market will be attractive to tenants if it's well-maintained and the owner provides the requisite services. Long-term leases at fixed rental rates tend to act as a cash flow cushion during economic downturns, and can usually be renewed at higher rates upon expiration—assuming a reasonably healthy economy and a lack of overbuilding. Rental roll-downs do occur at times, but the long-term trend for office rents has been up. Rents may be expected to rise, on average, with inflation, which can generate reasonably good returns for the office owner, including, of course, the office REIT.

Investors should remember that since the sector is very cyclical, they should keep a close eye on long-term trends in office building supply and demand.

◆ **Industrial properties.** An industrial building can be freestanding or situated within a landscaped industrial park and can be occupied by one or more tenants. It has been estimated that the total square footage of all industrial property in the United States is approximately 10 billion square feet, of which about half is owned by the actual users. Ownership is highly fragmented, and the public REITs own only about 1 percent of all industrial real estate. Industrial properties include:

◆ Distribution centers
◆ Bulk warehouse space
◆ Light-manufacturing facilities
◆ Research and development facilities
◆ Small office, or "flex," space for sales, or administrative and related functions

Ownership of industrial properties has generally provided stable and predictable returns, particularly in relation to office properties. According to *Industrial REIT Peer Group Analysis,* a research report published in June 1996 by Apogee Associates, LLC, approximately 80 percent of tenants renew their leases, and default rates are low. The report goes on to say that demand for industrial space has exceeded the demand for office space since 1981. Rents have generally grown slowly but steadily at a rate equal to or better than office properties, having declined, overall, only during the early 1990s, when this sector had its own overbuilding problem, and in 2001–2004, when a fall-off in demand created an excess supply of space. Vacancy rates, according to the report, have historically been lower than those of office properties. The long-term norm for industrial property vacancy is approximately 7 percent but is higher during recessionary periods; industrial property vacancy rates rose to over 10 percent in the period 2002–2004.

The industrial property market has had a good track record of being able to quickly shut down the supply of new space as soon as the market becomes saturated.

One big advantage of the industrial building sector is that, since it doesn't take long to construct and lease these units, there is a faster reaction time than in some of the other sectors, and consequently there generally has not been excessive overbuilding. A significant portion of new space is built in response to demand from new or existing users. "Built-to-suit" activity has thus been an important contributor to new development in this sector.

Hamid Moghadam, CEO of AMB Property Corp., believes that speed and cost-effectiveness are becoming essential criteria for industrial space users. He believes that goods will move from manufacturer to end-user at much more rapid rates, and that distribution facilities, principally in major transportation hubs, that offer the advantages of prime location and speed of movement will be much preferred by space users. If this is indeed a long-lasting trend, some portion of the older industrial facilities in the United States—primarily warehouses used principally for storage—may become less attractive to existing and prospective tenants, thus affecting future rental and occupancy rates.

Two of the largest industrial property REITs, ProLogis and AMB Properties, have been allocating a significant portion of their capital to foreign investments, including Europe, Asia, and Mexico. Their objective is to take advantage of customer relationships and to capitalize on increasing global trade and the need to modernize and consolidate distribution facilities.

The industrial property sector had been in equilibrium for a number of years, with new supply meeting demand, but showed weakness beginning in 2001 as a result of the recession that primarily impacted business and capital spending. Industrial property markets began to firm in 2004 as occupancy rates improved with increased space absorption, and rents began to increase in some markets by mid-2005.

Principal risks in this sector include declining economic and business conditions, dependence on the tenants' financial health, obsolescence, and, of course, overbuilding. While the $2 million–$10 million cost of developing an industrial property is not insignificant, it is low enough that merchant developers are often able to build spec buildings that may, in time, create an excess of available space.

A key advantage the industrial property sector owner enjoys is that, unlike the office, apartment, or retail sectors, this sector requires only modest ongoing capital expenditures to keep the buildings in good repair. Space demand has not been terribly volatile, and lease renewal rates have been high during most economic periods. Finally, industrial property REITs capable of developing new properties can often create substantial additional value for shareholders.

REITs that specialize in industrial sector properties can be very good investments, particularly if their managements have longstanding relationships with major industrial space users, and if they concentrate on strong geographical areas.

HEALTH CARE

Health care REITs specialize in buying and leasing various types of health care facilities to health care providers. Such facilities include skilled nursing facilities, "congregate" and assisted- and independent-living facilities, hospitals, medical office buildings, and rehabilitation/trauma centers. These REITs don't operate any of their properties themselves and thus maintain a very low overhead; they are leased to health care provider companies on a "triple-net" basis.

Health care REITs were launched in the late 1980s and did well for many years until hitting a rough spot from 1998 to 2000.

Health care REITs' revenues come from lease payments from the operators. There is generally a base rent payment or, for mortgage loans, an interest payment, and there are additional payments if revenues from the facility exceed certain preset levels or are based on an inflation index, such as the CPI. In this respect, the leases (or mortgages, as the case may be) are similar to those in the retail sector that provide for periodic rent increases.

In fact, however, the provisions of most health care leases are such that the facility owners have not traditionally enjoyed substantial increases in percentage rents on an annual basis; as a result, health care REITs have had to look to new property acquisitions or mortgage loans (and, to a limited extent, new developments) to fuel cash flow growth. Thus, access to the capital markets has been very important to these REITs. Unfortunately, this access—which had been strong for many years throughout most of the 1990s—was cut off beginning in 1999, resulting from a precipitous slide in the stock prices of the health care REITs that began early in 1998. This, in turn, was caused by financial problems experienced by a large portion of the lessees who operated the properties and paid rents to the REIT and by excessive development of assisted-living properties. Indeed, five of the seven largest publicly traded companies that operated skilled nursing and assisted-living facilities filed for bankruptcy by early 2000, due to a government-mandated reduction in payment for certain procedures performed for Medicare patients, coupled with excessive debt leverage.

Most of the health care REITs were forced to cut their dividends, although the strongest among them suffered only a flattening in their cash flow growth and a lack of access to equity capital. But by 2001, the stock prices of several health care REITs had improved to the point that they could again sell new shares, raising equity with which to make new investments.

Despite their modest internal growth prospects and their tenants' reliance upon government reimbursement in the skilled nursing subsector, health care REITs have certain favorable investment attributes that make them worth considering by those investors who are willing to accept lower growth rates as a trade-off for unusually high dividend yields. There is almost no new supply of skilled nursing facilities in the United States, and the supply of new assisted-living facilities has abated substantially in recent years. And, unlike virtually all other real estate types, the business is very recession-resistant. Although a substantial part of many health care REITs' revenues are derived, indirectly, from government reimbursement programs, most of them have diversified their investment portfolios away from skilled nursing facilities where government reimbursement is most problematic. Finally, the average age of the U.S. population continues to rise, generating the need for more health care services and facilities in which to provide these services.

The long-term negatives of an investment in this sector include a heavy reliance upon the capital markets to fund growth, the risks of adverse changes in government reimbursement programs, the financial health of the various operator/lessees, periodic overbuild-

WHAT TO LOOK FOR IN HEALTH CARE REITS

◆ Conservative balance sheets (which facilitate additional capital raising at rates that will generate profits from new investments)
◆ An emphasis on stable sectors, such as hospitals, skilled nursing facilities, assisted-living properties, and medical office buildings
◆ Diversification in both facility operators and geographical location
◆ Access to equity capital
◆ Capable management teams who watch their properties and operations carefully

WHAT TO LOOK OUT FOR IN HEALTH CARE REITS

◆ Adverse reimbursement legislation and regulations
◆ Single-use facilities with questionable land values
◆ Overbuilding in assisted-living facilities
◆ Increasing competition from lenders and other private investors

ing in the assisted-living sector, increased regulation of health care facilities and providers, and the ever-looming threat of class action suits and other litigation. Also, as most of the investment returns on health care REITs come from their dividend yields, they tend to be somewhat more sensitive to interest rate changes than the shares of other equity REITs.

The box above may be of use to investors when considering a health care REIT.

The long-term prospects for health care REITs depend on the stability and growth prospects for the U.S. health care industry and, in particular, the segments served by their lessees. Government reimbursement programs will continue to be important, as will new developments in the assisted-living and independent-living segments.

SELF-STORAGE

As anyone who's ever lived in one knows, there's one universal problem with apartments. It's stuff. Where do you put your stuff? Generally, there's no attic, no basement, and no private garage—and that means no storage. Well, that's where self-storage facilities come in.

Usually they're built on the edge of town, perhaps near the highway, or next to an industrial park. The units normally range from 5 × 5 feet to 20 × 20 feet. These facilities were developed experimentally during the 1960s and have slowly but steadily increased in popularity. They are rented by the month, allowing renters to store such items as personal files, furniture, and even RVs and boats. Even businesses occupying expensive office space use them to store items not needed regularly. They are particularly useful for those who are relocated on a regular basis by their employers, and by those who enjoy traveling across America in their recreational vehicles.

As recently as the mid-1990s it was believed that private individuals rented approximately 70 percent of the available space, with commercial users and military personnel accounting for most of the balance. However, while reliable statistics are unavailable, industry experts believe that commercial and industrial use may be approaching 50 percent of the total.

Self-storage was a mediocre investment in the late 1980s because of the same overbuilding problems that so bedeviled apartment, office, and other real estate owners at that time. The industry's health, however, recovered substantially in the 1990s, and occupancy and rental rates have improved.

The reasons for the recent recovery are twofold: Development of new units has moderated since the period of overbuilding, and the facilities are becoming more popular. From a longer-term perspective, these properties may also be benefiting from recent trends, such as a more mobile workforce and increased use of apartments and condos by new retirees.

Although industry-wide data have been difficult to obtain, estimated average occupancy rates nationwide are believed to have increased dramatically from 78 percent in 1987 to over 90 percent by early 1998. However, a significant number of new storage developments were built in response to more favorable industry conditions since then and, according to industry expert R. Christian Sonne, of Self Storage Economics, industry-wide occupancy in early 2004 had fallen to below 85 percent. However, by early 2005, according to Mr. Sonne, it had risen to approximately 87–88 percent. Rental rates have increased steadily over the last fifteen years. A typical 10×10 foot storage space rented for approximately \$45 per month in 1988. In 2004, according to Self Storage Economics, the average asking price for a space of that size was \$85 per month.

Absorption of space has been steady in this sector. The self-storage REITs experienced slower growth during the economic slowdown beginning in 2001, and had to provide increased concessions to attract new renters. However, industry conditions have firmed, beginning in the latter part of 2004. At the end of that year, there were five self-storage REITs, of which Public Storage was the largest.

Notwithstanding the growth of these major players, the industry is still highly fragmented and is dominated by many "mom-and-pop" owners. This, of course, presents substantial opportunities to the sector's publicly held REITs, which have more sophisticated management and greater access to capital for new acquisitions. Not only do the REITs have the opportunity to acquire properties at attractive returns, but the acquiring REIT can also target particular metropolitan markets to increase its physical presence and marketing effectiveness, often using television and radio advertising. Recently, however, property prices have risen and the REITs have been less active acquirers; data compiled by Self Storage Economics suggest that acquisition cap rates have fallen to the low- to mid-8 percent range, down from 10 percent several years ago. This has reduced acquisition volumes, and caused a modest increase in development activity. The long development and fill process of 2–3 years will dilute near-term earnings growth, but still promises attractive investment returns.

What about cycles? This sector is less affected than others by economic cycles, and many operators were able to increase rental rates even during the 1990–91 and 2001 recessions; however, lower levels of occupancy during economic contractions will normally require free rent and other concessions to attract renters.

There is a good case to be made for self-storage facilities being recession resistant since, in a recession, individuals as well as businesses cut costs by reducing the space they occupy. A reduction in living or office space often entails an increased need for storage space.

Still, as with any other investment, self-storage REITs aren't a sure thing. The largest risk, once more, is overbuilding, which hurt this sector when all real estate was hurting in the late 1980s. Costing only $3 million–$5 million apiece to build, self-storage facilities are not expensive, and, for this reason, supply can often exceed demand if financing is widely available for new projects. Weak economic conditions could also, at times, reduce discretionary spending and thus demand for the units.

That being said, internal and, to a more modest extent, external growth prospects appear to be favorable, and national or regional economic recessions are likely to be less of a problem for this industry than others.

HOTEL REITS

The hotel sector of the commercial real estate industry has been highly cyclical. Hotels were horribly overbuilt in the 1980s and into the early 1990s, but recovered strongly beginning in the 1993–94 time frame. Partly as a result of this recovery, between August 1993 and the end of September 1996, ten hotel REITs went public, raising almost $1.1 billion, and follow-on offerings raised significant additional proceeds. Nevertheless, more recent history has illustrated a key feature of this property type: It is prone to overbuilding. A large number of rooms were added in the late 1990s, from limited-service to luxury hotels, and this new supply took its toll in 2001 when room demand began to wane due to the recession and cutbacks in business spending. This negative trend was greatly exacerbated by the September 11 terrorist attacks, which caused consumers to shun travel. It wasn't until 2004 that the hotel industry began to recover. Of particular concern is that hotel cycles can be very deep and violent since room rates and occupancy levels can be very volatile and many operating costs cannot be pared back, while there are simply no long-term leases to protect owners' cash flows. This sector is not for the faint of heart. Nevertheless, profit growth for hotel owners can be spectacular in the early years of a recovery cycle, particularly if new construction levels are low.

Investors in this sector have also had to contend with some conflicts of interest issues. Although under the REIT Modernization Act a hotel REIT may form a taxable subsidiary to lease hotels from the REIT—potentially a very significant benefit to shareholders—day-to-day hotel management must be performed by an outside company. Some management companies have been owned or controlled by the REIT's major shareholders and executive officers, which creates obvious conflicts. However, the largest issues have arisen in the past when the companies leasing the REIT's hotel properties have been sold; in a number of such transactions, substantial premiums have been received by the REIT's controlling persons (as owners of the leasing company) but not shared with the REIT's shareholders.

Limited-service hotels are those that do not offer dining, conference services, or other amenities, and charge modest room rates. Upscale and luxury hotels, including those at convention destinations and vacation resorts, offer a full range of amenities for the business and leisure traveler and charge much higher rates; they are also more expensive to build, due to higher land costs, longer building periods, and higher construction costs. Extended-stay inns offer more amenities than limited-service hotels, and often cater to the business traveler on assignment who may need a room for extended periods. The performance of each of these hotel types will vary with supply and demand conditions, and the state of the economy. The luxury hotels did very well in the late 1990s, while limited-service hotels struggled with increasing amounts of new supply. However, in the early years of the twenty-first century, new supply in the upscale and luxury sectors (it takes more time for these properties to be completed), coupled with a recessionary economy beginning in 2001 and the tendency for lodgers to trade down during difficult economic times, caused the REITs which own limited-service hotels to perform somewhat better than their peers.

Whether investors should consider a hotel REIT depends upon their views of the economy, the level of new hotel construction, and their forecasts for spending and travel patterns of businesses and consumers—this sector is more economically sensitive than any other.

The substantial cutback in travel plans by both businesses and consumers beginning in 2001 put substantial pressure on occupancy rates and rental rates, leading to significant declines in cash flows for the hotel REITs and even numerous dividend cuts. The good news for hotel REIT owners today is that room demand has recovered, and the room supply situation is favorable: Most observers expected the new supply of rooms to increase at the rate of just 2–2.5 percent over the next several years, which should bode well for hotel owners as demand returns to higher pre-2001 levels.

MANUFACTURED-HOUSING REITS

Half a century ago, an enterprising landowner brought a number of trailers, together with their owners, to a remote spot out in the boondocks, semi-affixed them to foundations, and called the project a "mobile-home park." Many of today's modern "manufactured-housing communities," however, bear little resemblance to yesterday's mobile-home parks. The homes are now manufactured off-site, rarely leave their new home sites, and generally have the quality and appearance of site-built homes. According to the Manufactured Housing Institute (MHI), 131,000 manufactured homes were shipped in 2004, which amounted to 9.8 percent of all homes sold that year (including site-built homes).

In view of rapidly rising home prices throughout the United States, manufactured homes clearly help to satisfy America's need for affordable housing. The MHI has estimated that the average cost per square foot of a manufactured home is 10–35 percent less than a site-built home, depending on geographic location. However, off-site home manufacturers became somewhat exuberant in recent years and made too many of them—and lenders were too generous, lending to many who could not afford to keep up the payments. This led to a large wave of foreclosures, and a glut of used homes placed on the market. The result was falling new home sales and rising vacancy rates, which negatively impacted the manufactured-home community REITs. The situation, however, now seems to have stabilized, and demand for these homes is beginning to improve.

The quality manufactured-home community today looks something like a blend of a single-family-home subdivision and a nice apartment community. According to the MHI, a unit's average selling price was $54,900 in 2003, compared with $246,300 for a site-built home (or approximately $183,400 if the land cost is excluded). The residents own their own homes but lease the underlying land, typically at \$150–\$500 per month, from the owner of the community. MHI data suggest that typical terms of financing for new manufactured homes include a 5–10 percent down payment, and a loan term of 15–30 years, depending upon the buyer's credit profile, size of the home, and the type of loan. The homeowners have amenities such as an attractive main entrance, clubhouse, pool, tennis courts, putting greens, exercise room, and laundry facilities. Some of the communities have catered to seniors, while others focus on younger couples. According to the MHI, in 2004 there were approximately 10.5 million manufactured homes in the United States, in which approximately 22 million people resided.

Owners of manufactured-home communities enjoy certain advantages not available to owners of apartment buildings. First of all, the business is very recession resistant, in large part because of the low turnover rate. Next, the community owner's capital expenditures are limited to upkeep of the grounds and common facilities and do not require any maintenance on the homes themselves. What is particularly advantageous is that, because of the difficulties of getting land zoned for this type of property and the long lead time involved in filling a new community with tenant-owners, overbuilding has rarely been a problem. Providing space to users of RVs and campers may become an increasingly important source of additional income for the manufactured-home community REITs.

Problems of owners and operators of manufactured-home communities include occasional flare-ups of calls for rent control in some areas and the difficult and time-consuming nature of developing or expanding communities. And, similar to apartment owners, the lure of single-family site-built homes and condos, financed with low-interest mortgage loans, will always remain part of the competitive landscape.

Investors in manufactured-housing REITs should expect stable and predictable cash flows, modest internal growth from slowly increasing rents, and, over time, increasing dividends.

Low turnover and low maintenance with rental increases of 3–4 percent annually, together with modest debt leverage, provide reasonably good growth in operating income. Furthermore, because of the fragmented nature of manufactured-home community owner-ship throughout the United States, recurring acquisitions can add an additional avenue for growth.

OTHER PROPERTY SECTORS

There are also other, smaller property sectors that REIT investors might want to consider. "Triple-net lease" REITs own properties leased primarily to single tenants who pay for all maintenance expenses, property taxes, and insurance. The cash flow growth for these types of REITs is likely to be significantly lower than those in other sectors, but the risk is low if the properties are not built for specialty tenants and if the credit quality of the tenants is strong; the yields on these shares are also significantly higher than that of the typical equity REIT. Like health care REITs, their shares are more sensitive to changes in interest rates.

There are also other "specialty" REITs, including a movie theater REIT, two timberland REITs, an auto dealership REIT, a student housing REIT, and even a prison REIT. The unique investment characteristics and operating dynamics of these unusual property types need to be carefully considered by the investor, along with such factors as strength of management, balance sheet, growth prospects, and conflicts of interest. National Golf, a golf course REIT, experienced substantial difficulties a few years ago when the company that leased most of its properties got into financial trouble. I'm patiently waiting for the day when a cemetery REIT is organized, sold to investors on the basis of the aging of the U.S. population, the key attraction, of course, being that tenants will not be able to leave.

SUMMARY

◆ It's possible to invest in nearly every kind of real estate imaginable: apart-ment and manufactured-home communities, retail properties, office/industrial buildings, self-storage facilities, hotels, nursing homes, hospi-tals and assisted-living communities, timberland—even theaters and car dealerships.

◆ The phases of the real estate cycle are depression, recovery, boom, and overbuilding and downturn, and these cycles, along with changes in capi-tal flows, can affect REITs' performance and their stock prices.

◆ Some apartment REITs own units in specific geographical areas, while others have holdings throughout the United States.

◆ The principal retail real estate sectors behave differently from one another, and each must be considered separately.

◆ Mall REITs are relatively new on the REIT scene; they are very much in the retail business.

◆ Following the bad news of the early 1990s, office properties performed well until hit by the recession of 2001, but will recover as demand for office space recovers—there is only moderate new supply in most locations.

◆ The industrial property market has had a good track record of reacting quickly and shutting down the supply of new space as soon as the market becomes saturated.

◆ REITs that specialize in industrial sector properties can be very good investments, particularly if their management teams have longstanding relationships with major industrial-space users and concentrate on strong geographical areas.

◆ Health care REITs were launched in the late 1980s and have generally performed well, except for having encountered rough weather in 1998–99.

◆ Investors in health care REITs need to monitor the financial strength of the lessees, changes in reimbursement policies, and increased regulation.

◆ Self-storage was a mediocre investment in the late 1980s because of overbuilding. The industry's health, however, recovered substantially since 1990, and occupancy and rental rates also improved significantly.

◆ There is a good case to be made for self-storage facilities being recession resistant since, in a recession, individuals as well as businesses cut costs by reducing the space they occupy. A reduction in living or office space can mean an increased need for storage space.

◆ Hotel REITs have had periods of both substantial strength and major weakness; they represent aggressive investments because of their cyclicity and volatile room and occupancy rates.

◆ Investors in manufactured-housing REITs should expect stable cash flows and modest internal growth from slowly increasing rental income.

◆ Self-storage REITs, health care REITs, and manufactured-housing REITs are fairly recession resistant.

HISTORY
And Mythology

PART

I

CHAPTER

REITs:
MYSTERIES
AND MYTHS

T HERE'S NO QUESTION about it: In spite of their growing acceptance, there have been lingering mysteries and myths that REITs haven't been able to shake off. This chapter addresses these misconceptions and lays the fading myths to rest once and for all.

CHANGING ATTITUDES TOWARD REITS

For many years, REITs were regarded as odd and uninteresting investments. Even their unusual name—REIT—implied that the standard criteria applicable to most investments didn't apply to them. Bruce Andrews, the former CEO of Nationwide Health Properties, noted that the term *trust,* as in real estate investment trust, implies that REITs are oddities, that they are not like normal corporations whose shares are traded on the stock exchanges. One of the main reasons that REIT stocks were suspect for so long is that many people who traditionally invested in real estate didn't really understand—or trust—the stock market, while most people who invested in the stock market were uncomfortable with, or had little understanding of, real estate. REITs just didn't fit into either category and therefore fell between the cracks.

All this has finally changed. In October 2001, Standard & Poor's admitted the largest REIT, Equity Office Properties, with an equity market cap at that time of $12 billion, into the S&P 500 index. Equity Residential Properties Trust, the largest apartment REIT, was admitted soon thereafter, and at the end of 2004, there were seven REITs in the S&P 500. At the end of 2000, when the equity market cap of all REITs was $139 billion, many REIT observers believed that, within ten years, REITs' total market cap would reach $500 billion. Well, at the end of 2004, that figure had already exceeded $300 billion.

Of course, the growth in the REIT industry will wax and wane from time to time. And there are lots of good reasons why many investors might want to own real estate directly, not via an investment in a REIT. Nevertheless, the advantages of ownership through a REIT are very substantial, and the size of the REIT industry will continue to grow with increased investment by both individuals and institutions who appreciate REITs' liquidity, substantial information disclosure, and opportunity for wider diversification among property types and geographical locations. And, it seems, public scrutiny of some of the largest commercial property owners in the U.S., the REITs, may be causing real estate to become less cyclical and thus more valuable. Weakness in most real estate markets and property sectors from 2001 through 2004 resulted from a major slackening in demand due, in large part, to a national recession, a subsequent boom in single-family residences, and severe cutbacks of capital spending by businesses, not the overbuilding that's been the main culprit in prior real estate cycles. Perhaps operating in a fishbowl, as public REITs do, imposes substantial development discipline, which even carries over to the private markets.

THE BIAS OF TRADITIONAL REAL ESTATE INVESTORS

Traditionally, most real estate investors have chosen to put their money directly into property—apartment complexes, shopping centers, malls, office buildings, or industrial properties—and not in real estate securities like REITs. In other words, bricks and mortar, not stock certificates. Direct ownership historically has provided the opportunity to use substantial leverage, since lenders have traditionally been willing to lend 60–80 percent of the purchase price of a building. Leverage is a wonderful thing—when prices and rents are going up.

Since the Great Depression, real estate values pursued a profitable upward bias, notwithstanding a few potholes along the way. Appreciation of 10 percent on a building bought with 25 percent cash down would generate 40 percent in capital gains. In addition, owning a building directly provided the investor with a tax shelter, via depreciation expenses, for other operating income. As a result, real estate continued to appreciate and provide easy profits, and most real estate investors tended to focus on what they knew—direct ownership.

Many individual real estate investors harbored a distrust for public markets (REITs included), which they saw as roulette tables where investors put themselves at the mercy of faceless managers—or worse, speculators and day traders whose income depended on volatility. These investors saw REITs as highly speculative and wouldn't touch them.

Then, of course, there was institutional investment in real estate. Originally, institutional and pension funds earmarked for real estate were invested in properties either directly (where their own property managers and investment managers were retained), or through "commingled funds" in which big insurance companies and others used funds provided by various institutional investors to buy portfolios of properties. Who managed these properties, supervised their performance, and answered for their results? The same sort of real estate investors who, of course, didn't trust the stock market—or, if they had no such qualms about equities, didn't believe that the performance of REIT shares would match that of direct real estate investments.

Furthermore, since REITs are traded as common stocks, the result was—catch-22—that a decision to invest in REITs could be made only by the "*equities* investment officer" rather than the "*real estate* investment officer" of the institution or pension fund. The institutions' common stock investment funds were placed and monitored elsewhere. Furthermore, various investment guidelines often precluded the equities investment officers from investing in REITs—even if they knew about them and wanted to pursue this sector of the market. And why should they bother? After all, REITs have always been a very small sector of the equities market and were not included in the S&P 500 index until 2001.

A further discouragement has been volatility. Real estate investors have complained that REITs, even though traditionally less volatile than the broader stock market, nevertheless do fluctuate in price. However, to be fair, any asset fluctuates in price. With illiquid assets that were held, not traded (and by relying upon occasional appraisals), the private-fund managers could maintain the illusion that the values of their assets were "steady as a rock," despite the continuous ebb and flow of the real estate capital markets. Every asset fluctuates in value, but owners are sometimes unaware of these changing valuations until they try to sell the asset.

Finally, institutions buy and sell stocks in large blocks, and it's been only recently that REIT shares have had sufficient liquidity to attract institutional investors. In fact, one of the most oft-quoted reasons why pension funds have been reluctant to invest in REITs is their lack of liquidity. The REIT market was so thinly traded prior to 1993–94, when the size of the REIT market began to expand geometrically, that it would have been extremely difficult for an institution to accumulate even a modest position without disrupting the market for any particular REIT stock.

THE BIAS OF COMMON STOCK INVESTORS

What discouraged common stock investors from buying REITs? The flip side of the coin is that REITs' only business is real estate and stock investors didn't invest in real estate; they focused primarily on product or service companies. Real estate was perceived as a different asset class from common stock; this problem was particularly acute in the institutional world.

REITs have also been perceived as real estate mutual funds, and not as active businesses—a perception precluding REITs from being admitted to the S&P 500 until 2001. An IRS ruling at that time confirmed that REITs are active businesses, but old perceptions die hard.

In addition, the public perception—wrong as it was—was that REITs were high-risk but low-return investments. There were many investors who had bought construction-lending REITs and real estate limited partnerships in the 1970s and 1980s and gotten badly burned. These investors did not take the trouble to distinguish between these ill-fated investments and well-managed equity REITs.

Also, for years investors had been told that companies that paid out a high percentage of their income in dividends did not retain much of their earnings and therefore could not grow rapidly. Since, to most common stock investors, growth is the hallmark of successful investing, they didn't want to invest in a company that couldn't grow. Finally, some of the blame for lack of individual investors' interest in REITs can be laid at the feet of stockbrokers.

REITs for a long time were perceived as stocks by real estate investors, and as real estate by stock investors.

Until about fifteen years ago, most major brokerage firms did not even employ a REIT analyst. And, since individual investors generally bought individual stocks only when their brokers recommended them, the REIT story fell on deaf ears. Mutual funds have been popular for many years, but only a handful of mutual funds were devoted to REIT investments—and those did not advertise widely. Many of those investors who did their own research and made their own investment decisions quite likely felt that REITs were too much of an unknown territory for them to venture into. Even income investors, for whom REITs would have been particularly suitable, invested primarily in bonds, electric utilities, and convertible preferred stocks.

REITs, of course, given their favorable investment characteristics, were bound to be noticed sooner or later. They are gradually but inexorably becoming well known to real estate and common stock investors alike, and REITs' long period of being neglected is now ancient history. Interest in REIT stocks will ebb and flow with changes in investor fads and preferences, but they are now firmly recognized as strong and stable investments that help to diversify a broad-based investment portfolio.

THE MYTHS ABOUT REITS

In addition to—and sometimes because of—the other obstacles REITs have had to overcome, some myths exist, myths that in the past scared off all but the bravest investors. Although these myths were based on misunderstandings of the investment characteristics of REITs, they discouraged many would-be investors. Let's confront them, one by one.

MYTH 1

REITS ARE PACKAGES OF REAL PROPERTIES

This myth, which probably sprang from investors' experience with the ill-fated real estate partnerships of the late 1980s, may be the single most significant reason for REITs' failure in the past to attract a substantial investor following. Although at one time REITs may have been only collections of properties, or "real estate mutual funds," they are much more than that today.

 REITs are more than just portfolios of real properties.

Organizations that merely own and passively manage a basket of properties—whether they be limited partnerships, trusts, or even corporations—must contend with several specific investment concerns. Management is generally not entrepreneurial and thus is often unresponsive to small problems that can, if left unattended, develop into big problems. Also, management does not usually have its compensation linked to the success of the properties and therefore has no particular incentive to be innovative despite today's competitive environment. Often, there is no long-term vision or strategy for creating value for the investors. Finally, inefficient management rarely has access to attractively priced capital, making it difficult for the entity to take advantage of "buyers' markets" or attractive purchase or development opportunities. An investment in such a passive company, although perhaps providing an attractive dividend yield, offers little opportunity for growth or expansion beyond the value of the original portfolio.

Conversely, a large number of today's REITs are vibrant, dynamic real estate organizations first, and "investment trusts" second. They are far more than collections of properties. Their management is savvy and highly motivated by their own ownership stake and other equity incentives. They plan intelligently for expansion either in areas they know well or in areas where they believe they can become dominant players, and they frequently have access to the capital necessary for such expansion. They attempt to strengthen their relationship with their tenants by offering innovative and cost-efficient services. To categorize highly successful real estate companies, such as AMB Property, Alexandria, Archstone-Smith, Avalon Bay, Boston Properties, the "Equities," General Growth, Kimco, Home, Macerich, Reckson, SL Green, Simon, Taubman, Vornado, or Weingarten, to cite just a few examples, as just collections of properties, or "mutual funds of real estate," is to underestimate them seriously. Yet this myth still persists, even among some institutional investors.

MYTH 2

REAL ESTATE IS A HIGH-RISK INVESTMENT

It's amazing how many people believe that real estate (other than one's own home, of course) is a high-risk investment through which investors can be wiped out by tenant defaults or declines in property values. And, they surmise that if real estate investing is risky, then REIT investing also must be risky. Let's analyze risk here.

▦ Three essential determinants of real estate risk are leverage, diversification, and quality of management (including the assets and property locations chosen for ownership by such management).

◆ **Leverage.** Leverage in real estate is no different from leverage in any other investment: The more of it you use, the greater your potential gain or loss. Any asset carried on high margin, whether an office building, a blue-chip stock, or even a T-note, will involve substantial risk, since a small decline in the asset's value will cause a much larger decline in one's investment in it. However, because real estate historically has been bought and financed with a lot of debt, many investors have confused the risk of debt leverage with that of owning real estate.

▦ Although real estate investments have often been highly leveraged, it is the high leverage rather than the real estate that is the greatest risk.

In fact, one could argue that if lenders will lend a higher percentage of a real estate asset's value than the Federal Reserve will allow banks and brokers to lend on a stock investment, then real estate must be less risky than stock investments.

◆ **Diversification.** Again, the same rule that applies to other investments applies to REITs: Diversification lowers risk. People who would never dream of having a one-stock portfolio go out and buy, individually or with partners, a single apartment building or shopping center. Things happen—an earthquake, neighborhood deterioration, excessive building, a recession—and all of a sudden the building is sucking up money like a sponge. Never mind that

ONE COMMON MISCONCEPTION

WHEN ONE REIT encounters difficulty, investors sometimes rashly conclude that REITs as an asset class are very risky. Yet no one would condemn the entire stock market just because the price of one stock had collapsed.

a similar apartment building in another location is doing well, or that an office building upstate is raking in cash. Diversification should be the mantra of every investor.

◆ **Management quality.** Then, of course, there is the issue of management. Good management is crucial—but that is not only true in real estate. If you look around at major U.S. non-REIT corporations, you can see, for instance, the value of a Jack Welch to General Electric, or how Bill Gates's vision brought Microsoft to where it is today. Incompetent management can ruin a major corporation or a neighborhood candy store. Real estate, like all other types of investments, cannot simply be bought and neglected; it requires active, capable management. And good management teams are able to select real estate for acquisition and ownership that is likely to appreciate, not depreciate, over time. Despite this, many otherwise intelligent investors have bought apartment buildings, small offices, or local shopping centers, often in poor locations, and tried either to manage them themselves in their spare time or to give control to local managers who have little incentive to run the property efficiently. What happens? The apartment building or strip center does poorly, and the investor loses money and jumps to the wrong conclusion—that real estate is a high-risk investment.

MYTH 3

REAL ESTATE'S VALUE IS ESSENTIALLY
AS AN INFLATION HEDGE

Real estate is really nothing more than buildings and land, and, like all tangible assets (whether scrap metal, oil, or used cars), its value will ebb and flow with local, national, and even global supply and demand. However, inflation is only one factor that affects market prices; others are national and local economic conditions, interest rates, prices of—and return expectations for—other assets and investments, unemployment levels, consumer spending, levels of new personal and business investment, supply of—and demand for—space, government policies, and even wars.

Part of the reason for the real-estate-as-inflation-hedge myth may come from the fact that real estate happened to do well during the inflationary 1970s, while stock ownership during the same period was not as productive. This, quite likely, was a simple coincidence.

According to *Stocks, Bonds, Bills, and Inflation 1995 Yearbook,* published by Ibbotson Associates, equities have been very good inflation hedges over many decades. So has real estate. But the reality is that neither the real estate market nor the equity market is substantially better or worse than the other in this regard.

Yes, there are times when inflation *appears* to help the real estate investor by boosting the replacement cost of real estate, but such inflation can also increase operating expenses such as maintenance, other management costs, insurance, and taxes and thus restrain a property's net operating income growth, which could negatively affect its market value.

The value of a commercial building is determined essentially by three principal factors: the net operating income the owner derives, or is expected to derive, from the property; the multiple of that income that the buyer is willing to pay for it (which, in turn, is based upon a myriad of factors); and its replacement cost. And these factors fluctuate in response to various market forces; the expected rate of inflation is only one of those forces.

High inflation can positively or negatively affect rental rates and net operating income. A positive influence resulting from inflation, at least in the retail sector, can come from the higher tenant sales that normally result from increased inflation and higher prices on goods sold to consumers. Although these higher sales can translate into higher rents for property owners, this benefit will be short-lived if the retailers can't maintain their profit margins. If stores are not returning profits, it will be difficult for the owners to raise rents. Similarly, higher inflation can help apartment owners by increasing tenants' wages and thus their ability to afford higher rents, but only if wages are rising at least as rapidly as the price of goods and services.

When supply and demand are in balance, inflation may enable owners to raise rents because, as the cost of land and new construction rises, rents in new buildings will have to be high enough to cover these higher costs. If the demand is sufficient to absorb the new units that are coming into the market, owners of preexisting properties will often be able to take advantage of the new properties' "price umbrella" and charge higher rents. Real estate is not an effective hedge against inflation, however, when there is a large oversupply of competing properties.

Higher inflation rates can also have a *negative* effect on the value of real estate, certainly over the short term. The Federal Reserve acts as a watchdog for inflation, and, when there is a perceived inflationary threat, the Fed will raise short-term interest rates. Higher interest rates are meant to slow the economy, but interest rates that rise too high can strangle it, causing a recession. Once a recessionary economy exists, a property owner will have difficulty raising rents and maintaining occupancy levels, and therefore will not be able to generate higher net operating income.

Now for the second part of the property-value equation: the multiples of net operating income that buyers may be willing to pay. The price of a property is often determined by applying a multiple to its existing or forward-looking annual operating income (or by using its reciprocal, the cap rate), but the multiples (or the cap rates) don't always stay the same. There is an argument that buyers will pay more for, or accept a lower cap rate on, real property during inflationary periods. Since investors view real estate as a hard asset, like oil and other commodities, they may be willing to pay a higher multiple for every dollar of operating income if they perceive that accelerating inflation will lead to higher rents.

The counterargument is that cap rates may indeed be influenced by inflation, but in reverse. Higher inflation will often drive up interest rates, which in turn will increase the "hurdle rate of return" demanded by investors in a property, and have the effect of increasing the required cap rate and thus *decreasing* the price at which the property can be sold. Conversely, property values may rise even with no inflation whatever, as interest rates decline in a zero-inflation environment. Property values certainly increased in 2003–04 when interest rates and inflation were at very low levels. Consider the following example:

If the demand for apartment units in San Francisco exceeds the available supply of such units, rents will increase and the apartment building owner's net operating income will increase. Thus, one might think that the value of the apartment community would also rise. However, if this demand for apartment space has been fueled by an over-heated economy, which brings on higher interest rates, the cap rate applied by a potential buyer of the property to the net operating income might also rise, perhaps even causing a *loss* in value of the asset.

On the other hand, if the supply of apartment units in San Francisco exceeds the demand by renters, as was the case from 2001 to 2004, rents and net operating income may fall—but the value of the apartment community may nevertheless rise, due to a lower cap rate applied to that net operating income. And all of this has little to do with inflation.

It is likely that replacement cost for a real estate asset will rise during inflationary periods, but this alone won't increase the property's market value if the profitability of the asset falls short of buyers' requirements; it means only that new competing properties are unlikely to be built until market values exceed replacement cost.

Market factors like supply and demand, along with interest rates, are almost always more important than inflation in determining property value. REIT investors should focus more on market conditions and management ability than on inflation.

MYTH 4

DIFFICULT REAL ESTATE MARKETS MEAN
BAD NEWS FOR REIT INVESTORS

Real estate has at some times been a terrific investment and, at other times, a terrible investment. Right now, all available information suggests that real estate, as an asset class, will fare reasonably well through the rest of the decade.

A favorite observation among stock traders, after a long bear market that has finally turned around and moved up strongly, is "The easy money has already been made." Despite weak real estate markets from 2001 through 2004, property values held up well due to real estate's popularity as an asset class. And now, although a recovery is under way, it is unlikely that in most sectors of the real estate industry, property owners will be able to generate growth in rental rates and operating income much in excess of the rate of inflation, which is 2–3 percent annually. Some pockets of opportunity will always surface from time to time, but today most real estate is in "strong hands," and distressed sellers are scarce. Thus, the easy money has been made here, too.

The rapid industrialization and intense competition occurring today in North America, Europe, Asia, and Latin America seem to be major and perhaps long-lasting phenomena. U.S. companies must now go toe-to-toe with foreign competitors virtually everywhere in the world. This, in turn, requires U.S. businesses to be very cost-efficient. Downsizings, restructurings, outsourcing of jobs, and layoffs have been the result. Companies are finding it difficult to raise prices, and employees are finding it equally difficult to get significantly higher wages. The bottom line for real estate investors is that, as long as these competitive trends continue, and if excessive supplies of new developments do not trash real estate prices and create opportunities for bargain hunters, it will be difficult for them to generate returns above long-term norms.

Nevertheless, if real estate investors can obtain initial investment returns of 5–7 percent from property acquisitions and enjoy operating income growth in line with inflation, REITs should remain very solid investments—competitive with other asset classes. Furthermore, many REITS may, at times, be able to take advantage of opportunities presented by challenging real estate environments, just as they take advantage of opportunities in favorable environments.

Excellent managements view difficult conditions and tenant bankruptcies as opportunities. United Dominion went on a buying spree during the apartment depression of the late 1980s and early 1990s, while Apartment Investment and Management and Equity Residential bought huge amounts of undermanaged apartment communities several years later and spread their operating costs over a much larger number of units. Nationwide Health and Health Care Property bought defaulted nursing-home loans from the Resolution Trust Corporation (RTC) at 16–18 percent yields. Kimco Realty bought the properties, and even the leases, of troubled retailers and found new tenants willing to pay higher rents. A number of years ago, Weingarten Realty actually *increased* its occupancy rates during the Texas oil bust, as many tenants vacated half-empty locations and migrated to Weingarten's attractive shopping centers. More recently, in 1999 Cousins Properties bought The Inforum, a 50 percent-leased office building in downtown Atlanta, for approximately $70 million. It invested an additional $15 million in improvements and signed a new lease for about 30 percent of the building. Within approximately two years, it was earning a return of about 12.5 percent on the total investment. These are but a few examples of how lemons can be turned into lemonade by imaginative and capable real estate organizations with access to capital.

Conversely, it can also happen that a great real estate market is *bad* for REITs. For example, many REITs saw their profit growth "hit the wall" in the mid-1980s, when real estate prices were skyrocketing. Not only were properties simply not available at prices that would provide acceptable returns, but owners were also facing competition from new construction. Before anyone realized what was happening, the cycle moved into the overbuilt phase and cash flow growth slowed markedly.

As we'll see in more detail later, REITs can grow their profits both internally, through rising operating income, and externally, through property acquisitions and new developments. Poor real estate markets may create external growth opportunities if distressed sellers are numerous, but it doesn't always happen this way; there were few distressed sellers during the last real estate recession, and there were numerous buyers. One never knows how any particular real estate or capital market cycle will play out, but the point here is that strong REIT organizations with access to ample capital may be able to take advantage of opportunities often created by tough real estate markets. While cash flow growth would slow temporarily in response to such difficult rental markets, these REITs' ability, at certain times, to buy sound properties at cheap prices enables them to create substantial value for their shareholders.

The extent to which a well-managed REIT can avail itself of the opportunities presented in a down market depends upon the amount and cost of available capital, the depth of the market weakness, and the extent of competition from other buyers.

Some of the best investment opportunities arise when a company or even an entire industry is overlooked or misunderstood by the great mass of investors. Legendary investors Warren Buffett and Peter Lynch made their reputations not by buying the growth stocks that everyone else was buying, but rather by taking advantage of solid companies with undervalued stocks, often caused by investors' lack of patience or foresight. Buffett's investment in Wells Fargo Bank some years ago was but one example among many.

The same principle applies to REITs. REIT stocks are "all-weather" investments for diversified portfolios, but are particularly attractive when nobody wants to own them. Investors' past fears and hesitations had, for a long time, left these lucrative investments largely undiscovered and, therefore, undervalued. REITs have become more popular in recent years, but myths and misconceptions die hard, and one never knows when investors will again trash them for all the wrong reasons. Those who understand them are unlikely to follow scared sellers to the exits.

MYTH 5

REIT STOCKS ARE FOR TRADING

How often have you read in a financial magazine or newspaper, "Is now the time to get into (or out of) REITs?" It seems that we are always being hit with that inane question. Why is it asked so often? I believe the reason is the existence of yet another myth that is often encountered with respect to REITs: That they are meant for investors to get into and out of from time to time, perhaps "cyclical" stocks that must be market-timed if one is to make any money in them.

This mind-set is, I believe, one of the most dangerous myths of all. It makes several assumptions, all of which are erroneous. These include: (a) REIT stocks must be bought and sold at the right time if one is to do well with them; (b) real estate and REIT stock prices, market conditions, interest rates, and capital markets can be successfully anticipated and timed by astute investors; and (c) that the reason for buying and selling REIT stocks is to score big wins and to avoid equally large losses. Wrong, wrong, wrong!

First, REIT stocks needn't be bought and sold frequently; indeed, they are the ultimate "buy and hold" investment. Their total return performance, averaged over many years, has been outstanding, and certainly competitive with the broader equities markets. More than 50 percent of their returns to investors come from the dividend yields, so investors get paid to wait for the additional reward of stock price appreciation that comes, over time, with earnings, dividend, and net asset value growth.

Second, the most wealth has been created by investors who buy and hold the stocks of excellent companies, for example, Warren Buffett. There is little evidence that traders or market-timers have been able to consistently make money in the stock market. And this is certainly true in REIT world. To successfully time the purchase and sale of REIT stocks, one must be able to forecast accurately the direction of interest rates (both long-term and short-term), real estate markets throughout the U.S., capital flows of both institutions and individuals, rates of inflation and unemployment, and all the other factors that determine real estate and stock prices. This cannot be done consistently and, for 99.9 percent of all investors, isn't worth the effort.

Finally, most intelligent investors do not invest in REIT stocks for quick and sizable capital gains, as one might seek to do in steel, airline, or technology stocks. REIT stocks are best owned for consistent dividend payments, modest price appreciation, over time, corresponding to increases in cash flows and asset values, and low correlations with other asset classes. The investors who do best with REIT stocks are those who have the most patience, are willing to ride out the occasional bear market, and are not expecting to hit home runs.

The claim that REIT stocks are best traded but not owned is truly a myth, and a dangerous one. Intelligent financial planners and advisers are telling their clients to decide on an appropriate allocation to REIT stocks within their diversified investment portfolios and to stick with them, perhaps rebalancing from time to time to maintain that allocation. We'll spend a bit more time on this topic later in the book.

SUMMARY

◆ For years, REITs have been shunned as "common stocks" by real estate investors and treated as "uninteresting real estate" by stock investors.

◆ Three essential determinants of real estate risk are leverage, diversification, and quality of management (including the assets chosen for ownership by such management).

◆ Although real estate investments have often been highly leveraged, it is the high leverage, rather than real estate itself, that is the major risk.

◆ Real estate as an investment can be hurt as much as helped by inflation.

◆ Market factors like supply and demand, interest rates, the existing and future strength of the economy, and investors' preferences and available investment alternatives are almost always more important than inflation in determining property value. REIT investors should focus more on market conditions and management ability than on inflation.

◆ Even if the near-term outlook for real estate is not good, REITs with access to capital will be able, at times, to grow their profits by taking advantage of favorable acquisition opportunities.

◆ REIT stocks are not "trading vehicles," and should be owned for dividend yields and modest capital appreciation over long periods of time.

CHAPTER

A History
Of REITs
AND REIT
PERFORMANCE

A S AN INVESTOR, you want to be equipped with as many analytical tools as possible. Knowing how a particular type of investment has behaved in the past is a crucial yardstick in determining not only *whether or not* you want to buy it, but also *how much* of it you want to buy relative to other assets in your portfolio. How have REIT stocks behaved during the more than forty years since they were conceived? Like a child, like a teenager, and like an adult, depending upon which stage of their development you examine. We'll take a look at those developments—specifically, how REITs performed in their infancy, how they created havoc in their wild adolescent years, and how they've matured into solid citizens of the investment world. We will also consider how REITs have behaved in response to different real estate and economic environments.

THE 1960s

INFANCY

The REIT structure was officially sanctioned by Congress and signed into law in 1960. It allowed individual real estate investors to "pool their investments" in order to enjoy the same benefits as direct real estate owners. Once the structure was created, it was only a few years until the first REITs were established, but these REITs were not "pretty babies" by today's standards.

According to a report by Goldman Sachs, *The REIT Investment Summary* (1996), only ten REITs of any real size existed during the 1960s. Most of them were managed by outside advisers, and all property management functions were handled by outside companies. Many of these management companies were affiliated with the REITs' advisers, which created significant conflicts of interest.

The REITs' portfolios were miniscule, ranging from $11 million for Washington REIT (one of the few survivors) to the $44 million REIT of America. Industry-wide real estate investments were very small at the beginning, amounting to just over $200 million. (For comparison, by late 2004, REITs owned real estate assets of approximately $535 *billion.*) These early REITs were small in size, and their insider stock ownership was negligible—typically less than 1 percent.

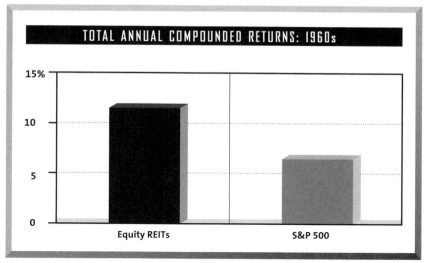

TOTAL ANNUAL COMPOUNDED RETURNS: 1960s

Despite these weaknesses, the Goldman Sachs report shows that these early-era REITs turned in a respectable performance, aided by generally healthy real estate markets in the 1960s. Cash flow (the early version of today's funds from operations, or FFO) grew an average of 5.8 percent annually, and the average dividend yield was 6.1 percent. The multiples of earnings (or cash flow) that investors were willing to pay for these early REITs remained steady, providing investors with an average annual total return of 11.5 percent—not a bad performance, considering that from 1963 to 1970 the S&P 500's total annual return averaged only 6.7 percent. Thus, despite their many handicaps, these upstart investments performed quite well.

THE 1970s

ADOLESCENCE AND TURBULENCE

The 1970s were tumultuous times for the economy, for the stock market, and for REITs. Inflation, driven by the OPEC-led explosion in oil prices, roared out of control, as evidenced by the Consumer Price Index (CPI), increasing 6.3 percent in 1973, 11 percent in 1974, 9.1 percent in 1975, and 11.3 percent by 1979.

Not content with such external hardships, the REIT industry was busy creating problems of its own. Between 1968 and 1970, with the willing assistance of many investment bankers, the industry produced fifty-eight new mortgage REITs. Most of these used a modest amount of shareholders' equity and huge amounts of borrowed funds to provide short-term loans to the construction industry, which, in turn, built hundreds of office buildings throughout the United States.

Such stalwart banks as Bank of America, Chase, Wachovia, and Wells Fargo, among many others, got into the act, and it seemed no self-respecting major bank wanted to be left out of sponsoring its own REIT. Largely as a result of these new mortgage REITs, the REIT industry's total assets mushroomed from $1 billion in 1968 to $20 billion by the mid-1970s.

When the office market—hammered by inflation-driven high interest rates—began weakening in 1973, the new mortgage REITs found that leverage worked both ways. Hurt by questionable underwriting standards, nonperforming assets rose to an alarming 73 percent of invested assets by the end of 1974, and share prices collapsed.

As a result of their negative experience with mortgage REITs, investors of the 1970s became disenchanted with the entire REIT industry for many years thereafter.

Ironically, aside from these mortgage REITs, nonlending equity REITs didn't do badly during the decade of the 1970s, since many real estate markets remained healthy. Federal Realty and New Plan, among others, made their first appearances and these retail REITs did well for investors for many years. While asset growth slowed, operating performance was reasonably good. During that decade, ten representative equity REITs charted by the Goldman Sachs study turned in a 6.1 percent compounded annual cash flow growth rate, with negative growth in only one year. Not surprisingly, those REITs with more than 5 percent insider stock ownership did much better than the others. These ten equity REITs also enjoyed an average annual compounded growth rate of 4.2 percent in their stock prices. This, when added to their dividend yields, produced a compounded total annual return of 12.9 percent during the 1970s, which compared very favorably with the total compounded annual rate of return of 5.8 percent for the S&P 500 index.

Nevertheless, as the decade drew to a close, REITs were still not

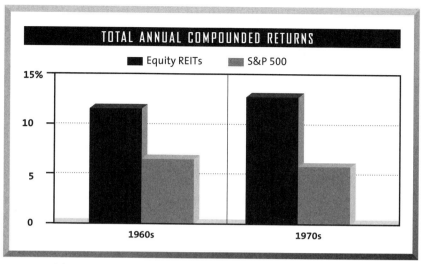

accepted by much of the investment community, since investor sentiment focused on the debacle of the mortgage REITs. By the end of 1979, the size of the REIT industry, as measured by equity market capitalization (number of shares outstanding × market price), was smaller than it was at the end of 1972. Most investors were not taking the time to distinguish between the steady, solid, equity REIT and its poor relation, the construction-loan mortgage REIT, and there was virtually no pension money allocated to the equity REITs during this time; they were unproven, illiquid, and still (in most cases) without independent management. Further, with only a few exceptions (notably Washington REIT, Federal Realty, and New Plan), few focused on specific property sectors in specific geographical regions. By the end of the decade REITs were still suffering growing pains and were not widely respected.

THE 1980s

THE OVERBUILDING OGRE
REARS ITS UGLY HEAD

The massive inflation of the 1970s had caused construction costs to mushroom, and, unless rents could be raised enough to provide a reasonable return on new investment capital, new construction would no longer be cost-effective. As occupancy rates rose, however, real estate owners (including, of course, the REITs) *were* able to increase their rents substantially. Yet, due to very high interest rates, new building was, at least for a time, deferred.

As the 1970s drew to a close, investors, reacting to high inflation, were looking for hard assets, such as gold, oil, and real estate.

The extraordinarily high mortgage rates of the early 1980s—ranging from 12.5 percent to 14.8 percent—substantially increased REITs' borrowing costs and eventually caused FFO growth to slow. According to the January 1996 *REIT Investment Summary,* per share FFO growth rates for Goldman Sachs's representative equity REITs declined from 26.1 percent in 1980 to 4.4 percent in 1983. However, FFO growth in the first half of the decade averaged a very respectable 8.7 percent, due to higher rents and little new supply of real estate. During the six years from 1980 through 1985, the group's total annual rate of return to shareholders was truly eye-popping, averaging 28.6 percent.

It says in Ecclesiastes, "To everything there is a season," and the good times, having had their season in the first half of the decade, were unfortunately no longer sustainable for the second half. Investors, both public and private, couldn't help noticing the outstanding returns achieved by real estate owners in the early 1980s; it was just too much of a good thing. They all just *had* to own real estate, and lots of it. What really put the icing on the cake, however, was that Congress passed the Economic Recovery Act of 1981, which created an attractive tax shelter for real estate owners. Authorizing property owners to use the vehicle of depreciation of their real estate assets as a tax shelter for other income prompted a real estate buying frenzy.

Almost immediately, major brokerage firms and other syndicators formed real estate limited partnerships and touted them as "can't-miss" investments, offering both generous tax benefits and capital gains. Of course, what happened was that the tax-shelter incentive inflated property prices to unsustainable levels, not supportable by rental revenues. REITs, offering greater stability but insignificant tax write-offs, were largely ignored. No one even considered the possibility that the tax laws might change (as tax laws always seem to do).

As megabillions poured into real estate, several unfortunate events occurred. First, REITs had to compete for capital with limited partnerships and private investors, who, in creating tax shelters, didn't have to show a positive cash flow. There was no contest: The latter could afford to pay a lot more for properties than the REITs could, thus limiting REITs' external growth prospects.

Second, as a result of the buying frenzy, real estate prices escalated. Even if REITs could have raised the acquisition capital, properties were being priced at levels that precluded their earning an adequate investment return. Third, and worst of all, with real estate being priced well above replacement cost, the developers got into the act—without regard for the law of supply and demand—and began a great amount of new construction. Virtually every developer who had ever built anything (and many who hadn't) visited his or her friendly banker, laid projections and budgets on the table, shouted, "Construction loan time!" and walked away with 90 percent financing.

Small wonder that within a few years real estate markets, beginning to feel the effects of overbuilding, weakened considerably. As if that weren't bad enough, Congress then decided to take away the tax-shelter advantage that had been such an impetus for investment, and passed the Tax Reform Act of 1986. Investors who were left holding properties that had already been performing poorly now lost the last reason they had for owning real estate. By the late 1980s, real estate was in big trouble.

During the 1980s, when investors were seeking the tax shelters offered by limited partnerships, real estate prices inflated to unsustainable levels.

As early as 1985, year-to-year growth rates in FFO for most REITs were peaking and beginning to decline. By the second half of the 1980s, the growth rate for the representative group of REITs in the Goldman Sachs study dropped to only 2.5 percent. Dividends continued to rise through the end of the decade, in most cases faster than FFO increased, and the payout ratios became extremely aggressive, causing shareholders to worry about potential dividend cuts. The average payout ratio for Goldman's group rose from

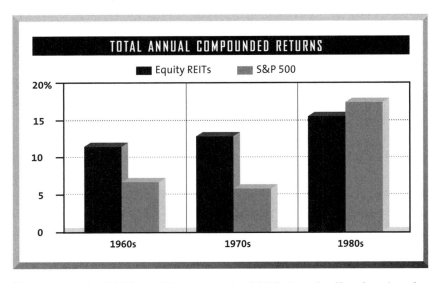

72 percent in 1980 to 98 percent in 1986. Ironically, despite the problems encountered by the REITs in these difficult years, their stocks didn't do badly. Total annual returns for Goldman's REIT group ranged from a high of 29.4 percent in 1985 to a low of 3.7 percent in 1988. They slightly underperformed the S&P 500 in 1985, 1988, and 1989, but bested it in 1986 and 1987. Nevertheless, these problems would eventually catch up with REIT stock prices in 1990.

THE 1990s

THE MODERN REIT ERA—PLUS GROWING PAINS

Emerging from the 1980s' real estate excesses, REITs did not begin the 1990s well. REIT shareholders suffered through a bear market in 1990 that cut their share prices down to bargain levels not seen since the 1970s. National Association of Real Estate Investment Trusts (NAREIT) statistics show that equity REITs' total return for 1990 was a *negative* 14.8 percent, making that the worst year since 1974, when their total annual return was a negative 21.4 percent. This was quite a shock to REIT investors, who had become cocky and over-confident; from 1975 until 1990, equity REITs had experienced only one year of negative total return—1987—when the figures were in the red by a scant 3.6 percent.

1990'S BEAR MARKET

REITs' big negative numbers in 1990 resulted from several factors: for office buildings and apartment communities, it was overbuilding, causing rising vacancies and stagnating or reduced rents; for retail, it was the continued inroads made by Wal-Mart and other discounters on the turf of traditional retailers. Dividend cuts by a number of REITs, which had found their payout ratios too high during such tough real estate climates, didn't help matters. Although a general markdown in real estate securities was warranted, investors overreacted (as they often do), and share prices fell below reasonable levels.

Excellent REIT bargains had sprouted up by the end of 1990, and these bear market lows set the stage for a major bull market that thrived from 1991 through 1993 and ushered in the great IPO boom of 1993–94.

The opening of the decade had been rough for REITs, but the investment vehicle itself by this time had nearly completed its metamorphosis. REITs of the late 1980s and early 1990s had come a long way from the REITs of the 1960s. Insider ownership increased and, thanks to the Tax Reform Act of 1986, which liberalized the rules pertaining to REITs, many REITs terminated their outside investment advisory relationships—and the major conflicts of interest that accompanied them—and internalized all their own leasing, maintenance services, redevelopment, and new construction. By the end of the 1990 bear market, a number of REITs, such as Health Care Property, Nationwide Health, Washington REIT, and Weingarten Realty, could boast experienced management teams and good track records. However, it would not be until 1993 that a large number of new, high-quality REITs would become available to investors.

1991–93: THE BULL RETURNS

A combination of factors caused equity REITs to do exceedingly well from 1991 through 1993. According to NAREIT data, total annual returns for 1991–93 averaged 23.3 percent. This outstanding performance was ample reward for the patient investors who had stuck with REITs through the bad times.

Why REIT stocks did so well following the tough years is easy to explain in hindsight. For one thing, investors overreacted terribly when they dumped REIT stocks in 1990; some of the gain came merely from getting prices back to reasonable levels. Perhaps a more important reason, however, was the bargain prices at which REITs were able to pick up properties in the aftermath of the depression-like and overbuilt real estate markets of the late 1980s and early 1990s. By 1991, many REITs were once again able to raise capital. They bought properties at fire-sale prices from banks that had foreclosed on billions of defaulted real estate loans, from insurance companies that wanted to reduce their exposure to real estate, from real estate limited partnerships that had crashed following the frenzy of the 1980s, and, last but certainly not least, from the Resolution Trust Corporation (RTC), which had been organized by Congress to acquire and resell real estate and real estate loans from bankrupt and near-bankrupt lenders. REITs were once more able to pursue aggressive acquisition programs, raising funds from both public offerings and additional borrowings, and investing them at very attractive rates of return.

The rebound from the low, bear market prices, REITs' ample access to capital with which to make attractive deals, and lower interest rates were all factors in driving the REIT bull market onward from 1991 through 1993.

Between January 1991 and the end of 1993, the Federal Reserve Board incrementally lowered interest rates in an effort to ease what had become a shallow but long recession. In January 1991, the yield on three-month Treasury bills was 6.2 percent. By the end of 1993, it had fallen to 3.1 percent. High-yielding REITs presented an irresistible lure to investors.

Since REIT shares were providing such high yields, investors renewed their romance with REITs during this period. Indeed, they were seen as an antidote to the puny short-term yields available on CDs and T-bills. These investors may not have known much about REITs, but that didn't stop them from buying with enthusiasm. Individual investors and a few adventurous institutions alike flocked to REIT investing, not only for the hefty yields but also for the prospects of substantial capital gains.

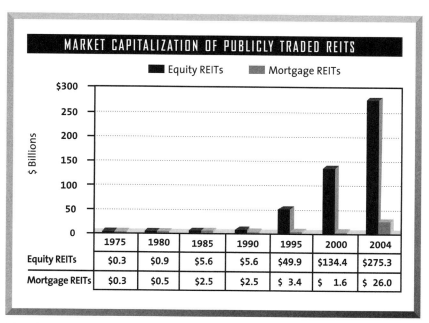

MARKET CAPITALIZATION OF PUBLICLY TRADED REITS

■ Equity REITs   ▨ Mortgage REITs

$ Billions	1975	1980	1985	1990	1995	2000	2004
Equity REITs	$0.3	$0.9	$5.6	$5.6	$49.9	$134.4	$275.3
Mortgage REITs	$0.3	$0.5	$2.5	$2.5	$ 3.4	$ 1.6	$ 26.0

THE GREAT 1993–94 REIT-IPO BOOM

The REIT industry was revolutionized by a tremendous boom in REIT initial public offerings (IPOs) that began in 1993. That year, according to NAREIT, 100 REIT equity offerings were completed, raising $13.2 billion, including $9.3 billion by fifty new REITs and $3.9 billion by fifty existing REITs. An additional $11.1 billion was raised in 1994, including forty-five new REIT IPOs raising $7.2 billion and fifty-two follow-on offerings by existing REITs raising $3.9 billion. The offerings in 1993 alone surpassed the total amount of equity that REITs had raised during the previous thirteen years, according to Merrill Lynch's August 1994 report, *Sizing Up the Equity REIT Industry.*

At the end of 1990, the estimated market capitalization of all publicly traded equity REITs was $5.6 billion. By the end of 1994, it exceeded $38.8 billion, thanks primarily to the REIT offering boom of 1993–94. The level of activity abated in 1995, as $8.2 billion in fresh equity was raised; there were only eight IPOs, garnering just $900 million.

While the 1994 slowing of the major bull trend in REITs' stock prices reflected a subpar year for their investors, the IPO boom of the

mid-1990s had a revolutionary effect on the REIT world: It was largely responsible for a huge increase in the number of REITs and property sectors in which investors could participate.

Unlike many small-stock IPO frenzies that occur from time to time in U.S. stock market history, the REIT-IPO boom brought the public some of the most solid and well-respected real estate operating companies in the United States, including, to name just a few, Developers Diversified, Duke Realty, General Growth Properties, Kimco Realty, Post Properties, Simon Property Group, and Taubman Centers. Furthermore, the number of property sectors in which REITs participated expanded widely. As a result of the success of these IPOs, these new sectors now included regional malls, outlet centers, industrial properties, manufactured-home communities, self-storage facilities, and hotels, all in addition to other property types such as apartments, neighborhood shopping centers, and health care facilities.

Why many of these companies went public has been the subject of much discussion. The cynics claim that, at many companies, insiders were taking the opportunity to cash out of some of their ownership interests at inflated prices at the expense of their new public shareholders. Although this claim undoubtedly had validity in some cases, there are more legitimate reasons to explain the phenomenon. In the early 1990s, the banks and savings and loan institutions had been so badly burned by nonperforming loans resulting from the real estate depression that they stopped providing the kind of real estate financing they had once routinely given. Cut off from their historical sources of private capital, many of these companies had good reason—some were forced—to seek access to *public* capital. Such public capital was expected to provide substantially greater financing flexibility. In addition, there was a growing perception in the minds of many managements that the "securitization" of real estate through REITs was becoming a major new trend and would help them to become stronger and more competitive organizations. A third reason might have been managements' desire to transform illiquid partnership ownership interests into publicly traded shares that could, from time to time, be more easily sold, transferred within the family, or used for estate-planning purposes. In this respect, these new REITs were not any different from other thriving enterprises that decided to go public as a way of solving financing, liquidity, and estate-tax issues.

The bottom line is that approximately ninety equity REITs did go public from 1992 through 1994, including some of the best real estate organizations in the country. As has been the trend from time to time in American business, some have been taken over by or have merged with other REITs, while a few have been bought out by private companies or institutional investors. Although there have been mediocre performers among them, a large number of this new generation of REITs can make a legitimate claim to being outstanding real estate companies that should provide investors with excellent returns for many years into the future.

1994–95: THE REIT MARKET TAKES A BREATHER

Even before the end of the IPO boom of 1993–94, the prices of many REIT stocks had cooled off considerably, particularly in the apartment and retail sectors. By the end of 1995, many REIT shares were trading at prices well below their 1993 highs, and this was despite the continuing impressive FFO growth in 1994 and 1995. Post Properties, for example, reported FFOs of $2.07, $2.25, and $2.53 in 1993, 1994, and 1995, respectively. Funds from operations thus increased by 22.2 percent from 1993 to 1995, yet Post's stock traded at $31 in October 1993 and had risen to only $31⅞ by the close of 1995.

Other sectors performed better, particularly in 1995. The prices as well as the P/FFO ratios of the industrial, office, and hotel REITs rose in response to investors' convictions that the overbuilt conditions plaguing these sectors from the late 1980s had dissipated, and that great acquisition opportunities were alive and well for those REITs with access to capital.

Thus, although the average total return of equity REITs was a disappointing 3.2 percent in 1994, according to NAREIT data, it recovered nicely in 1995, up 15.3 percent. Whereas the equity REITs' 1994 performance was similar to that of the S&P 500 that year (up 3.2 percent), it was outdone by non-REIT common stocks in 1995, when the S&P 500 rose by a whopping 37 percent.

By 1996–97, securitization of real estate through REIT offerings had become well established.

1996–97: THE REIT BULL MARKET RESUMES

Following the solid year in 1995, the year 1996 was an exciting one for REIT investors. NAREIT's Equity REIT Index logged in a total return of 35.3 percent. Although 1997 wasn't as spectacular, the NAREIT Equity REIT Index nevertheless managed to turn in a well above par total return of 20.3 percent. Why were REITs able to perform so well in these two years?

There are several possibilities, which may illustrate certain factors that may drive REIT stock pricing and performance from time to time. One is that investors were anticipating faster FFO growth than in the recent past, driven by attractive acquisition and development opportunities and REITs' greater access to capital. Faster perceived growth rates often translate into higher stock prices, whether within or outside of REIT world. Second, the strong performance may have resulted from investors' perception that real estate cap rates may have begun a long downward cycle, perhaps resulting from reduced risks of owning real estate due to milder real estate cycles, a lower longer-term rate of inflation, lower interest rates, and stronger real estate property performance. Lower cap rates translate into higher real estate prices if net operating income is stable, and higher real estate prices, of course, boost REITs' net asset values.

Yet another reason for the outsized performance may have been the lower interest rates on corporate and government bonds prevailing at that time, and expensive stock prices following several years of strong performance. REITs thus looked like a good investment alternative when compared with expensive assets elsewhere. Finally, at least during the early phases of the recovery, REIT prices may have been pushed higher by new demand from institutional investors who were beginning to appreciate the improved quality of many REIT management teams and REIT stocks' greater liquidity.

It was probably due to a combination of these factors that REIT stocks performed so well in 1996 and 1997. But let's be honest: Some of that performance, especially during 1997, was probably due to momentum investors hopping on board the "REIT express" simply because the stocks were performing well. This phenomenon occurs from time to time in the world of equities, and REIT investors will just have to learn to live with some extra volatility resulting from short-term traders moving into and out of REIT world at times.

Traditional real estate advisers for large institutional pension funds have been setting up new businesses devoted solely to the management of REIT portfolios. Institutional buying (and selling) has had a major impact on the REIT market.

1998–99: THE BEAR RETURNS

Following their stunning performance in 1996 and 1997, perhaps it was not surprising that REIT shares would come under pressure the following year. However, the severity of the decline in 1998 was unforeseen. Equity REITs suffered a total return of –17.5 percent in 1998, its worst performance since 1974. This poor showing was followed by another negative year in 1999, when REIT equities fell by 4.6 percent, also on a total return basis (per NAREIT data), and marked the first time since 1973–74 that the REIT industry incurred two consecutive down years.

One of the advantages of history is that causative events often become clearer with the passage of time. There appear to have been several forces that caused the 1998–99 bear market in REIT shares. First, lots of "hot money" was invested in REITs in 1996–97 by non–real estate and non-REIT investors, riding the wave of REITs' new popularity as they did in 1993. "Momentum investing" has been a popular investment strategy since the latter part of the 1990s, and REIT shares certainly had lots of momentum in 1996 and well into 1997. Near the end of 1997, when it appeared that the party was over, many of these new REIT investors exited in a hurry and hastened the downward movement in REIT share prices.

The thirst for REIT securities while the party was going strong was slaked by an extraordinary amount of new REIT equities issued to the public. This time, unlike in 1993–94, most of the new shares were issued by existing REITs in secondary offerings. According to NAREIT statistics, there were 318 separate equity offerings in 1997, which raised a total of $32.7 billion; of these, only 26 were IPOs

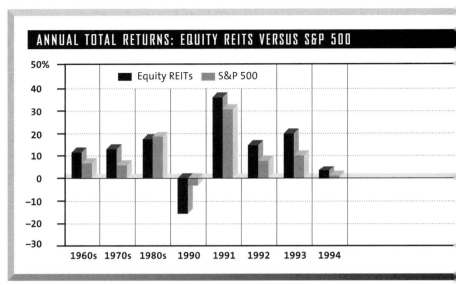

ANNUAL TOTAL RETURNS: EQUITY REITS VERSUS S&P 500

Legend: Equity REITs, S&P 500

(X-axis: 1960s 1970s 1980s 1990 1991 1992 1993 1994)
(Y-axis: 50% 40 30 20 10 0 -10 -20 -30)

(raising $6.3 billion). Although the bull market topped out in late 1997, a slew of offerings almost as large as in 1997 was completed in 1998, most of them early in the year. By the end of 1998, REITs had raised an additional $21.5 billion in fresh equity via 314 offerings, of which 17 were IPOs. Unit investment trusts were formed by many of the large brokerage firms; designed for the ostensible purpose of enabling their smaller clients to participate in the continuing REIT bull market with a minimum of commissions and fees, the net result was that lots of new REIT shares were dished off to investors who didn't have a long-term commitment to REITs as an asset class, and eventually most of these passive funds were liquidated.

The volume of offerings was just too much for the REIT industry's base of shareholders to absorb without having a major adverse impact upon REIT share prices. The total raised in both years—$54.2 billion—amounted to 69 percent of the equity market capitalization of all equity REITs at the end of 1996 ($78.3 billion).

When the supply of anything greatly exceeds demand, prices fall; REIT shareholders learned that lesson in economics in 1998 and 1999.

Many investors who abandoned REIT shares during those years may also have perceived that FFO growth would slow significantly.

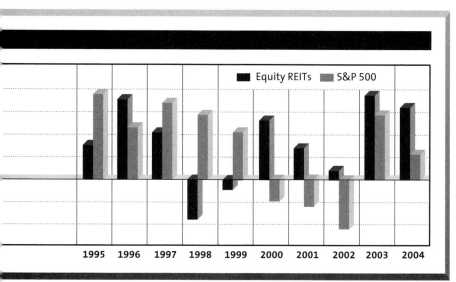

SOURCE: IBBOTSON

The buzzwords heard in 1996 and 1997 were phrases such as "new era" and "thinking out of the box," suggesting that many of the leading REIT management teams would no longer be limited to REITs' traditional per share FFO growth rates of 4–6 percent annually. This perception, however, was dashed when the shares began to fall; no longer would these "gazelle REITs" be able to run faster than any REIT had run before, and analysts began to mark down their estimates of earnings growth. At the same time, investing in high-tech stocks became fashionable, and REIT shares, offering prospective long-term total returns of 10–12 percent annually, just could not compete with the new darlings of the investment world; indeed, the Nasdaq Composite Index skyrocketed approximately 150 percent from the beginning of 1998 through the end of 1999.

Finally, the managements of many REITs did themselves no favors during those years. Some of them issued so-called forward equity contracts, which allowed them to raise equity immediately and deliver the promised shares to the buyers at a later date. The theory was that the share prices would be higher at that time, meaning a smaller number of shares could be issued when delivery was required; in fact, however, share prices fell and a significantly higher number of shares had to be issued. It also dawned on many investors that many REIT managements, when raising all that equity through secondary offerings, may not have really understood their

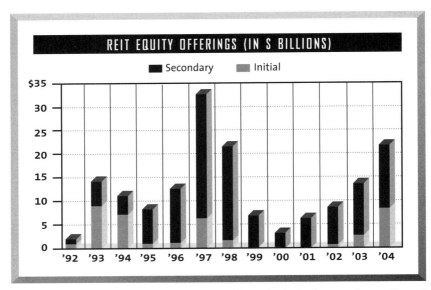

cost of capital. They were "expanding their balance sheets" and acquiring almost any property that was available—in what some have called the "Great REIT Pie-Eating Contest"—at prices that were unlikely to deliver the returns their shareholders expected.

2000–2004

CREDIBILITY AND MARKET ACCEPTANCE

Eventually, as a result of the deep and painful bear market, REIT prices became extraordinarily cheap by the end of 1999, in many cases trading at discounts of 20–25 percent below their estimated net asset values. At the same time, real estate markets were acting quite well, with occupancy and rental rates moving higher in response to the strong economy, and boosting REITs' FFO growth and asset values. Furthermore, the technology stocks were topping out; indeed, March 2000 was to be the high-water mark for the Nasdaq and most tech and telecommunications stocks, not to mention the dot-coms. Value investing again became popular, and REITs were quintessential values as we entered 2000. REIT shares began to rise early that year, commencing a major bull market that continued throughout 2004. By the end of 2000, equity REITs had posted outstanding returns—up 26.4 percent on a total return basis, according to NAREIT. This newfound popularity of REIT shares was not a one-year wonder. Total returns for equity REITs, per NAREIT, were 13.9 percent, 3.8 percent, 37.1 percent, and 31.6 percent in 2001, 2002, 2003, and 2004, respectively.

Before looking for an explanation for such strong performance, let's first take a quick look at the commercial real estate markets during that time period. And here, at first glance, appears to be a "disconnect" between weak real estate "space" markets and strong real estate capital markets. Those who projected falling REIT stock prices on the basis of deteriorating space markets were confounded during this entire period. Let's first review the space markets before seeking an explanation for this apparent paradox.

With the exception of *retail* real estate, which performed well during this entire time frame, commercial real estate markets struggled; the adverse conditions generally began in 2001, and didn't begin to stabilize until the latter part of 2004. Owners of apartment communities and office buildings were hit the hardest. For apartments, the culprits were the 2001 recession, poor employment growth (even during the recovery phase), and low interest rates, which made single-family homes (with cheap mortgage financing) very formidable competitors. Office owners were hammered by substantial reductions in hiring, capital expenditures and, most importantly, space needs by most U.S. businesses following the boom times of the late 1990s; substantial amounts of office space were just not renewed when leases expired, and office owners had to offer large concessions and substantial tenant improvement allowances to attract new tenants and even to re-sign existing tenants.

As a result, rents and occupancy rates for both apartment communities and office buildings tumbled, and net operating income for most commercial property owners declined—in some cases significantly. Average apartment vacancy rates rose from 3 percent in 2000 to a peak of 6.8 percent in late 2003–early 2004, and comparable community net operating income remained negative from 2001 to 2004. Conditions were no better in the office sector, as same-property net operating income turned negative in 2002, worsened substantially in 2003, and remained weak, although improved, in 2004.

And yet, as noted above, REIT stocks performed very well during this time period, especially in 2003 and 2004. Were investors nuts?

LESSONS FROM THE '98-'99 BEAR MARKET

THE YEARS 1998 AND 1999 marked the first time in almost twenty-five years, going back to 1974–75, that equity REIT shares suffered back-to-back negative returns. The decline in 1998 was particularly horrendous—off 17.5 percent on a total return basis—and was greater than in any single year since 1974. Another loss, of 4.5 percent, followed in '99. Coming on the heels of two spectacular years for REIT stocks (total returns in 1996 and 1997 were +35.3 percent and +20.3 percent, respectively), investors were shell-shocked by the length and violence of the decline. The 17.5 percent negative return for 1998 was *after* dividend payments; on a price-only basis, equity REIT stocks fell 22.3 percent (and they fell an additional 12.2 percent on a price-only basis in 1999).

The shock effect may have been so severe because new REIT investors had not expected these equities to be so volatile; after all, REITs' upside potential wasn't expected to match that of tech or telecom equities, but the downside risk was also supposed to be quite modest. Meanwhile, to add insult to injury, real estate itself was performing well.

Thus, REIT investors were traumatized, and many deserted this asset class for what they perceived as greener pastures elsewhere. Those of us who believe REIT shares fill an important role in a diversified investment portfolio might want to heed the words of George Santayana, "Those who do not remember the past are condemned to repeat it," and note some lessons from history—in this case the 1998–99 REIT bear market:

1 A few months before the bear market began, in October 1997, the typical REIT stock traded at a 30 percent premium over estimated net asset value. Because REITs, by law, are unable to retain much in the way of retained earnings, and due to the capital-intensive (and perhaps even commodity-like) nature of the real estate business, very few REIT organizations are able to consistently grow their profits in the double-digit range. **Lesson: Investors should be careful about paying large NAV premiums even for the very best and fastest-growing REIT organizations.**

2 Investors believed, as we headed into 1998, that extraordinary REIT FFO growth of the type demonstrated in 1996–97 by many REITs such as Crescent, Starwood, Vornado and others, deserved premium pricing multiples; however, as REITs' growth rates reverted to the mean in the following years, so did their multiples. **Lesson: Beware of paying high multiples**

of earnings if the cause is temporarily high FFO or AFFO growth rates.

3 Hordes of new investors, both individual and institutional, embraced REIT investing in '96 and '97, creating unprecedented demand for additional REIT shares; with the help of the investment bankers, these were obligingly delivered—primarily in the form of REIT secondary offerings. But a large number of these new investors were buying REIT shares only because they were moving—"momentum investing" was very popular in the latter part of the '90s—and exited quickly when the shares stopped rising. **Lesson: Although REIT stocks are all about real estate, and their long-term returns will thus be very dependent upon the profitability and values of quality commercial real estate, they are equities as well, and thus subject to the shifting fashions and investment styles prevalent in the investment world from time to time—their popularity will ebb and flow. Corollary Lesson: Expect REIT prices to remain more volatile, over the short- and medium-term, than directly owned real estate.**

4 Many REITs bought huge amounts of assets and expanded into many new markets as a result of the easy availability of equity capital from 1996 through early 1998, but these REITs frequently did not get bargain prices, nor did they invariably have lots of expertise in their new markets. The decline in REIT shares during the bear market can be partially attributable to investors' disappointment with the REITs' prospective returns on these new investments; many of them have since been sold, and REITs exited many of their new markets. **Lesson: REIT organizations must generate investment returns that meet or exceed their long-term cost of capital and understand that capital deployment decisions are among the most important that a REIT can make.**

5 A number of well-regarded REIT organizations pursued some very aggressive acquisition strategies from 1995 through 1997, often making extensive use of short-term debt and exotic hedging techniques such as forward equity transactions. These REITs, which had been very popular with investors due to their high growth rates, became overextended and found themselves having to issue new equity at give-away prices in order to repay maturing debt. **Lesson: Conservative REIT investors should understand the risks of aggressive external growth strategies, particularly when short-term debt is used to finance long-term assets such as real estate. A sound and conservative balance sheet reduces risk.**

INVESTING IN REITS

Did they simply fail to understand the fact that, for most REITs, FFO growth was negative and that dividend coverage was becoming very tight due to these very adverse real estate markets? Not at all. Students of the stock market know that stock prices do not necessarily correspond to current economic or business conditions, or even to the operating results of individual companies. Markets are often driven by factors that sometimes have little to do with near-term profits, and this phenomenon was alive and well not only for REIT stocks, but also for commercial real estate generally, from 2001 through 2004. So let's speculate a bit on the causes for this.

Perhaps there were many of them. I suspect that the fact that REIT stocks began their bull market in March 2000, the very month in which technology stocks peaked, was no coincidence. Indeed, 2000 marked the beginning of a period in which investing for current yield became very popular. This may have been a reaction to the horrendous investment losses in tech, telecom, and dot-com stocks, or it may have been due to a "back to basics" philosophy in which investors wanted to be paid a substantial portion of their total return expectations in the form of current income. In any event, REIT stocks, bearing some of the highest dividend yields in the equities markets (outside of preferred stocks, limited partnerships, and other exotica) certainly benefited from this trend.

This preference for yield is not irrational, and may be partially attributable to the fact that ever-increasing numbers of baby boomers are approaching retirement age and may prefer to have a substantial portion of their retirement needs funded out of current cash flows (in the form of dividend payments). And pension funds and other institutional investors are increasingly facing a similar problem, that is, providing monthly pension or other retirement checks to growing numbers of retirees. Capital gains in the stock market can't always be counted on, and so current income, either from real estate cash flows or REIT dividend payments, may have been seen as relatively more desirable in recent years than in the past.

A related factor is that many of the REITs' investment attributes beyond high yield had also become popular. REIT stocks' movements haven't correlated well with other asset classes, and this low correlation probably attracted new investors who wanted to smooth out the fluctuations in their diversified investment portfolios. REIT cash flows are stable and predictable, and this low-risk attribute may have found new favor with investors who have been shell-shocked by negative "earnings surprises" that can decimate the value of a stock virtually overnight.

Another issue is that commercial real estate (including REITs), as an asset class, has generally performed well in recent years, notwithstanding the normal cyclical ups and downs. Real estate market information is better, deeper, and more available; markets are more disciplined and efficient; and assets are more liquid. As a result, many investors—both individual and institutional—may have been wondering why they don't own more real estate, either directly or through REIT stocks. After all, if real estate can deliver returns similar to equities, with somewhat less risk and with low correlation to the performance of other investments, why not own more of it? So it's not unreasonable to assume that a substantial portion of REIT stocks' superior performance during this time period was due to investors beefing up their real estate/REIT allocations.

I would be remiss if I didn't also note that, in the minds of many, REIT executives have done a superior job of managing their companies throughout the downturn in real estate markets. They have also deployed their capital well, maintained investment discipline, boosted corporate disclosure, and improved corporate governance. These enhancements in credibility, together with increased liquidity in REITs' shares, could have been a material contribution to rising REIT stock prices during this period.

The increasing popularity of commercial real estate as an investment during this time period has, of course, boosted property prices (and has reduced real estate cap rates). This, in turn, has caused REITs' net asset values to increase. As a result, much of the increase in REIT stock prices during the 2003–2004 time frame has been merely reflective of higher valuations for commercial real estate generally. Whenever market values increase substantially, we will hear talk about a pricing "bubble." However, interest rates on government and corporate bonds during this entire period have been relatively low, and the "spread" between these yields and real estate cap rates hasn't been out of line versus historical norms. As a result, REIT stocks were not wildly overpriced at the end of 2004, given prevailing levels of interest rates. Substantial interest-rate spikes, of course, would negatively affect the value of all asset classes, includ-ing REITs and commercial real estate.

RECENT TRENDS

Before leaving this chapter on the performance of REIT shares over the years and what drove that performance, let's take a quick look at some of the trends that were very much in evidence in REIT world during the last ten years.

Merger and acquisition activity began to pick up substantially in 1996 and 1997 with rising stock prices, as DeBartolo Realty, Colum-bus Realty, Evans Withycombe, Paragon Group, ROC Communities, Wellsford Residential, Beacon Properties, and several other compa-nies were acquired by the end of 1997. M&A activity continued over the next several years, though not at the pace that some had predict-ed. Large deals completed since 1998 have included the mergers of Avalon Properties and Bay Apartment Communities, Archstone and Charles Smith Residential, Camden and Summit, Equity Residential and Merry Land, Equity Office and both Cornerstone Properties and Spieker Properties, Duke Realty and Weeks Corp., General Growth and Rouse, and Simon and Chelsea. In addition, a number of REITs were taken private or bought by private investors, for example, Bradley Realty, Cabot Industrial Trust, Irvine Apartment Communi-ties, Pacific Gulf, and Urban Shopping Centers.

Due largely to this activity, the number of equity REITs declined from 178 at the end of 1995 to 151 at the end of 2001. Since then, additional mergers were offset by new IPOs, and there were 153 equity REITs at the end of 2004. Thus, while the size of the average REIT has grown considerably over the last ten years (see below), the actual number of REITs has declined due to consolidation activity. There is still much debate on the extent of future consolidation activity in REIT world. No doubt there will be more of such activity, but there are significant obstacles making it difficult for one REIT to acquire another on an economic basis. This topic is discussed further in Chapter 12.

SIZE INCREASES

Another trend in REIT world has been the increasing size of the typical equity REIT. On December 31, 1994, there were only four

REITs with equity market capitalizations of over $1 billion. Due to a combination of increasing stock prices, merger activity, and equity offerings (offset to a modest extent by REIT share repurchases), there were seventy-four REITs with equity market caps of more than $1 billion by March 2005, and thirteen equity REITs had equity market caps exceeding $5 billion. Simon Property Group, with an equity market cap of $13.7 billion as of March 1, 2005, recently surpassed Equity Office Properties ($12.2 billion) as the largest REIT. The increased size of the largest REITs, along with an Internal Revenue Service ruling to the effect that REITs are active businesses, led to the decision in October 2001 to include REITs within the S&P 500 index, and by the end of 2004 a total of seven REITs had become part of the S&P 500. This event has enhanced the credibility of the entire REIT industry, and has caused non-REIT equity investment managers to consider investments in REIT shares.

CAPITAL RECYCLING

Three other trends surfaced in recent years, at least two of which were in response to the REITs' bear market of 1998–99. With REITs losing the ability during that time, and throughout 2000, to raise equity capital, they needed a mechanism to take advantage of particularly attractive development—and even acquisition—opportunities. An intelligent method of financing these projects is to sell off portfolio properties with limited upside, or even to exit entire markets that are viewed as less attractive on a long-term basis, and to use the proceeds, net of debt repayment, to finance the new projects, or even to repurchase outstanding common shares, at—it is hoped—much higher returns than would be generated by the assets sold.

This "capital recycling" strategy was adopted by a large number of REITs and was a significant departure from the way in which most REITs had done business in the past; indeed, until recently, selling off any asset was viewed by REIT executives as tantamount to selling off one's first-born child. The significance of REITs' willingness and ability to recycle assets to create more value and faster growth rates for their shareholders should not be underestimated, as it constitutes a new business model by which REIT management teams can continue to grow at very respectable rates even without access to the equities markets. And, even assuming such access, equity is the most expensive form of capital.

SHARE REPURCHASING

Another new development in the REIT industry is the willingness of many companies to repurchase their shares, most often in open market transactions, when they're selling at particularly cheap prices. Many management teams have begun to understand that, at certain times, more value can be created for shareholders, particularly when adjusted for risk, by buying in stock than by making that neat acquisition or even doing that dynamite development project. Although the pace of repurchase activity declined from 2000 through 2004, due to the rise in REITs' share prices, the dollar volume of shares bought in by REIT organizations has been substantial.

According to a Merrill Lynch report, from the beginning of 1998 through the end of 2000, forty-eight REITs announced stock buyback programs totaling $6.7 billion, of which $4.1 billion had been bought in by year-end 2000; this represents 4 percent of the equity market capitalizations for those companies who announced share buybacks. It appears that the share repurchase program has become a very useful tool within the REIT industry to create value for shareholders, particularly when share prices have been unduly punished by investors seeking more rapid growth elsewhere. Some REITs, such as Archstone-Smith, Boston Properties, and Cousins Properties, have even paid special dividends to shareholders out of asset sale proceeds.

JOINT VENTURES

Another recent trend is the willingness of many REIT organizations to form joint ventures (JVs) with institutional investors to own, acquire, and/or develop investment-grade commercial properties. These joint ventures can take many forms, including the transfer of mature or recently developed properties to the joint venture, the acquisition of existing properties, and the development of new ones. The deals have one thing in common: the opportunity for the REIT to leverage the talent of its in-place management, and often its development expertise, to generate good returns on new investments by forming partnerships with institutions who have the capital and the desire to invest alongside the REIT.

These JVs allow the REIT to control more assets (and retain tenant relationships) and to generate somewhat higher returns by collecting management and development fees, often with additional incentive fees for particularly attractive returns to the JV. They can, however, be complex and make projections more difficult for the analyst, and can be destructive of value for the shareholders if not organized and implemented carefully. Furthermore, some investors worry that the REIT may be giving away too much upside, particularly in development projects. But if the interests of the REIT and the institutional investor are properly aligned, there is sufficient incentive for the REIT to engage in the targeted activity, the debt incurred by the JV is not excessive in relationship to the REIT's own debt, there is a logical and mutually acceptable exit strategy, and there is a good working relationship on both sides, the JV concept can be used effectively to create higher income streams and additional value for the REIT's shareholders. JVs have been implemented successfully by a number of REITs, including AMB Property, Carr America Realty, Cousins Properties, Developers Diversified, Kimco, Mills Corp., ProLogis, Public Storage, and Regency Centers, among many others.

SUMMARY

◆ The first REITs, in the early 1960s, ranged from about $10 million to $50 million in size, their property management functions were handled by outside management companies, and their combined assets were only about $200 million.

◆ As a result of their negative experience with mortgage REITs, investors of the 1970s became disenchanted with the entire REIT industry.

◆ During the 1980s, when investors were seeking the tax shelters offered by limited partnerships, real estate prices became inflated; this limited REITs' external growth prospects.

◆ REITs' performance improved substantially in the early 1990s because they were able to pick up property at bargain prices resulting from the bear market in real estate beginning in the late 1980s.

◆ The IPO boom of the 1990s had a revolutionary effect on the REIT world: It was largely responsible for a huge increase in the number of REITs and property sectors in which investors could participate.

- ◆ The hot market for REIT stocks in 1996 and 1997 was driven, in part, by new REIT investors looking for attractive yields and substantial growth prospects.
- ◆ In 1996–97, institutional money managers started to invest in REITs, and the trend of public securitization of real estate had become indelibly established.
- ◆ REIT investors suffered through a two-year bear market in 1998–99, caused by excessive equity issuances, questionable allocation of capital, and slowing growth rates—but the bull market returned with a vengeance in 2000 despite weak real estate "space" markets.
- ◆ New trends seen in the REIT industry in recent years include capital recycling, stock repurchases, and joint venture strategies—all intended to enable management to increase shareholder value.

CHOOSING REITs and
Watching Them
Grow

PART II

CHAPTER

7

REITs:
HOW THEY GROW

NCREASES IN the value of a company are, of course, the driving force behind increases in its stock price over time. There are a number of ways to measure increases in company value, but measuring and valuing streams of income and cash flows is perhaps the most commonly used metric in the world of equities. And it is the only metric presently sanctioned by today's accounting rules, as a company's assets must be carried on its books at historical cost, less depreciation, not at current fair market value.

As a result, rising earnings are a key driving force for a company's share price. Steadily rising earnings normally indicate not only that a REIT is generating higher income from its properties, but may also suggest that it is making favorable acquisitions or completing profitable developments. Furthermore, higher income is generally a precursor of dividend growth. In short, a growing stream of cash flow means, over time, higher share prices, increased dividends, and higher asset values. Value can be created in a REIT by investment activities that don't show up in current income or cash flow, but these latter metrics are most easily quantifiable.

THE SIGNIFICANCE OF FFO AND AFFO

Investors in common stock use net income as a key measure of profitability, but the custom in REIT world is to use funds from operations (FFO). The historical preference for FFO rather than net income relates to the concept of depreciation. The Securities and Exchange Commission (SEC), under federal securities laws, requires that all publicly traded companies file audited financial statements. On a financial statement, the term *net income* has a meaning clearly defined under generally accepted accounting principles (GAAP). Since most REITs are publicly traded companies, net income and net income per share can therefore always be found on a REIT's audited financial statement. For a REIT, however, these net income figures are less meaningful as a measure of operating success than they are for other types of companies. The reason is that, in accounting, real estate depreciation is always treated as an expense, but in the real world, not only have most well-maintained quality properties retained their value over the years, but many have appreciated substantially. This is generally due to a combination of increasing land values (on which the structure is built), steadily rising rental and operating income, property upgrades, and higher costs of construction for new competing properties. Thus a REIT's net income under GAAP, reflecting a large depreciation expense, has been determined by most REIT investors to be less meaningful a measure of REIT cash flows than FFO, which adds back real estate depreciation to net income.

Using FFO enables both REITs and their investors to partially correct the depreciation distortion, either by looking at net income before the deduction of the depreciation expense or adding back depreciation expense to reported net income.

When using FFO, there are other adjustments that should be made as well, such as subtracting from net income any income recorded from the sale of properties. The reason for this is that the REIT can't have it both ways: In figuring FFO, it cannot ignore depreciation, which reduces the property cost on the balance sheet, and then include the capital gain from selling the property above the price at which it has been carried. Furthermore, GAAP net income is normally determined after "straight-lining," or smoothing out contractual rental income over the term of the lease. This is another accounting convention, but, in real life, rental income on a multiyear property lease is not smoothed out, and it

---

FUNDS FROM OPERATIONS (FFO)

HISTORICALLY, FFO HAS been defined in different ways by different REITs, which has only exacerbated the confusion. To address this problem, NAREIT (National Association of Real Estate Investment Trusts) has attempted to standardize the definition of FFO. In 1999, NAREIT refined its definition of FFO as used by REITs to mean net income computed in accordance with GAAP, excluding gains (or losses) from sales of property, plus depreciation and amortization, and after adjustments for unconsolidated partnerships and joint ventures. Adjustments for unconsolidated partnerships and joint ventures should be calculated to reflect funds from operations on the same basis.

often starts low but rises from year to year. For this reason, many investors, when examining FFO, adjust reported rent revenue to reflect current contractual rent revenue.

Although most REITs and their investors believe the concept of FFO is more useful as a device to measure profitability than net income, it is nevertheless flawed. For one thing, most commercial property will slowly decline in value year after year, due to wear and obsolescence, and structural improvements are generally necessary if that property value is to be retained (e.g., a new roof, or better lighting). Merely adding back depreciation, then, to net income, when determining FFO, can provide a distorted and overly rosy picture of operating results and cash flows.

The very term *depreciation* allows yet another opportunity for distortion when it comes to items that might be considered part of general maintenance, such as, for example, an apartment building's carpeting or curtains, even dishwashers. The costs of such items often might not be expensed for accounting purposes; instead, they might be capitalized and depreciated over their useful lives. But, because the depreciation of such items is a real expense, when such "real estate" depreciation is added back to arrive at FFO, the FFO will be artificially inflated and thus give a misleading picture of a REIT's cash flow. Practically speaking, carpeting and related items, to use our example, really do depreciate over time, and their replacement in a building does not significantly increase the property's value. These are real and recurring expenses.

Additionally, leasing commissions paid to leasing agents when renting offices or other properties are usually capitalized, then amortized over the term of the lease. These commission amortizations, when added to net income as a means of deriving FFO, will similarly inflate that figure. The same can also be said about tenant improvement allowances, such as those provided to office and mall tenants. Usually, these are so specific to the needs of a particular tenant that they do not increase the long-term value of the property.

Short-term capital expenditures cannot be considered property-enhancing capital improvements, no matter how they are accounted for, and they should be subtracted from FFO to give an accurate picture of a REIT's operating performance.

ADJUSTED FUNDS FROM OPERATIONS (AFFO)

AFFO IS THE FFO as used by the REIT, adjusted for expenditures that, though capitalized, do not really enhance the value of a property, and is adjusted further by eliminating straight-lining of rents.

Unfortunately, not all REITs capitalize and expense similar items in similar ways when announcing their FFOs each quarter. Also, some include investment write-offs and gains from property sales in FFO, while others do not. With only FFO as a gauge, investors and analysts are still lacking consistency in terms of the way adjustments to net income are reflected. Furthermore, there is no uniform standard to account for recurring capital expenditures that do not improve a property or extend its life, such as expenditures for carpeting and drapes, leasing commissions, and tenant improvements.

The term born of this need is *adjusted funds from operations* (AFFO), which was coined by Green Street Advisors, Inc., a leading REIT research firm.

Although FFO as a valuation tool is more useful to REIT investors than net income under GAAP, NAREIT maintains that "FFO was never intended to be used as a measure of the cash generated by a REIT, nor of its dividend-paying capacity." Adjusted funds from operations, on the other hand, is a much better measure of a REIT's operating performance and is a more effective tool to measure free cash generation and the ability to pay dividends. Unfortunately, AFFO is normally not specifically reported by a REIT, and the investor or analyst must calculate it on his or her own by reviewing the financial statements and related footnotes and schedules. And, even when AFFO is disclosed, different REITs define it differently. The following is an oversimplified, but perhaps useful, way of looking at this methodology.

Revenues, including capital gains, *minus*:
◆ Operating expenses and write-offs
◆ Depreciation and amortization
◆ Interest expense
◆ General and administrative expense   = NET INCOME

Net Income *minus:*
◆ Capital gain from real estate sales
plus:
◆ Real estate depreciation   = FFO

FFO *minus:*
◆ Recurring capital expenditures
◆ Amortization of tenant improvements
◆ Amortization of leasing commissions
◆ Adjustment for rent straight-lining   = AFFO

The problem encountered by investors in using FFO and its derivatives was discussed by George L. Yungmann and David M. Taube, vice president, financial standards, and director, financial standards, respectively, of NAREIT, in an article appearing in the May/June 2001 issue of *Real Estate Portfolio.* They note, "A single metric may not appropriately satisfy the need for both a supplemental earnings measure and a cash flow measure." They suggest using a term such as *adjusted net income* (which is GAAP net income prior to extraordinary items, effects of accounting changes, results of discontinued operations, and other unusual nonrecurring items) as a supplemental earnings measurement. Each REIT would then be free to supplement this "ANI" figure by reporting a cash flow measure such as FFO, AFFO, or other terms sometimes used by REITs and analysts such as *cash available for distribution* (CAD) or *funds available for distribution* (FAD).

Of course, when comparing the earnings and FFO figures reported by two different REIT organizations, it's important to compare apples to apples, in other words, we don't want to compare the P/FFO ratio of one REIT to the P/AFFO ratio of another, and we should try to apply similar FFO or AFFO definitions to the REITs being compared.

In valuing a REIT, although net income should not be ignored, AFFO (when properly calculated) is the most accurate means for determining a REIT's free cash flow.

Thus, some analysts and investors, when determining AFFO, look at the actual capital expenditures incurred by a REIT during a reporting period, while others apply a long-term average to smooth periods of unusually high or low capital expenditures. There is no "right" or "wrong" approach but, again, it's important for the investor to compare apples to apples.

Now that we have established the differences between these important terms, we will use, in the balance of this chapter, either FFO (funds from operations) or AFFO (adjusted funds from operations), keeping in mind that virtually all REITs report the former, although it is less meaningful to investors.

When we discuss the price/earnings ratio of a REIT's common stock, we will use either the P/FFO ratio or the P/AFFO ratio, with the understanding that, although we are trying to be as consistent as possible, sometimes true consistency is not attainable, and we must therefore be aware of how these supplements to net income reporting under GAAP are calculated by or for each REIT.

THE DYNAMICS OF FFO GROWTH

What makes REIT shares so attractive, compared with other high-yield investments like bonds and preferred stocks (and, to a lesser extent, utility stocks), is their significant capital appreciation potential and steadily increasing dividends. If a REIT didn't have the ability to increase its FFO and its dividend, its shares would be viewed as not much different from a bond, and they would be bought only for their yield. Because of the greater risk, of course, the yields on the stocks of growth-challenged REITs would normally be higher than those of most bonds and preferreds, and their prices would correlate with the fluctuations of long-term interest rates and investors' perceptions of these REITs' ability to continue paying dividends.

FFO should not be looked upon as a static figure, and it is up to management to continue to seek methods of increasing it.

We can sometimes find REITs that *do* trade as bond surrogates because of investor perception that they have very little growth potential. Some of these pseudo-bonds can be of high quality because of the stability of their stream of rental income, while others can be compared to junk bonds because of their high yields but

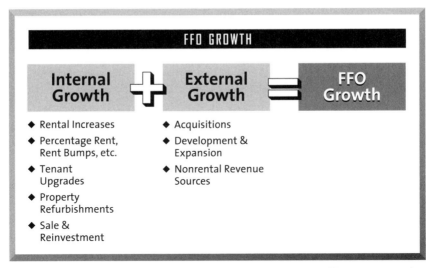

uncertain flow of rental revenues. These "junk-bond" REITs may be traded, sometimes profitably, by bottom fishers and speculators, but such yield chasers are playing a dangerous game.

Long-term investors should be looking at REITs with dividends that are not just safe but also have good long-term growth prospects. Wouldn't you rather own a REIT that pays a current return of 4 percent and grows 6 percent every year than one that pays 7 percent and doesn't grow at all?

Sometimes it's possible to get the best of both worlds—a 7 percent yield *and* 3–4 percent annual growth. But, with REITs, as with everything else in the investment world, there's usually no such thing as a free lunch. A REIT that yields more than 7 percent often suggests that investors perceive very low growth or that the shares are particularly risky.

All right, then, how does a REIT generate growth in FFO, and what should you look for? First of all, it is very important to look at FFO growth on a per-share basis. It does the shareholder no good if FFO grows rapidly because the REIT has issued large amounts of new shares. Such "prosperity" is meaningless—like a government printing more money in times of inflation. Remember, also, that REITs, by definition, must pay their shareholders at least 90 percent of their taxable net income each year but, as a practical matter, most REITs pay out considerably more than this, as depreciation expense is also normally taken into account when setting the dividend rate. So, if REITs want to achieve external growth through acquisitions or new developments, where is the cash going to come from? They will sometimes go to the capital markets, which means selling more shares, and such new capital is not always available— and can, at times, be very expensive in terms of dilution to net asset values. While it is indeed true that REITs can generate cash from the sale of existing assets, retention of a modest portion of their free cash flows, and the formation of joint ventures, raising capital externally has traditionally been a very important driver of above-average FFO growth. All of this means that internal growth—which can be accomplished without having to raise more equity or to take on additional debt—is very important to a REIT and its shareholders.

FFO can grow two ways: externally—by acquisitions, developments, and the creation of ancillary revenue streams, and internally—through a REIT's existing assets and resources.

REIT investors and analysts need to understand exactly how much of a REIT's growth is being achieved internally and how much is being achieved externally. External growth, through new developments, acquisitions, and the creation of ancillary revenue streams, may not always be possible, because of a lack of available, high-quality properties at attractive prices, inability to raise capital, or the high cost of such capital. Internal growth, on the other hand, since it is "organically" generated through a REIT's existing resources, is more under management's control (though it is subject to real estate market dynamics).

INTERNAL GROWTH

Internal growth is growth via an improvement in profits at the property level, through increased rental revenues (higher rents and occupancy rates) and reduced expenses at one or more of the specific properties owned by the REIT. Controlling corporate overhead expenses is also important. Since it is not dependent on acquisitions, development, or outside capital, it is the most stable and reliable source of FFO growth.

Before we examine the specific sources of REITs' internal growth, however, we should review one of the terms that analysts use in reference to internal growth. The term is *same-store sales* (or, a related term, same-store net operating income)—a concept taken from retail but also used in nonretail REIT sectors. In a retail operation, same-store sales refers to sales from stores open for at least one year, and excludes sales from stores that have closed or from new stores, since new stores characteristically have high sales growth.

Although the term *same-store sales* was originally a retail concept, it, and its companion, same-store net operating income, have been borrowed for use by other, nonretail REIT sectors to refer to growth that is internal, rather than from new development or acquisition.

Once you consider what the same-store concept means in retail, you can see how it might be applied to various REIT sectors. Most REITs report to their shareholders on a quarterly basis same-store rental revenue increases (and net operating income, or NOI, on a same-store basis). Same-store rental revenues (which include changes in occupancy), reduced by related expenses, determines same-store NOI growth, which presents a good picture of how well the REIT is doing with its existing properties as compared to the similar prior period.

Property owners, including REITs, use different tools to generate growth on a same-store basis. These tools include rental revenue increases, ancillary property revenues, upgrading the tenant roll, and upgrading—or even expanding—the property. Those REITs that are more aggressive and creative in their use of these tools are more likely to achieve, over time, higher internal growth rates. Of course, the strategic location of the properties, and their quality, are also highly important.

RENTAL REVENUE INCREASES

The most obvious type of internal growth, the ability to raise rental rates and revenue, regardless of property sector, is probably a REIT's most important determinant of internal growth.

Rental rates can be increased over time if a property is desirable to tenants, and higher occupancy rates can lead to even higher rental revenues. Nevertheless, raising rents is not always possible, and there are periods in virtually every sector's cycle when such revenues actually fall rather than rise. Anyone who owned office buildings in the early 1990s or in the first few years of the twenty-first century knows there's no guarantee the rent can be raised—or even maintained at the same level—when the lease comes up for renewal. Even if the rent is raised slightly, if the tenant receives huge tenant improvement allowances as an inducement to lease the space, the lease may still not be very profitable. In addition, unit rent increases can be wiped out by high vacancy rates, rental concessions, and heavy marketing and advertising costs. These problems were faced, most recently, from 2001 to 2004 in most property sectors, when high vacancy rates put the tenants in the driver's seat in negotiating rents on new leases. Many factors, such as supply and demand for a particular property or property sector (including, of course, location and obsolescence), the current economic climate, and the condition of (and amenities offered by) a property can enhance or restrict rental revenue increases. During recessions, of course, vacancy is likely to rise. When occupancy slippage occurs, owners have difficulty raising, and sometimes even maintaining, rents until the economy recovers.

Most retail shopping center owners have been able to raise rental rates at a healthy rate, even during the difficult real estate markets of 2001–2004, as leases have come up for renewal—despite the steady pace of retailer bankruptcies, the challenges from Wal-Mart and others, and the threat coming from the rise of e-commerce. In malls, tenants have signed new, more expensive leases to replace the leases signed during prior years when sales volumes were significantly lower than they are now. In the long run, however, rent increases will generally not be able to outpace the rise in same-store tenant sales, as tenant occupancy costs as a percentage of sales have been quite consistent over the years. Rental rate increases have been a bit more difficult for neighborhood shopping center and outlet center owners, due to heavy competition and the in-roads made by Wal-Mart and its wanna-bes, and there is no guarantee, of course, that retail real estate owners will always be able to increase rents.

The apartment sector had been in equilibrium for many years, with demand offsetting new supply, but poor job growth in the early years of the twenty-first century, coupled with low interest rates that encouraged new construction and stoked demand for single-family housing, put renters in control. Apartment occupancy rates and net operating income declined, but started to grow again beginning in the latter part of 2004. Investors in this sector should expect long-term internal growth roughly in line with inflation.

Office rents suffered during the period of massive overbuilding in the late 1980s and early 1990s, but the cycle bottomed out earlier than most had anticipated. Rent growth was strong from the mid-1990s through 2000, but then rents declined substantially from 2001 through 2004, and most observers don't expect meaningful rent growth until at least 2006 in most markets. The cycle for industrial properties was similar, although less pronounced. Rents declined more significantly in some of the erstwhile hot high-tech markets.

Self-storage facilities have enjoyed steady rental growth since the early 1990s, although growth slowed substantially from 2001 to 2004. Their popularity, coupled with only moderate building over the last few years, has enabled owners of these facilities to increase rents frequently, and, even with a slowdown in the pace of rent increases, should still be able to do reasonably well over time.

Hotel owners fared well during the strong economic recovery that began in earnest in 1993, seeing big jumps in room rates (and even, in most cases, occupancy rates). But from 2001 to 2004, both rents and occupancy slipped badly—as would be expected during a very weak economy, especially in the business sector, exacerbated by the September 11 terrorist attacks. This property sector hit bottom in 2004, and revenue and income growth were accelerating throughout 2005.

Health care REITs enjoy the protection of long-term leases, which also offer a bit of upside based upon revenues generated by the operator. The key here, as we saw in the late 1990s, is the financial strength of the lessees; defaulting tenants are often not easily replaced at the same or higher rents. Base rents for these facilities should remain fairly stable. The assisted-living market, however, will be somewhat more volatile, as barriers to entry are lower.

Although it may be an oversimplification, most real estate observers seem to think that owners of well-maintained properties in markets where supply and demand are in balance will, over time, continue to get rental revenue increases at least equal to inflation. We are talking here only about broad-based industry trends; some REITs will get better rental increases upon lease renewal than others, based upon many factors related to supply and demand for specific properties in specific locations, as well as property quality and location. Management's leasing capabilities are also very important. Trying to determine which REITs and their properties have better than average potential rental revenue and NOI growth is one of the challenges—and some of the fun—of REIT investing.

HOW TO BUILD RISING FFO INTO THE LEASE

Many property owners have been able to obtain above-average increases in rental revenues by using methods that focus on tenants' needs and their financial ability to pay higher effective rental rates. These methods include percentage rent, rent bumps, and expense sharing and recovery.

PERCENTAGE RENT

"Percentage-rent" clauses in retail-store leases enable the property owner to participate in store revenues if such revenues exceed certain preset levels.

A retail lease's percentage-rent clause might be structured so that if the store's sales exceed, for example, $5 million for any calendar year, the lessee must pay the landlord 3 percent of the excess, in the form of additional rent. The extent to which lessees will agree to this revenue sharing depends on the property location, the market demand for the space, the base rent, and the property owner's reputation for maintaining and even upgrading shopping centers to make them continually attractive to shoppers. This concept has been carried over into the health care sector, where REITs have structured most of their leases (and even their mortgages when the REIT provides mortgage financing) so that the owner shares in same-store revenue growth above certain minimum levels. In some cases, the rent increases are capped at predetermined levels.

RENT BUMPS

"Rent bumps" are contractual lease clauses that provide for built-in rent increases periodically. These are sometimes negotiated at fixed dollar amounts and sometimes based upon an index of inflation such as the Consumer Price Index. Office and industrial-property owners who enter into long-term leases are often able to structure the lease so that the base rent increases every few years, thus providing built-in same-store NOI growth. The rent-bump provision is also popular with owners of health care facilities, who use them in leases with their health care operators, and with retailers, who use them to match leasing costs with projected longer-term revenues from the stores' operations.

EXPENSE SHARING

"Expense sharing" or "cost recovery" is a way in which owners have persuaded their lessees to share expenses that at one time were borne by the landlord, and have included "cost-sharing" or common area maintenance (CAM) recovery clauses in their leases to offset rising property maintenance, and even improvement, expenses.

In the case of office buildings, the lessees might pay their pro rata portion of the increased operating expenses, including higher insurance, property taxes, and on-site management costs. Similarly, retail owners have, over the last several years, been able to obtain reimbursement from their lessees for certain common-area maintenance operating expenses, such as janitorial services, security, and even advertising and promotion.

Many savvy apartment community owners have put separate electric and water meters, or even separate heating units, into their apartments, with a twofold benefit. The owner is protected from rising energy costs, and the tenant is encouraged to save energy.

Cost-sharing lease clauses improve NOI, and thereby FFO, while tending to smooth out fluctuations in operating expenses from year to year. The degree to which they can be used depends on a property's supply/demand situation and location, as well as the property owner's ability to justify them to the lessee. The large mall REITs, such as Simon Property Group, may, on the basis of their size and reputation for creative marketing, be able to get lease provisions a weaker mall owner could not.

OTHER WAYS TO GENERATE
INTERNAL GROWTH

There are two principal ways to improve a property in order to capture higher rental rates: One is by upgrading the tenant mix; the other is by upgrading the property, through renovation or refurbishment. Both can be effective.

TENANT UPGRADES

Upgrading the tenant mix is largely a retail opportunity, and creative owners of retail properties have been able to increase rental revenues significantly by replacing mediocre tenants with attractive new ones. Retailers who offer innovative products at attractive prices generate higher customer traffic and boost sales at both the store *and* the shopping center, and successful tenants can afford higher rents.

This ability to upgrade tenants is what distinguishes a truly innovative retail property owner from the rest. Kimco Realty, which boasts one of the most respected management teams in the retail REIT sector, maintains a huge database of tenants that might improve its centers' profitability. This resource, along with the strong relationship Kimco has with high-quality national and regional retailers, allows it to upgrade its tenant base within an existing retail center on a continual basis. Regency Centers, another retail REIT, has been following a similar strategy, establishing long-term relationships with strong national and regional retailers. In the factory outlet center niche, Chelsea Property Group, which was acquired by Simon in 2004, has been a leader in replacing poorly performing tenants with those who can draw big crowds, enhancing the value of the property and providing higher rent to the property owner. Most mall owners have, for many years, been following this formula as well, and are always looking for opportunities to replace or downsize weaker tenants. For them, when a Montgomery Ward's goes out of business, or a May's store closes, it is not a problem but an opportunity.

Tenant upgrades are even more important during weak retailing periods. Late in 1995 and into 1996, many retailers, having been squeezed by sluggish consumer demand and inroads made upon them by Wal-Mart and other discount stores, filed for bankruptcy. A similar situation prevailed from 2001 to 2003. Those mall owners who replaced poorly performing apparel stores with restaurants and other unique retailing concepts prospered; those who did not encountered flat-to-declining mall revenues, vacancy increases, and declining or stagnating rental rates upon lease renewal. A good and productive mix of tenants is just as important as a good location.

PROPERTY REFURBISHMENTS

Refurbishment is a skill that separates the innovative property owner from the passive one. This ability can turn a tired mall, neighborhood shopping center, office building—even an apartment community—into a vibrant, upscale property likely to attract new tenants and customers.

Successfully refurbishing a property has several benefits. The upgraded and beautified property attracts a more stable tenant base and commands higher rents and, for retail properties, more shoppers. The returns to the REIT property owner on such investments can often be almost embarrassingly high.

Federal Realty, another well-regarded retail REIT, has been generating outstanding returns from turning tired retail properties into more exciting, upscale, open-air shopping complexes. Acadia Realty, a smaller retail REIT, has been doing very innovative refurbishments. In the apartment sector, Home Properties and United Dominion, among others, have been buying apartment buildings with deferred maintenance problems or with significant upgrade potential at attractive prices, then successfully upgrading and refurbishing them with new window treatments and upgraded kitchens. Alexandria Real Estate, which focuses on the office/laboratory niche of the office market and provides space for pharmaceutical and biotech companies, has been expanding its redevelopment strategy and is believed to be earning returns in excess of 12 percent on such projects. The lesson here for investors is that REITs with innovative management can create value for their shareholders through imaginative refurbishing and tenant-upgrade strategies.

SALE AND REINVESTMENT

Sometimes investment returns can be improved by selling properties with modest future rental growth prospects, and then reinvesting the proceeds elsewhere, including acquisition of properties which are likely to generate higher returns, new development projects, or even stock repurchases, preferred stock redemptions, and debt repayment. REITs should "clean house" from time to time and consider which properties to keep and which to sell, using the capital from the sale for reinvestment in more promising properties. This may still be considered internal growth, since new projects are financed by the sale of existing properties and does not require new capital.

Truly entrepreneurial managements are always looking to improve investment returns, and sale and reinvestment is one conservative and highly effective strategy. As noted in Chapter 6, this practice has become popular with REIT organizations ever since the capital markets slammed shut on them in mid-1998, and is now referred to as a "capital recycling" strategy.

For example, a property might be sold at a 7.5 percent cap rate, with a prospective long-term return of 8.5 percent annually, and the net proceeds invested in another (perhaps underperforming) property that, with a modest investment of capital and upgraded tenant services, might provide a long-term average annual return of 10–11 percent or more within a year or two. Funds reinvested in well-conceived and well-executed development projects can be equally profitable, as we'll discuss below. Sometimes a REIT will decide to exit an entire market if it doesn't like its long-term prospects, and will sell all its properties located there. This approach to value creation does not require significant use of a REIT's capital resources, since the capital to acquire new properties or to develop them is created through the sale of existing properties.

Again, as with tenant upgrading and property refurbishing, capital recycling is something to watch for. Most REIT managements are always alert for new opportunities and should have no emotional attachments to a property just because their REIT has owned it for a while or because it's performed well in the past. For example, just in the apartment sector, Archstone-Smith, Avalon Bay, Camden, Equity Residential, Post Properties, and United Dominion have all been substantial sellers of mature assets in recent years. There may be a short-term cost in terms of temporary earnings dilution, as higher-quality assets usually trade at lower entry yields than the lower-quality assets disposed of and as the sale proceeds are used temporarily to pay down debt, but the long-term benefits of this strategy will be substantial if executed with good judgment and intelligence.

CONCEPTS OF NOI AND IRR

Before we leave this discussion, let's fill in our knowledge—and help us prepare for what follows—with a couple of very important concepts in real estate, net operating income and internal rate of return. The term *net operating income* (NOI) is normally used to measure the net cash generated by an income-producing property. Thus, NOI can be defined as recurring rental and other income from a property, less all operating expenses attributable to that property. Operating expenses will include, for example, real estate taxes, insurance, utility costs, property management, and, sometimes, recurring reserves for replacement. They do not include items such as a REIT's corporate overhead, interest expense, value-enhancing capital expenditures, or depreciation expense. Therefore, the term attempts to define how much cash is generated from the ownership and leasing of a commercial property. Investors might expect NOI on a typical commercial real estate asset to grow about 2–3 percent annually, roughly in line with inflation, during most economic periods.

The term *internal rate of return* (IRR) helps the real estate investor to calculate his or her investment returns, including both returns *on* investment and returns *of* investment. It is used to express the percentage rate of return from all future cash receipts, balanced against all cash contributions, so that when each receipt and each contribution is discounted to net present value, the sum is equal to zero when added together. To put it more simply, it's the rate of return that an investor expects when making the investment, or, with hindsight, the rate of return obtained from the investment. For example, if the real estate investor requires a 10 percent return on his or her investment, he or she won't buy the offered property if the net present value of all future cash receipts from that property, including gain or loss on its eventual sale, isn't likely to equal or exceed 10 percent. Of course, this requires some sharp-penciled calculations (these days, done with Excel spreadsheets!), including many assumptions concerning occupancy and rental rates, property expenses, growth in net operating income, and what the property will be worth when sold at some assumed future date.

One of the reasons that so many real estate investors lost a bundle of money in the early 1990s is that the IRR assumptions they made when buying commercial real estate in the late 1980s were wildly optimistic. Perhaps the *real* value of IRR calculations for potential acquisition opportunities is not the resulting percentage derived from a single mathematical exercise. Rather, the value is that they let the prospective property buyer test the sensitivity of percentage returns under differing sets of performance assumptions, that is, "To what extent will my prospective IRR return be reduced if my occupancy rate averages 90 percent rather than 93 percent in years three, four, and five following the investment?"

As we've seen here, REITs' internal-growth opportunities are as numerous as their property types. In the hands of shrewd management, these options can be maximized so that results pay off for both the REIT and its investors. However, internal growth isn't the only way REITs can expand revenues, funds from operations, and dividend-paying capacity. There is another.

EXTERNAL GROWTH

Let's assume, for purposes of discussion, that a high-quality REIT can obtain annual rental revenue increases slightly better than the rate of inflation, say 3 percent, and that expenses and overhead growth can be held to less than 3 percent. Let's assume further that with modest, fixed-rate debt leverage, such a REIT can increase its per share FFO by 4.5 percent in a typical year. Finally, let's assume that the well-managed REIT can achieve another 0.5 percent annual growth through tenant upgrades, refurbishments, and other internal means. How do we get from this 5 percent FFO growth to the 6–8 percent pace some REITs have been able to achieve for a number of years? The answer is through *external* growth, a process by which a real estate organization, such as a REIT, acquires or develops *additional properties* or engages in additional business activities that generate profits for the organization's owners. Let's look at the ways in which this can occur.

ACQUISITIONS

THE EXTENT OF A REIT's acquisition opportunities is dependent upon many factors, including a REIT's access to the capital markets and the cost of such capital, the strength of its balance sheet, levels of retained earnings, and the prevailing cap rates and prospective IRRs on the type of property it wants to acquire. We would like the acquired properties to have meaningful NOI growth potential, which, together with the initial yield, will provide internal rates of return equal to, or ideally in excess of, the REIT's true weighted average cost of capital.

External growth can be generated through attractive property acquisitions, development and expansion, and activities such as joint ventures and other real estate businesses.

ACQUISITION OPPORTUNITIES

The concept of acquiring additional properties at attractive initial yields and with substantial NOI growth potential has been applied successfully for many years by such well-known REITs as AMB Property, Equity Residential, Home Properties, Macerich Corp., Simon Property Group, United Dominion Realty, Washington REIT, Weingarten Realty, and many others.

For example, a REIT might raise $100 million through a combination of selling additional shares and medium-term promissory notes, which, allowing for the dilution from the newly issued shares and the interest costs on the debt, might have a weighted average cost of capital of 8 percent. It would then use the proceeds to buy properties that, including both their initial yields and the additional growth from rent increases and some capital appreciation over time, might generate internal rates of return of 10 percent. The net result of such transactions would be a pickup of 200 basis points over the REIT's average cost of capital. We must keep in mind, however, that near-term FFO "accretion" (obtaining initial yields on a new investment that will increase per share FFO over the near term) is much less important to investors than being able to find and acquire properties able to deliver longer-term internal rates of return that equal or exceed the REIT's true cost of capital. And this, at certain times, can be very difficult, making acquisitions problematical.

Acquisition opportunities are rarely available to a REIT that cannot raise either equity capital (perhaps because of undesirable prior company performance, an unproven track record, or a history of poor capital allocation by management) or debt capital (when its balance sheet is already heavily leveraged). Furthermore, investors do not want their company to sell new equity if doing so would cause dilution to FFO or to estimated net asset values (NAV) of the company. Dilutive acquisitions are not popular with REIT investors.

The early 1990s were a golden acquisition era for apartment REITs, which may be why so many of them went public during that time. The most seasoned apartment REIT at that time, United Dominion, could raise equity capital at a nominal cost of 7 percent, and debt capital at 8 percent. It could then acquire apartment properties at well below replacement cost in the aftermath of the real estate depression of the late 1980s that provided it with entry yields of 11 percent or more and internal rates of return that were even higher. (The sellers were troubled partnerships, overleveraged owners, banks owning repossessed properties, or the Resolution Trust Corporation.)

At first glance it may seem odd that properties could become available at such cheap prices and high investment returns, but if a type of property in a particular location has few willing buyers but lots of anxious sellers, the purchase price will be low in relationship to the anticipated cash flow from the property, and internal rates of return to the property buyer will be extraordinary. At the bottom of property cycles we often see such supply/demand imbalances, since, with abundant foreclosures, not only are owners anxious to cut their losses, but property refinancings are unavailable, and confidence levels are low. This is not, however, always the case; in the early years of the twenty-first century, despite very weak real estate markets, owners were able to refinance assets at low interest rates, few of them were overburdened with debt, and there were lots of willing buyers for underperforming properties.

The extent of acquisition opportunities for REITs thus depends upon real estate pricing and prospects from time to time, includ-

THE COST OF EQUITY CAPITAL

THE COST OF equity capital is often a misunderstood concept. What does it really cost a REIT and its shareholders to issue more shares?

There are several ways to calculate such cost of equity capital. "Nominal" cost of equity capital refers to the fact that a REIT's current earnings (FFO or AFFO) and its net assets must be allocated among a larger number of common shares, while "true" or "long-term" cost of equity capital considers such dilution over longer time periods and gives credence to shareholders' total return expectations on their invested capital. What's important for investors, however, is that they focus not just on the initial accretion to FFO from an acquisition, but also upon the longer-term internal rate of return (IRR) expectation from an acquired property, and they should compare expected total returns against an estimated weighted average cost of capital. *(For more information on cost of equity capital, see Appendix E.)*

ing the prevalence or absence of competing buyers, as well as each REIT's cost of capital—both equity and debt. Attractive acquisition prospects will be few when real estate prices are high and thus offer poor returns relative to historic norms; this often results from an abundance of potential buyers all waiting to snap up the next property coming onto the market, as well as overly rosy forecasts for rental growth. This situation has been prevalent during the last ten years, when finding great acquisitions has been difficult. Most REIT investors want their REIT to find the unusual acquisition opportunity at a bargain price—they believe that little value can be created when a REIT pays simply a fair price for an asset (unless it can manage it much more efficiently than anyone else or earn a substantially higher return through a joint venture strategy).

Even if reasonably attractive opportunities are available, the REIT cannot take advantage of them if its cost of capital exceeds the likely returns. To use an excessively pessimistic example, let's assume that investors expect 15 percent returns from their investment in a particularly fast-growing REIT (we'll call it *Gazelle REIT*), and that Gazelle REIT wants to buy a package of quality properties that is expected to deliver an internal rate of return of 10 percent.

Even if the REIT finances the acquisition using 50 percent debt at a 7 percent interest rate, it's a "no-go" from the investors' standpoint.

Why? Gazelle REIT's weighted average cost of capital will be 11 percent, which exceeds the expected 10 percent return. However, if Gazelle REIT's cost of equity capital were 11 percent rather than 15 percent, the weighted average cost of capital would be 9 percent, and the deal would probably be attractive.

The importance of attractive investment opportunities to a REIT's FFO growth rate and stock price cannot be overemphasized.

Many REIT executives talk about FFO accretion, or the difference, or *spread*, between what the REIT can earn on its invested capital (for example, the cash flow that a newly acquired apartment will provide to the REIT buyer) and the REIT's cost to obtain that invested capital. But we need to be very careful here. The true cost of capital for any company that uses long-term debt is a combination of the cost of equity *and* the cost of debt. The cost of debt capital is fairly straightforward—it is simply the interest that the REIT pays for borrowed funds. However, we should use long-term interest rates, since drawdowns under a credit line and other forms of short-term debt are temporary and must be repaid relatively quickly; furthermore, they are subject to interest-rate fluctuations. Calculations should be based on rates for debt that will be outstanding for seven to ten years, which will usually be higher than short-term interest rates. Using the short-term rate would distort the picture, making it seem that the REIT is able to borrow short term at 4 percent to buy 7 percent cap-rate properties, at times when the cost of long-term debt is actually 7 percent—a very attractive piece of fiction, but a fiction nonetheless.

The true cost of equity capital is much less straightforward and depends upon investors' total return expectations over time. This is not a readily identifiable number and must be assessed by each REIT—yet it is crucial to the REIT's decision on whether to raise additional capital. The arcane but important topic, cost of equity capital, is discussed in more detail in Appendix E.

A final point on acquisitions. When professional real estate organizations like REITs acquire a property, they are often able to operate and manage it more efficiently and profitably than the prior owner did. Thus, such a REIT can often obtain above-average internal growth from acquired properties, beyond the initial yield, by controlling expenses and spreading them over more units, even assuming no change in rents. The largest apartment REIT, Equity Residential, has often been able to generate better profit margins than those selling apartment assets to it.

What REIT investors need to remember on the issue of acquisitions is this:

◆ Investors should want a REIT to acquire properties that are likely, through initial yield and growth prospects, to generate internal rates of return that will equal or exceed the REIT's weighted average cost of capital. For most REITs, that cost is approximately 9–10 percent.

◆ A REIT whose shares trade in the market at a relatively high P/ FFO ratio will generally have a lower *nominal* cost of equity capital (though not necessarily a lower *true* cost of equity capital) than a REIT trading at a lower ratio. A lower nominal cost of capital enhances the REIT's ability to find and make acquisitions that are, in the short term, accretive to FFO, but that is merely a short-term advantage. If the long-term total returns on acquisitions do not meet or exceed the REIT's cost of capital, the shares will fall to the extent that disappointed investors punish the REIT for destroying shareholder value.

DEVELOPMENT AND EXPANSION

Some REITs can increase external FFO growth by developing entirely new properties, whether they are apartments, malls, neighborhood shopping centers, office buildings, or any other property sector.

Until the REIT-IPO boom of 1993–94, very few public REITs had the capability of developing new properties from the ground up. To do that takes specialized skill and experience. Today, REITs with those attributes are not uncommon, and we see them in almost all sectors. A well-conceived development program requires capital as well as know-how. New properties require financing during the twelve to twenty-four months (and sometimes even longer) required to build them out and fill them with new tenants. Having development capabilities is a key advantage in most real estate markets, for they allow REITs to grow externally when tenant demand is strong and space is tight, a time when, because cap rates are then often low, finding attractive acquisitions is very difficult. Successful developments typically provide 8–10 percent initial returns on a REIT's investment when the property is stabilized, that is, when it is largely filled with new tenants, usually a much higher figure than returns on the acquisition of existing properties of comparable quality. Furthermore, the REIT's net asset value will be significantly enhanced, since, when lower cap rates are applied to newly developed and nearly fully leased properties, extra property value is created, which, over time, will also enhance the price of the REIT's stock. At times these development "spreads" can exceed 200 basis points, which can create substantial value for the REIT's shareholders. Some mall REITs, for example, have been able to develop new malls that provide 10 percent stabilized yields and could be sold at 7 percent cap rates; that's value creation!

Such capability also allows a REIT to capitalize on unique opportunities. For example, many years ago, Weingarten Realty was able to obtain a parcel of property directly across the boulevard from Houston's Galleria, one of the premier shopping complexes in America, and build an attractive new center in that location. More recently, Macerich has redeveloped the Queens Center in New York, and is generating 11 percent returns on its investment. Boston Properties, Cousins Properties, Duke Realty, Kilroy Realty, ProLogis, SL Green, and others have been getting close to double-digit returns from developments and redevelopments in the office and industrial sectors. Apartment development returns have declined in recent years along with the cap rates, but Avalon Bay and some of its peers are still developing up to 200 basis-point spreads over cap rates. Finally, a few REITs, including AMB Property, ProLogis, and Simon, are even developing properties overseas, including Europe and Japan.

Although a REIT can contract with an outside developer to acquire ownership of a new project, it will not be as profitable because of the outside developer's need to generate its own profit.

However, the REIT's risks will be lessened to the extent the outside developer assumes the risk of construction cost overruns and some of the lease-up risk. The prospective returns, and the risks, will be higher if the REIT fully develops its own projects, particularly when there is little or no pre-leasing.

Those investors willing to assume somewhat higher risk should consider REITs with successful track records of property development, since they have yet another avenue for increasing per-share FFO growth and NAV increases.

Property development certainly has a downside—the risks. What can go wrong? Plenty. There are three areas of risk in development: construction risk, tenant risk, and financing risk. Cost overruns can significantly reduce expected returns. This can happen particularly when a builder lacks experience with a unique property type or develops in a new locality, as was the case at Post Properties in 2000, or if the REIT relies extensively on unproven local contractors. Next, the projected rents or anticipated occupancy level might come in under estimates, a particular risk if the development occurs when a favorable property cycle ends abruptly as it did in 2001. Over-building is also a real danger to rental and occupancy estimates, as it can put lots of competing space into the same market. Some apartment development projects in the San Francisco Bay Area fell short of projected returns for BRE Properties because of a sudden falloff in demand, due to the reversal of fortunes of many high-tech and manufacturing companies in the national recession in 2001. The third risk—involving financing—arises because permanent debt financing is usually unavailable until a project is complete and leased, which could be two or three years away. Who knows what interest rates will look like that far down the road? A large increase in interest rates can siphon off much of the profits in any development project.

The bottom line is that REIT investors and managements alike should expect higher returns from development in order to be compensated for taking greater risks. What remains to be seen is whether development-oriented REITs that are capable of creating substantial value via their development expertise, even when the extra risk is accounted for, will be given adequate pricing premiums by investors to reflect their ability to create extra value for shareholders. The jury is still out on that question.

A parallel method of external growth closely related to new development is the expansion or redevelopment of existing successful properties. Some development capability is required here, but the risks are significantly smaller for two reasons: The existing property has proven itself, and the cost of adding space is less than developing a new property from scratch. Furthermore, while the *total* profit potential from an expansion or redevelopment may be less than that from an entirely new "ground-up" project, the *percentage* return on invested capital from the expansion is often higher. Successful expansions and redevelopments can be done in any property type, but a strong location tends to bring more success to the project.

Nothing beats seeing a REIT announce it's adding phase 2 or phase 3 to an existing successful property. This generally indicates that the existing property is doing well, that management has had the foresight to acquire adjacent land, and that the risk/return ratio is favorable. Many well-regarded REITs in various property sectors have the ability to add expansion properties, sometimes even when they don't have full development capabilities.

MORE EXTERNAL GROWTH AVENUES

Although property acquisitions, developments, expansions, and redevelopments are the primary vehicles for a REIT to grow externally, they are not the only ways. As noted earlier, a number of REITs have been able to form joint ventures (JVs) with institutional partners to acquire, own, and, at times, even develop properties. Although these JV structures can make a REIT's business strategy and financial structure more complex and create risks not present when assets are owned outright, they do generate additional fee income streams for the REIT, and this can augment FFO growth and create extra value for shareholders. Each JV strategy should be examined on its own merit, of course, as investors will want the benefits to more than offset both the risks and the additional complexity.

REITs have other avenues for external growth as well. Thanks to the REIT Modernization Act, they can engage in real estate–related businesses that can often generate substantial additional revenues and net income. One of the REITs that has been most adept at this business strategy is Kimco Realty. It has formed several businesses that take advantage of its core competencies in real estate acquisition, development, and management, including the acquisition of rights to restructure leases of bankrupt retailers, providing financing for certain retailers and dispensing of their surplus space, as well as developing properties for them. Indeed, a number of development-oriented REITs, particularly in the office and industrial sectors, such as Duke Realty, ProLogis, and Catellus, have also been developing properties for others on a fee basis.

And some REITS, such as Vornado Realty, have been making opportunistic real estate–related investments in which they do not own the underlying property; a few are even making "mezzanine" loans, which are certainly risky but also potentially very profitable. SL Green, a leading office REIT, had long carried on a successful higher-risk lending business in the New York City office sector. In 2004 it organized a new mortgage REIT, Gramercy Capital, which is now engaged in the same business.

There are risks in these nontraditional businesses, of course, and as they generate revenues from nonrental sources they may cause a REIT's FFO growth to be more lumpy and less predictable. But they should be viewed as a tool for the creation of additional value and external growth for the REIT's shareholders, and all tools can be used well or misused. Every such nontraditional business engaged in by a REIT should therefore be examined closely and judged on its own merits.

SUMMARY

◆ Using FFO and AFFO enables both REITs and their investors to estimate disposable cash flows by correcting for real estate depreciation.

◆ FFO should not be looked upon as a static figure, and it is up to management to continue to seek methods of increasing it.

◆ AFFO is the most useful means for estimating REITs' recurring free cash flows, but there is no uniform standard by which it is calculated.

◆ FFO and AFFO can grow two ways: externally, by acquisition, developments, and engaging in related joint ventures and other businesses, and internally, through a REIT's ability to improve profitability of its existing assets.

◆ Internal growth is the most stable and reliable source of FFO growth since it does not depend on new capital or acquisitions but only on controlling expenses, increasing occupancy rates, and raising rental rates at the property level.

◆ Investors should try to understand concepts such as *net operating income* and *internal rate of return,* as they help us to understand how REITs can create—or destroy—value when making acquisitions or doing developments.

◆ External growth can be generated through attractive property acquisitions, development and expansion, and developing fee-related and investment businesses.

◆ The importance of attractive investment and development opportunities to a REIT's FFO growth rate and stock price cannot be overemphasized, but the risk profiles of external growth strategies should be carefully monitored by investors.

CHAPTER

Spotting the
BLUE CHIPS

A S WITH ANY TYPE of investing, a number of selection approaches can be used in the REIT world, depending on our investment goals and styles. We can look for companies of the highest quality, buy them, and hold them patiently over the long term. Or we can take more risk and go for large gains in more speculative stocks, or those selling at deep discounts to net asset value. We can also try to pick up REITs that are in the doghouse and hope for a turnaround. It's also possible to stress very small REITs, searching for little-known gems. It's just a question of investment style.

INVESTMENT STYLES

Some non-REIT investors have done well by buying and owning the large, steadily growing companies with excellent long-term track records, such as General Electric, Procter & Gamble, or Wal-Mart. Peter Lynch calls these stocks "stalwarts." Other investors have looked for companies growing at very rapid rates, such as Cisco, Yahoo!, or eBay. "Contrarian" or "value" investors buy shares whose prices are temporarily depressed by bad news that is expected to eventually dissipate, or where hidden asset values will eventually be discovered. Some investors like to buy "small-cap" shares in growing companies most people have never heard of. All of these approaches can work—for REITs as well as for other stocks—if the investor is disciplined and patient and exercises good judgment. There is no consensus as to which style works best, and a Warren Buffett–type guru of the REIT world has yet to emerge (although the "sage of Omaha" himself has bought REIT shares on occasion).

The most conservative investors are likely to emphasize blue-chip REITs. Those seeking quality and safety above all else certainly will. And it is vital for *all* REIT investors to know what makes a blue-chip REIT different from the rest, since it's the blue chips that set the standards by which all others should be measured. Before we take on the blue chips, however, we'll examine a few of the others.

GROWTH REITS

Some believe that the term *growth REIT* is a contradiction; by their very nature, REITs cannot grow per-share earnings at rapid rates. Real estate is a high-yield but slow-growth enterprise, and REITs must, by law, pay out most of their cash flow to shareholders and thus cannot retain much of their earnings to plow back into the business to generate growth. Yet there have been times in the past when some REITs have been viewed as growth stocks, and this will undoubtedly happen again.

Growth REITs, then, are those viewed by investors as having the ability to increase funds from operations (FFO) much faster than historical norms of 4–6 percent annually, even at rates exceeding 10 percent. This growth potential may be because a specific sector is enjoying the boom phase of its property cycle, when rental rates and occupancies are rising rapidly, or because their management's strategy is to implement a very aggressive acquisition or development program. This pattern of growth in a REIT normally requires substantial regular infusions of new equity and debt capital to expand the business and property portfolio. If the newly raised capital is used to acquire properties that are cheaply priced and offer strong rental and net operating income (NOI) growth prospects, management ends up looking very clever. Another approach to rapid growth is through a program of building a number of new properties and selling them to others or to a joint venture. If, however, acquisition or development opportunities abate, such a REIT's earnings growth will slow; the REIT will be hard-pressed to meet investors' lofty expectations, and its stock price will decline substantially. Much, of course, depends upon the extent of premium pricing accorded to a growth REIT and the extent of the disappointment.

As long as a growth REIT can stay one step ahead of investors' expectations, it can deliver exciting returns, but it's very important to estimate when the growth rate may slow significantly.

Several hotel REITs were in a high-growth phase in the mid-1990s. Starwood Hotels and Patriot American Hospitality, for example, enjoyed above-average internal growth, while acquiring billions of dollars in new hotels. Their FFOs increased rapidly. Those who bought them in 1995 and 1996 enjoyed hefty gains for a while, but those who bought in later or held on too long saw much or most of their gains dissipate in later years. Patriot American, now Wyndham International (and no longer a REIT), was a disaster for shareholders, having overextended its balance sheet with excessive acquisitions. Even mortgage REITs can be growth REITs at certain times, raising lots of capital and making large volumes of new loans. Growth-oriented REIT investors will seek out rapid-growth opportunities and may, with good market timing, "beat the market." The key is knowing when to get out.

VALUE OR "TURNAROUND" REITS

If you're a value investor, there are often a number of depressed REITs to choose from—these are REITs that are selling for very low valuations relative to their peers or at large discounts to net asset value. This might be because they're below the radar screens of most investors, or because they own marginal properties, or because they are in the doghouse, due to management's miscues. Or their balance sheets may be frighteningly ugly. They might be excellent short- or even long-term investments if they're cheap enough or if you can get them just prior to a turnaround in their performance. Carr America Realty is a good example. This office REIT was languishing shortly after it went public and had no access to capital to take advantage of the recovering office markets. The stock was selling at cheap prices despite excellent management. However, a short time later Security Capital Group, a multi-billion-dollar real estate investment organization, agreed to acquire a controlling interest in Carr America, and those who bought before the Security Capital Group transaction were extremely well rewarded.

Investors can do very well buying a depressed REIT in hopes of a turnaround—but they should be aware of the risk. It's very difficult to know when an investment has bottomed out.

Many apparently cheap REITs have potentially serious pitfalls that include unsustainably high dividends, high debt leverage, and suspect managements; some even present substantial conflicts of interest issues. REITs like this can be compared to junk bonds— high risk *sometimes* brings high rewards, but sometimes just brings further woes. Proceed with caution.

It is possible for investors to do very well with a turnaround REIT, but it's important to remember that some of these investments never make a comeback if management continues to destroy shareholder value. And it's particularly important to do extensive homework before venturing into these REITs, including detailed balance sheet and asset analysis, as well as checking for conflicts of interest between the management and the shareholders.

BOND-PROXY REITS

Another type of REIT that is often appealing to some investors is one that I refer to as a bond proxy. It generates relatively slow FFO and dividend growth, but, because of its moderate debt and stable properties, it has a reasonably secure dividend, one that is usually higher than that of most REITs. Adjectives like *reliable* and *consistent* describe these REITs. They might include certain health care, retail, and apartment REITs that do not have aggressive growth strategies. Those seeking bond proxies should look for conservative, capable, and dedicated management, with moderate debt levels and a substantial, well-covered dividend. Growth, of course, is likely to remain modest. Another in this category might be a "triple-net" lease REIT, one that is locked into leases with creditworthy tenants for long periods of time, such as Realty Income Corp.

Bond-proxy REITs provide high dividend yields, in the range of 6–7 percent, but they have less well-defined growth prospects compared with other REITs. Investors are trading higher prospective total returns for higher current income.

Many of these REITs might be quite suitable for those investors to whom stable, high income is more important than capital appreciation. However, most investors will do better, over time, to defer the reward of high current dividends in favor of the higher-potential, long-term total return of the blue-chip REITs, which have greater growth prospects.

THE VIRTUES OF BLUE-CHIP REITS

So far, we've discussed growth, value, and bond-proxy REITs. Now we'll introduce the stalwarts of REITdom—the blue-chip REITs. But first, a caveat: There is no objective definition of "blue-chip REIT," so you will have to accept mine until you develop your own. Blue-chip REITs take you safely through the ups and downs in the sector's cycles and will, over reasonably long time periods, deliver consistent, rising, long-term growth in FFO and dividends. Because they are financially strong and widely respected, they will, in most periods, have access to the additional equity and debt capital that can fuel above-average growth. They will not always provide the highest dividend yields or even, in many years, the best total returns, nor can you frequently buy them at bargain prices—but they should provide years of 7–10 percent total returns, with only modest risk.

The quality attributes of blue-chip REITs should be the standard by which all REITs are measured. Those qualities include:

◆ Outstanding proven management
◆ Access to capital and its effective deployment
◆ Balance sheet strength
◆ Sector focus and strong regional or local expertise
◆ Substantial insider stock ownership
◆ Modest dividend payout ratio
◆ Absence of conflicts of interest.

A blue-chip REIT may not boast all of these attributes, but it will have most of them.

THE SUPREME IMPORTANCE OF MANAGEMENT

Strong management is the single most important attribute of blue-chip REITs.

Good management is what separates mere collections of properties from superior businesses whose stock-in-trade just happens to be real estate. Even if its management is mediocre, a REIT will do reasonably well when its sector is healthy—a rising tide lifts all boats. The rapidly rising rents and occupancy rates enjoyed during a sector's boom cycle will generate strong internal growth for the entire sector, such as was the case for the apartment REITs throughout much of the 1990s, office REITs from 1995 through the end of the decade, and retail REITs from 2000 through 2004.

The true test of quality is when difficult property markets return, often bringing excellent buying opportunities as well as pain in their wake. That is when strong property-level management, good asset location, strong leasing skills, and good access to capital make the difference. When real estate is depressed, strong companies are able to retain most of their tenants while sometimes being able to pick up sound, well-located properties cheaply—properties that can, with intelligent and imaginative management, be put back on track and produce excellent returns for shareholders. Excellent management teams should be able to guide their REITs through the downside of the real estate cycle and emerge even stronger.

When shopping for solid blue chips, it's important to focus on REITs whose managements have been able to build sound portfolios with only a modest amount of debt, who have been able to invest shareholder capital wisely, who know how to measure risk, and who can raise reasonably priced capital to take advantage of acquisition or development opportunities when they arise. These are REITs whose managements have been able to achieve internal growth by upgrading properties and tenant rolls, while maximizing rental revenues and reducing the rate of operating and administrative expense growth. And they have guided us through cyclical weakness in their markets with minimal damage. Now all we have to do is learn how to recognize them.

FFO Growth in All Types of Climates

We've discussed buying opportunities in depressed real estate markets. But there are other advantages that superior managements offer: They know which tenants are looking for space, and in which locations. They make sure that the lease rates in acquired properties are supported by underlying real estate values, which enables them to find replacement tenants who can afford equal or higher rents if the original tenants don't make it. Superior managements will keep on top of tenant rosters, always looking to replace the weak with the strong and reducing the risk of tenant defaults. Defaults are disruptive to cash flow, not only because of lost rent and "down time" but also because changing tenants midlease might require that expensive improvements be made for the new tenants.

Experienced management teams will be continuously scanning for market weakness that they can use to their advantage.

One example of a REIT that's been able to take advantage of difficult retailing environments is Kimco Realty, a neighborhood shopping center REIT we have met previously. Retailers are engaged in a very competitive business, and some of them who own their own stores need extra capital when business trends deteriorate. Capitalizing on such difficulties, Kimco bought a package of retail stores in early 1996 from a retailer, Venture Stores, that was trying to restructure its business. The stores were bought at prices well below market and leased to Venture at an estimated yield to Kimco of almost 13 percent. Investors should look for blue-chip REITs, such as Kimco, that have the ability to do well even in difficult environments by making unusually attractive acquisitions, upgrading tenant quality, continuing to generate above-average rental growth, and pursuing business opportunities that create value for shareholders.

Extra Growth Internally

There are times when attractive acquisitions are not available to a REIT (e.g., when expected rates of return would be below the REIT's weighted average cost of capital), and often there just aren't many development opportunities that are likely to provide an acceptable risk-adjusted return. Such a time was 1998 through 2000. Not only were real estate markets very competitive and very late in their cycles, but REIT stock prices were such that capital raising was prohibitively expensive. Several years ago Robert McConnaughey, managing director and senior portfolio manager of Prudential Real Estate Securities at the time, stated, "The low-hanging fruit has already been picked. We are no longer in an environment where anyone can find bargains, as we have been in a recovery mode for five years now." During such periods it becomes more important than ever to create higher internal FFO growth rates, and to accomplish this REITs must be creative. Home Properties, for example, provides a community atmosphere at its seniors-oriented apartment complexes, which enables the tenants to feel that they're getting value for their rent dollars. One result is low turnover. Equity Residential and

United Dominion, large and highly diversified apartment REITs, have been able to generate healthy profit margins through highly efficient property management. Weingarten Realty and Regency Centers have been able to build and maintain an extensive database of tenants' space requirements. As a result of their long-standing relationships with hundreds of national, regional, and local retailers, they have been able to refer to this database to fill vacant space quickly, whether in established properties or in new acquisitions. A number of mall REITs also have this capacity.

We discussed earlier how a REIT is often able to charge higher rents for enhanced properties. There is no guidebook written on how to most effectively improve the appearance and desirability of specific properties, nor on how to reduce operating costs, but innovative management will always find a way to generate above-average NOI growth at the property level, and this is a major contributor to rising FFOs over time.

Another key advantage of blue-chip REITs in the area of internal growth is that their properties are situated in strong locations, often where it is difficult for competing properties to be developed. Excellent management teams figure out ways to build or acquire in these locations. This, too, enables the REIT to generate strong same-store NOI growth over an entire market cycle, thus enhancing FFO growth rates and asset values.

External growth opportunities are important, but internal growth is more stable and dependable.

"The Art of the Deal"

One unique characteristic of a high-quality management team is that, from time to time, it can make an unusual but very profitable real estate deal. A prime example of this is the 1995 Vornado coup involving Alexanders. Alexanders was a department-store chain in the New York City area that filed for bankruptcy in 1992. It owned seven department store sites and a 50 percent interest in an adjacent regional mall. According to a Green Street Advisors' March 17, 1995, report, these sites were very valuable, including a full square block in midtown Manhattan. In March 1995, Vornado bought a 27 percent stock interest in Alexanders from

Citicorp for $55 million, a purchase price estimated at 20 percent below the prevailing market price. Vornado also lent $45 million to Alexanders, at a weighted average interest rate of 16.4 percent. Vornado structured the deal to earn fees for managing, leasing, and developing Alexanders' real estate. This not only enabled Vornado to increase its FFO significantly, but also to increase its per-share net asset value (NAV). Vornado has frequently made unusually attractive real estate deals, including its acquisition in 1997 of the Mendik Company, which owned 4.0 million square feet (net) of office properties in midtown Manhattan.

Another instance of what Donald Trump called "the art of the deal" is the 2002 acquisition of the Westcor portfolio of shopping malls in and near Phoenix, Arizona, by Macerich Company. Many investors at that time criticized Macerich for overpaying for these quality assets, but their return on invested capital has been outstanding. Kimco Realty has made its reputation on the strength of many such favorable deals, including both large property portfolios and "one-off" smaller deals.

Investors should look hard for REITs with management teams that can add value by finding and making unusually attractive deals that are not widely marketed. Almost anyone with the capital can buy real estate at market prices; only a few can steal it.

Attracting the Best Tenants

A well-managed REIT should not be entirely at the mercy of the quality and creditworthiness of its tenants. Even in difficult environments, it should be able to take space vacated by a financially troubled tenant and re-lease it at rates comparable to or better than before. Most retail REITs with good managements were not hurt in the retail contraction of the late 1980s and early 1990s, nor were they significantly affected by the 1995–96 or 2000–2001 waves of retail bankruptcies. Office and industrial REITs with strong underwriting standards and assets in excellent locations should also be able to "back-fill" vacant space quickly in most economic environments.

Nevertheless, a REIT's ability to attract a roster of high-quality tenants is very important, particularly in retail sectors such as malls and neighborhood shopping centers. In a shopping center, having productive tenants means higher traffic, which means higher sales—for all the stores. For the owner of the center, such retail prosperity means that the tenants will be able to afford their rent bumps and will generate the sales overages built into their leases. It also justifies higher rental rates when it's time to renew the leases. Productive centers mean higher operating profits for their owners and higher asset values.

A retail REIT's management wants to do everything possible to attract shopping traffic. More traffic means more sales, and more sales means less tenant turnover.

Better-quality tenants, whether in retail space, industrial properties, or office buildings, will usually be looking to expand, and if a management enjoys good relationships with these tenants, they will turn to the REIT management when they're ready for additional space. For example, ProLogis's business plan is for continual development of long-term relationships with America's major corporations, with the prospect of acquiring and developing additional properties for these companies both here and abroad. ProLogis is one of the few REITs with a significant overseas development business, which may give it a competitive edge with some major industrial space users.

The very best management teams perform well even when their tenants do not.

In the mid-1980s, when the downward spiral in oil prices sent Texas into a virtual depression, retail sales in Houston weakened considerably, and retail store occupancy rates fell below 90 percent in the oil patch. However, Weingarten Realty, a blue-chip REIT, came out of the downturn completely unscathed, retaining occupancy rates of 93–95 percent. Weingarten was able to continue to do well, despite the horrendous economic conditions, by retaining excellent relationships with its tenants, owning centers in strong locations, and anchoring its centers with stores that catered to consumer necessities, such as drugstores and supermarkets.

Cost Control

It has always been axiomatic in business that the low-cost provider has an edge on the competition. That has never been more true than in today's highly competitive business environment. Outstanding REITs build very cost-efficient internal property management teams, while also keeping overhead costs—administration, legal services, accounting, and so forth—under tight control.

We spoke about REITs' availing themselves of buying opportunities in a depressed market, but what about buying properties in a healthy market? Well, rich or poor, it's nice to save money. If the property-management team is highly efficient at keeping operating costs down, then it will be in a position to outbid competing buyers for high-quality properties and still generate highly satisfactory returns on those properties. For example, let's assume a reasonably attractive apartment building located in an upscale suburb of Maryland is available for $7 million. It has an annual rent roll of $1 million and might cost the typical property owner $500,000 in property-management expenses. That would leave the owner with an unleveraged profit of $500,000, a return of 7.1 percent ($500,000 divided by $7 million) on the asking price. This would be considered a reasonably attractive return by 2005 standards. But suppose that a REIT had a management team so efficient (aided, perhaps, by owning multiple properties in the same community) that it could manage the building at a cost of only $400,000 annually, providing $600,000 in annual net operating income. At the same asking price of $7 million, the return would then be 8.6 percent, which would be a home-run acquisition.

But it isn't only property-management expenses that need to be kept under control; overhead must be kept down as well. Let's take a REIT that owns $10 million of properties (at current market value) that generate unleveraged NOI of 9 percent, or $900,000 per year. If the overhead costs amount to 1 percent of assets, or $100,000 per year, the REIT's funds from operations (FFO) (excluding interest expense—remember, we're talking about no debt leverage) will be $800,000, or 8 percent on current asset values. Compare this with a second REIT whose overhead costs amount to only 0.5 percent of assets, or $50,000. The second REIT will generate $850,000 in FFO, providing an 8.5 percent return, half a percentage point over the first REIT.

Cost control is an often overlooked factor when evaluating REIT managements, but, over a significant period of time, the management that can contain its costs will have a substantial competitive edge, not only with tenants but also with prospective investors.

Track Record of Value Creation

Patrick Henry said, "I have but one lamp by which my feet are guided, and that is the lamp of experience." One of the most obvious but often neglected methods of determining the quality of management is to review the REIT's historical operating performance. Does the REIT have a long and successful track record of increasing FFOs and NAVs on a per-share basis? Does it have a history of steady, increasing shareholder dividends? How long has the REIT been a public company, and has it weathered various real estate cycles? Has its management found ways to deliver acceptable performance even when its real estate markets have been depressed or when it's had a lot of competition from new developments? How has it invested the capital that's been entrusted to it by shareholders and new investors? How does it truly create value for its shareholders?

REITs have been around for forty-five years, but the number of REITs that have established unblemished track records of consistent and substantial growth through a complete property cycle is somewhat limited. Recall, as we discussed in an earlier chapter, that most of today's REITs were not even in existence—certainly not as public companies—prior to 1993, and thus have only recently been tested in severely depressed real estate markets such as existed in the 2001–2004 period.

Nevertheless, many of the REITs that have gone public since 1993 are among the most outstanding names in the real estate industry, and most of them had operated successfully for many years as private companies before their IPOs. Furthermore, a large number of them have shown their ability to create value for shareholders as public companies. While they may have only recently been battle-tested in troubled real estate markets, they have had to contend with stop-and-go capital markets, periodic bouts of overbuilding in some markets, and changing demands of investors. Although there have been stumbles along the way, many have allocated their capital wisely. There are many REITs with very capable managements and well-conceived growth strategies that have figured out ways to generate extra FFO growth and create shareholder value, even during periods of difficult real estate and capital markets.

Examples of such REITs include (but are not limited to) Archstone-Smith, Avalon Bay Communities, Camden Property, Equity Residential, Essex Property, and Home Properties in the apartment sector; CBL & Associates, Developers Diversified Realty, General Growth Properties, Kimco Realty, Macerich Company, Pan Pacific Realty, Regency Centers, Simon Property Group, and Tanger Factory Outlets in retail; and AMB Property, Alexandria Real Estate, Boston Properties, Carr America Realty Corp., CenterPoint Properties, Duke Realty, Equity Office Properties, Kilroy Realty, Liberty Property, Prentiss Properties, ProLogis, and SL Green Realty in the office and industrial sectors. Older REITs with similar—and even longer—impressive track records include Cousins Properties, United Dominion Realty, Vornado Realty Trust, Washington REIT, and Weingarten Realty.

Today's REITs are still in the process of proving that they can maintain successful long-term track records as public companies through good cycles and bad. There are hopeful signs, however. Most REITs were less aggressive on the development front prior to the most recent economic and cyclical downturn, and have been heavily focused on early lease renewal and intensive property management. They have also pruned their portfolios when necessary, at attractive prices, and have been disciplined on the acquisition front.

ACCESS TO, AND EFFECTIVE USE OF, CAPITAL

In determining which REITs deserve the "blue-chip" label, we also need to look at access to capital and how it is deployed. Since a REIT must pay out 90 percent of its annual net income to shareholders, access to capital to fund external growth like acquisitions and developments is important in determining a REIT's potential long-term returns to shareholders. Likewise, how a REIT chooses to allocate its precious capital is vital to shareholders' assessment of a REIT's long-term value as an investment.

The better a REIT's track record, and the greater the respect investors have for a REIT's management team, the more likely it is to have a solid balance sheet and the ability to raise new capital upon which a satisfactory return can be earned. Although most REITs could raise capital from 1996 through early 1998, very few were able to do so from then until 2001. Part of the reason for the shutdown of available capital to the REIT industry from 1998 to 2001 is that many REITs were perceived as having done a poor job in allocating the capital that was given to them in prior years.

The owner of a typical commercial property might expect that when the market is in equilibrium his or her property will generate increased net operating income only at the rate of inflation, say 2–3 percent, unless the returns are leveraged by taking on debt; this extra leverage could get the internal FFO growth rate to 3–4 percent. However, if the owner has access to additional equity capital, it will be able to buy additional properties or complete new developments, assuming a return exceeding the cost of capital that will allow for meaningful external growth. Simply put, this is one of the principal reasons why many outstanding REITs will, over many years, be able to report FFO growth of 6–8 percent per year, on average.

Access to capital and using capital wisely are key factors in separating the blue-chip REITs from the rest.

The value of acquiring properties providing internal rates of return greater than the cost of capital has already been addressed. Similarly, in the case of new development, obtaining returns that are less than the cost of capital to finance that return is pointless. To make sense, the spread must be positive—thus the importance of low-cost capital.

Even though capital might *seem* expensive in absolute terms, if a REIT is able to buy properties at high enough returns or to create

VALUE CREATION

VALUE CREATION can be defined as the positive difference between the true cost of capital and the long-term return obtained from the use of that capital discounted to net present value. It can be manifested in higher income and greater net asset values. This concept can be extended to all business enterprises.

new developments that yield even more than the cost of the capital, the spread between capital cost and its ultimate return can still make the project attractive. Of course, the careful REIT investor, as well as the REIT's management, will want to weigh the risks involved in any new development project. A new development *should* deliver returns greater than that of an acquisition, given the higher risks inherent in any development project.

Some REIT investors use the term *franchise value* to refer to the ability of a REIT to generate returns on new opportunities that exceed their cost of capital. There are times, such as in the early 1990s, when it's easy for almost any REIT to obtain such returns, due to an abundance of opportunities in the real estate markets. Conversely, there are other times, as in the late 1990s and the early years of the twenty-first century, when few REITs can avail themselves of these opportunities. And there are yet other times when some REITs operating in some sectors are able to do so.

But the blue-chip REITs, due to imaginative management and multiple strategies for creating value (along with a strong balance sheet), have better value-creating opportunities than other REITs no matter what the status of the economy or the real estate markets. A company like Kimco Realty is able to develop when retailer demand is strong, and also to take advantage of the real estate of troubled retailers when business is poor. REITs such as Kimco are believed to have superior franchise value and should be sought by investors when their shares are priced at reasonably attractive levels. (See Chapter 9 for a discussion of REIT valuations.)

As noted earlier, in 1998–99 some REITs were perceived by investors as having done a poor job of deploying new capital raised from investors by secondary stock offerings in prior years, and from additional debt financings, as well as from retained earnings. To the extent that a REIT raises fresh capital (or uses existing capital) and does not generate a return on the money that at least equals its cost, it may be said to have destroyed shareholder value. Or, to put it another way, it has done a poor job of allocating its capital.

The blue-chip REIT, conversely, allocates its precious capital wisely. Capital can be allocated by a REIT in various ways, including acquisitions of single properties or portfolios, the purchase of entire companies (such as other REITs), engaging in new property developments or joint ventures, repurchasing its own stock, paying down debt, or even investing in new business ventures. This last can be done indirectly via stock ownership or directly by starting up a new business (perhaps in the form of a taxable REIT subsidiary, or even launching a new REIT, such as SL Green has done with Gramercy Capital).

The overriding issue for investors is to determine whether such capital has been allocated in a way that will generate strong returns for its shareholders, particularly when the risks of any such allocation are factored into the equation. Is that acquisition at market rates, or did the REIT get a deal? What's the upside potential—and prospective IRR—from the acquisition? Is the new development likely to succeed, and to what extent—and is it worth the risks? Is management stepping outside of its field of expertise? When buying another company, what kind of premium is being paid, and how long will it take for the REIT to earn back that premium in the form of cost savings or a higher growth rate? Is it a good time to retire debt, or should the balance sheet be "expanded" to take advantage of an apparent abundance of opportunities? Did management use good judgment when it financed that new business, and will it augment the growth rate of its core business? Is raising new equity even necessary—can growth be financed exclusively through a joint venture strategy?

These are the kinds of questions that investors need to ask themselves when trying to identify that blue-chip REIT. Of course, most of these questions can only be answered with hindsight, and sometimes it can take quite some time before the answers are known. Nevertheless, to the extent that a REIT proves that it can be trusted to allocate its capital wisely and effectively, it will not only be able to access additional capital, if needed, with which to generate higher growth rates but will also be accorded a higher stock market valuation by investors.

BALANCE SHEET STRENGTH

A third factor in ferreting out blue-chip REITs is the balance sheet. Property owners, perhaps since biblical days, have used debt to partially finance their acquisitions. At certain times, such as when an individual buys a single-family residence, the amount of debt has dwarfed the amount of equity put into the property. Not too long ago, developers, too, were able to obtain 90 percent, even 100 percent, financing.

Debt leverage increases both the risks and rewards of owning real estate.

Due to the stability and predictability of real estate cash flows, all property owners, including REITs, can justify a moderate amount of leverage to carry their properties and to finance acquisitions. For this reason, many years ago, when Washington REIT boasted that it had reduced its debt to almost zero, most investors were not impressed, since such low debt levels usually result in subpar FFO growth rates. What *is* impressive to investors is when a REIT carefully manages a moderate amount of debt in order to increase the rate of return on its properties and boost FFO, yet keeps the balance sheet strong enough to take advantage of new opportunities.

A strong balance sheet enables a REIT to leverage ongoing business expansion, when needed, by raising new equity capital and additional debt. Conversely, even a REIT with strong management, faced with the best development or acquisition climate in the world, will nevertheless be shut out of the capital markets and find itself unable to take advantage of the opportunities if it has a weak balance sheet.

Debt Ratios and Interest-Coverage Ratios

What determines a strong balance sheet? First, a modest amount of debt relative either to its total market cap or to the total market value of its assets; second, strong coverage of the interest payments on that debt, and other fixed charges, by operating cash flows; and third, a manageable debt maturity schedule. Let's talk about debt levels first.

◆ **Debt ratios.** Suppose a REIT has 100 million shares of common stock outstanding (including partnership units convertible into shares), and its market price is $10 per share, for a total equity capitalization of $1 billion. It also has $100 million of preferred stock outstanding, and indebtedness of $300 million. The debt/market-cap ratio can be determined by dividing debt ($300 million) by the sum of the common equity cap ($1 billion), the preferred stock ($100 million), and the debt ($300 million), resulting in a debt/market-cap ratio of 21.4 percent.

Debt/Market-Cap Ratio =
Total Debt / (Common Stock Equity + Preferred Stock Equity + Total Debt)

Some analysts, such as Green Street Advisors, prefer using a ratio based on the estimated asset values of a REIT, instead of the debt/total-market-cap ratio. For example, if a REIT had $100 million in debt and total asset values (an estimation of the fair market values of its properties) of $300 million, its debt/asset-value ratio would be $100 million divided by $300 million, or 33 percent. This method, which focuses on the *asset value* of a REIT rather than its *share valuation* in the stock market, has two advantages: It is more conservative (since REITs most often trade at market valuations in excess of their NAVs), and it avoids rapid fluctuation (since a REIT's share price bounces around from day to day). Advocates of this formula feel that a REIT's leverage ratio should not be adversely affected by a temporary rise or decline in its stock price if the price movement has nothing to do with operations or property values. Nevertheless, the debt/asset-value ratio is less frequently utilized than the debt/total-market-cap ratio as it involves a subjective factor (estimated asset values).

Sometimes the formula is tweaked just a bit, to include preferred stock in the numerator along with debt. In this approach, we'd use debt plus preferred stock as a percentage of total market cap or total asset value. The basis for this is that preferred stock, like debt, increases a company's sensitivity to changes in property values and market conditions.

Just what is the right amount of debt leverage for a REIT? First, let's look at some averages. At the end of 1995, Robert Frank, who has followed the REIT industry for many years, estimated that REITs' median debt/total-market-cap ratio was 30 percent and the average was 34 percent (*Barron's*, December 18, 1995). According to SNL Securities and NAREIT, this percentage has increased moderately since then, rising to an average of approximately 43 percent by the fourth quarter of 2003. Some sectors use more debt than others.

DEBT/MARKET-CAP-RATIO GUIDELINES

SOME GENERAL GUIDELINES regarding a debt/market-cap ratio:

◆ Anything over a 55 percent debt/total-market-cap ratio makes some REIT investors uncomfortable, particularly in the more volatile sectors, such as hotels, where cash flows are not protected by long-term leases.

◆ A ratio under 40 percent is almost always conservative and indicates a strong balance sheet, subject to the other tests described in this section.

◆ If competition is heating up or there is a danger of overbuilding, even a 50 or 55 percent ratio might be risky.

Mall REITs, for example, have used more leverage than REITs in other sectors (48.3 percent as of the fourth quarter of 2003, per SNL Securities and NAREIT data), which is justified by the stability of their lease income from national retailers.

Financial leverage means that, if things go well, you've increased your profits; if things go badly, you've increased your losses. Under adverse economic conditions, a high debt level can be a time bomb waiting to explode. Mall owners have been able to use substantial debt leverage because their business has generally been very steady and predictable; most national retailers have always expressed a need to be located in malls, and so mall rents have continued to edge higher over time, while occupancy rates have been stable at the higher quality malls. If this situation should change, yesterday's reasonable leverage and manageable debt might be tomorrow's overly aggressive leverage and crippling debt. The reverse may also be true in some sectors. When a sector is in recovery mode, and rents are rising quickly, a higher amount of debt leverage may be appropriate.

The answer, then, to the debt/market-cap or debt/asset-value question is that there is no answer that is "right" at all times. Thus, there is no universally appropriate debt ratio which, if exceeded, would make a REIT overleveraged. It depends on the REIT's sector, the properties' quality and locations, the existing and prospective business conditions, and the supply/demand situation concerning the REIT's properties. Each company must be analyzed on its own merits.

SOURCE: NAREIT

INTEREST-COVERAGE AND DEBT RATIOS AT Q4 2003

REIT SECTOR	INTEREST-COVERAGE RATIO	DEBT/MARKET CAP
Apartments	2.8	44.2%
Neighborhood Shopping Centers	3.9	37.6%
Malls	3.4	48.3%
Manufactured Homes	2.4	47.9%
Health Care	3.8	31.0%
Hotels	5.3	42.7%
Office	3.1	46.5%
Industrial	4.4	38.7%
Self-Storage	3.8	32.4%
Diversified	3.9	39.9%

◆ **Interest-coverage ratios.** Another way to determine whether debt levels are reasonable or excessive is to look not at the *aggregate amount* of debt (excluding or including preferred stock), but rather at the amount by which all debt interest payments are *covered* by the REIT's NOI. (Net operating income, you will recall, is prior to interest payments, income taxes, depreciation, and amortization.) This measurement is often expressed as the ratio of NOI, or "EBITDA," to total interest expense. Sometimes analysts look at, in addition to interest expense, other fixed charges such as dividend payment obligations on outstanding preferred stock or scheduled debt repayments. The ratio, so defined, would be referred to as the *fixed-charge coverage ratio*, and is a more conservative test than the interest-coverage ratio.

EBITDA means:
Earnings Before Interest, Taxes, Depreciation, and Amortization.

For example, if Aggressive Office REIT has annual NOI of $14 million and carries debt of $100 million, which costs it $9 million in annual interest expense, then its interest-coverage ratio would be $14 million divided by $9 million, or 1.56.

Many analysts prefer to measure debt this way instead of looking at the debt/total-market-cap ratio or the debt/asset-value ratio, since this measurement gives a picture of how burdensome the debt service is in relation to current operating income. In other words, if the REIT is doing very well with its properties at a particular time and can obtain fixed-rate financing at reasonable rates, even though the total debt level is high, the REIT may find it easy to service the debt. This measurement also avoids one obvious problem with the debt/total-market-cap ratio (but not with the debt/asset-value ratio), which is that, when a REIT's stock price declines, the debt/total-market-cap ratio rises.

However, advocates of interest-coverage ratios seem to ignore the fact that real estate markets do change over time, and managements don't always make perfect decisions. To use the interest-coverage-ratio method to the exclusion of either debt/total-market-cap or debt/asset-value ratio is to ignore the fact that a REIT's NOI may be temporarily high because of favorable economic or market conditions. If, for instance, a recession or overbuilding causes rental revenues to decline and NOI is reduced, what might have been a comfortable coverage ratio will now be very aggressive. Again, the risk is that the REIT will be forced to raise equity capital at the worst possible time—when investors are already nervous about future prospects.

A careful REIT investor will look at both debt/total-market-cap (or debt/asset-value) and interest-coverage ratios or fixed-charge coverage ratios in order to determine whether a REIT might be overleveraged or underleveraged.

Like debt/total-market-cap or debt/asset-value ratios, there is no magic-number cutoff that will tell us whether a REIT has taken on so much debt that interest expenses are too high in relation to current operating income. Generally speaking, an interest-coverage ratio of below 2.0 will often be cause for some concern in most real estate sectors, and blue-chip REITs will rarely have ratios that low.

To give you a reference point, the chart above shows, as of the fourth quarter of 2003, the average interest-coverage ratios and the average debt ratios for the principal REIT sectors.

Variable-Rate Debt
The next component that we need to examine is variable-rate debt. Variable-rate debt subjects the REIT and its shareholders to signifi-

---

FIXED-RATE DEBT

THE ADVANTAGE OF fixed-rate debt is that it sets a specific interest rate for the entire duration of the debt instrument. In addition, if the borrower is allowed to prepay the debt should interest rates fall substantially after the debt is incurred, the borrower will have the opportunity to reduce interest costs. In recent years, many REITs have taken on a sort of semi–variable-rate debt in which the interest rate is capped at a level somewhat higher than the current rate of interest. These caps can be expensive, their price depending upon the length of the cap and width of the interest-rate band. Generally, in spite of the cost, capped–variable-rate debt is worth paying for because it is an insurance policy against the possibility of interest rates spiking up due to higher inflation or an overheated economy. However, all such caps, and related "swaps," have termination dates.

---

cantly increased interest costs in the event that interest rates rise. Mike Kirby at Green Street Advisors has made the point that REIT investors will invest in a REIT for its business and real estate prospects, and don't want to see their expectations dashed because a REIT's management team guessed wrong on the direction of interest rates. Mr. Kirby is absolutely correct; it's clearly a negative for a REIT investor when the REIT is loaded up with variable-rate debt that exposes the REIT's FFO to the risk of rising interest rates. It's not that a good REIT cannot have *any* variable-rate debt; it's a question of how much is too much. Given the large portion of a REIT's total expenses that is comprised of interest expense, substantially higher interest costs could cause a significant reduction in FFO and even, on occasion, result in a dividend cut. Conversely, fixed-rate debt is a positive, since it allows REIT investors to be able to predict future FFO growth without having to guess whether rising interest rates will throw all forecasts askew.

Hotel REITs occasionally argue that some variable-rate debt is appropriate for them, as interest rates tend to rise when the economy is strong, and vice-versa. Hotels generally do quite well in strong economies, so variable-rate debt can serve as a hedge in weak economies, that is, lower room revenues are partially offset by lower interest expenses.

The strategy of some REITs has been to inflate FFO growth by using cheaper, variable-rate debt to finance property acquisitions, and so we have seen it used, often excessively, from time to time. The economics of a property acquisition should be analyzed on the basis of financing with equity and fixed-rate debt, as near-term "accretion" from variable-rate debt is just temporary. Thus, the *quality* of a REIT's FFO and its growth rate are suspect when the REIT relies heavily upon variable-rate debt, and this quality—or lack thereof—should be reflected in the multiples of earnings which investors are willing to pay for REIT shares. Fortunately, we are seeing modest levels of variable-rate debt at most of today's REITs, particularly the blue-chip REITs.

Despite the negatives, with entities like REITs, which often seek additional capital, *some* variable-rate debt is inevitable, and even desirable. The typical pattern is for a REIT to establish a line of credit that can be used on a short-term basis and then paid off through either a stock offering; the placement or sale of longer-term, fixed-rate debt; or the sale of assets. Borrowing under such credit lines is almost always at a variable rate. The key is the *amount* of such variable-rate debt in relation to a total enterprise value such as the REIT's estimated NAV or its market cap. On February 7, 2003, a Green Street Advisors report noted that REITs' variable-rate debt, as a percentage of REITs' asset values, then averaged 8.7 percent.

If variable-rate debt exceeds 10–15 percent of the value of the REIT's assets, the REIT will be exposed to significant negative earnings surprises should interest rates escalate.

Maturity of Debt

It's axiomatic that real estate, being a long-term asset, should be financed with long-term capital.

Short-term debt (which must be repaid within one or two years) exposes the borrower to significant risk. When the loan comes due, if for any reason the lender is unwilling to "roll it over" or extend the loan to the REIT borrower, and if no other source of financing can be found, the REIT will be forced either to sell off assets at whatever price is offered or to file bankruptcy proceedings. Second, if interest rates have risen in the meantime, the debt will have to be refinanced at the higher rate. Finally, the mere threat of a failure to extend financing can cause a severe drop in the REIT's stock price, thus precluding altogether its raising additional equity capital as an alternative to extending the debt, or, at the very least, making such capital prohibitively expensive.

Nationwide Health Properties, today a well-respected health care REIT, had this problem in its early years. Under its original management team it took on a lot of short-term debt, which the lender was unwilling to roll over at its due date. The REIT (then known as Beverly Investment Properties) was required, unfortunately, to sell off significant amounts of assets and to reduce its dividend. And several years ago, Patriot American Hospitality (now known as Wyndham International) took on an excessive amount of short-term debt as a result of a hotel acquisition binge. It could not roll the debt over and had to sell new equity at prohibitively expensive terms. The dividend was eliminated, and the company gave up its REIT status.

Accordingly, REIT investors must be mindful of the maturity dates of a REIT's debt. Some analysts look at the average debt maturity, and intelligent investors prefer that most of a REIT's debt not mature for several years. They prefer to see long-term financing (of at least seven years' average duration) at fixed interest rates.

Wise REIT managements will refinance expensive debt well before maturity, if this can be done with modest prepayment penalties, and seek as long a maturity as possible.

The above-cited Green Street Advisors report notes that, among the REITs in Green Street's universe, the amount of short-term debt (defined as the difference between cash balances and debt maturing within two years), as a percentage of asset value, averaged approximately 5.9 percent.

THE IMPORTANCE OF SECTOR AND GEOGRAPHICAL FOCUS

Many, many years ago, during the infancy of the REIT industry, some brokers and asset managers claimed that a healthy REIT is one that is well diversified in sector and in geographical location, since such a REIT diversifies the risks of owning real estate. That is a very misleading statement.

There are many idiosyncrasies in local real estate markets involving demand for space in the "best" locations, the nature and identity of the strongest tenants, the amount of amenities required to make space competitive, and, with respect to property development projects, a whole host of zoning and entitlement procedures. And each property sector has its own unique set of characteristics. To buy, manage, and develop properties well requires a deep familiarity and extensive experience with property sectors and specific locations.

The investor should diversify—but by buying shares in a number of REITs, each doing business in a different sector and location, not by trying to buy one REIT that is diversified within itself.

A good example of specialized REIT management is that of Bay Apartment Communities, which merged with Avalon Properties in 1998 to form Avalon Bay Communities. Bay, which went public a number of years ago, had been an active developer and owner of apartments in northern California since 1970. It never owned other types of properties. Management survived the depression-like conditions in California in the early 1990s and built an excellent track record in developing and refurbishing high-quality apartments. Until its forays into Southern California and the Pacific Northwest, this REIT had not owned a single apartment unit outside of northern California. Avalon Properties, with which Bay merged, also had an excellent reputation for owning, managing, and developing apartment communities in the northeast and middle Atlantic states. Avalon Bay remains a strong competitor on both coasts, having a deep knowledge of local markets.

Local, specialized knowledge gives a REIT several advantages in its markets. Its management will be more likely to hear of a distressed seller who must unload properties. It will therefore be able to take advantage of unusual opportunities, and similarly, it may be able to close a deal before it's put out for competitive bidding. If it has development capabilities, it will know the best and most reliable contractors and will be familiar with the ins and outs of getting zoning permits and variances. It will be very much aware of local economic conditions and to which neighborhoods the city or region's growth is headed. If it is a retail REIT, it will have good access to the up-and-coming regional retailers. The bottom line is that, in most real estate sectors, REITs that focus intensively on specific geographical regions have a significant edge in the competitive business of buying, managing, and developing real estate.

If it's important for a REIT to concentrate on a specific geographical area, it is even more important to specialize in one property type.

Successful real estate ownership and operation is more competitive than ever. Each type of commercial real estate has its own peculiar set of economics, and it's far more likely that a management familiar with its sector's idiosyncrasies and supply/demand issues will be better able to navigate through rough waters—and take full advantage of subtle opportunities—than a management that tries to adjust to the shifting economies of several different property types. Only a very few, such as Cousins Properties, Washington REIT, and Vornado Realty, have managed to do well with multiple asset types.

For all these reasons, most blue-chip REITs will be specialized in both sector and location. There are, however, some exceptions in both general and individual cases. Health care REITs, for example, should not seek geographic concentration; since nursing homes depend on state reimbursement regulations, having too many properties in one state means exposure to the vagaries of that state's reimbursement policies. Mall REITs, while not requiring diversification, nevertheless have little need for geographic concentration and their lack of geographic focus shouldn't be a significant issue with investors. Mall economics are similar in most areas of the United States, and a large percentage of mall tenants are national retailers, for example, Gap Stores. And self-storage REITs, such as Public Storage, have not been at a disadvantage when using a national market strategy.

To make matters more confusing, many high-quality REITs have been taking on a regional, or even national, character. It can be advantageous for a retail, health care, or even an apartment, office, or industrial REIT, to have locations in several neighboring states because of the importance of size, market dominance, and tenant relationships. Duke Realty is a prime example. It operates in many Midwest and Southeast states, and because of its relationship with strong regional companies, its geographical diversification is often an advantage.

In other cases, quality REITs simply outgrow their home base. For many years known as the dominant neighborhood shopping center owner in Houston, Weingarten Realty has been entering new markets, such as other locations in Texas, Louisiana, Arizona, and Nevada. In 2001 it acquired nineteen California assets from a liquidating REIT, Burnham Pacific, and now has assets throughout the Southwest. Spieker Properties (which merged with Equity Office Properties in 2001), long a "local sharpshooter" in northern California office properties, expanded into Southern California and the Pacific Northwest in the latter part of the 1990s—very successfully. Some veteran REIT investors may decry such wanderlust, but at some point a well-run and growing real estate company like each of those just mentioned will look for new promising markets. If Weingarten, for example, applies the same degree of care and foresight to its California and other western markets that it's applied in its original markets, investors need not be overly concerned—but it must have experienced local management in place.

Finally, we are now seeing the presence of strong national REITs, with assets in numerous markets throughout the United States, often clustered in major markets, such as AMB Property and Prentiss Properties. A slightly different approach was taken by Boston Properties, which owns large office assets in four key markets—New York City, Washington, D.C., Boston, and San Francisco. The key to the success of these REITs will be the strength of their management teams in each of their local markets, together with the ability of corporate headquarters to walk the fine line between providing adequate guidance and allowing for local incentives and creativity. While it is still too soon to tell how successful these national strategies will be, early results are encouraging.

And yet, all else being equal (and it rarely is), we must give a great deal of credit to, for example, CenterPoint Properties, which has remained a very successful local sharpshooter in the greater Chicago area, and be more skeptical of an office or industrial REIT with assets in twenty-eight different markets across the United States. Large size can, indeed, be a competitive advantage for certain property types, but my belief is that the strong and highly focused local or regional player has a greater ability to create more value for its shareholders.

REIT investors should be careful about investing in companies that are very spread out, whether by property sector or geographical location, unless they become market leaders in their areas of concentration.

Before we leave the subject of specialization versus diversification, let us address how an investor can diversify a REIT portfolio (which is also discussed further in Chapter 10). This is far easier today than it was before the REIT-IPO explosion of 1993–94, but not as easy as it was several years ago before so many REITs expanded geographically. Yet we can still buy a package of high-quality REITs, each specializing in a particular property sector and operating in a particular geographical region. For example, if you like apartments in the Sun Belt, consider Amli or Camden; if you like California and the Northwest, take a look at BRE or Essex. On the East and West Coasts, check out Archstone-Smith or Avalon Bay. Investors can do the same thing in retail properties, office buildings, or industrial properties, although today many of the larger REITs do have properties in many widespread locations. While it's true that investors will have a hard time finding an apartment REIT operating only in the Great Lakes area or an office REIT with properties located exclusively in the Rocky Mountain states, the range of property types and sectors covered by blue-chip REITs is sufficient to allow the individual investor as much diversification as is needed. Another way to diversify is through REIT mutual funds, or even "exchange-traded funds," which we discuss in Chapter 10.

INSIDER STOCK OWNERSHIP

Few investment techniques exist upon which both academics and investors seem to agree wholeheartedly. After painstaking research, academics often come up with conclusions that contradict principles most investors hold dear. One exception, however, about which these opposites concur is insider ownership. Significant stock ownership in a company by its management often has a strong bearing on the company's long-term success.

That profit is the best incentive is basic capitalism, and a management that has a high percentage of ownership in the REIT it manages will be making money for shareholders while it's making money for itself.

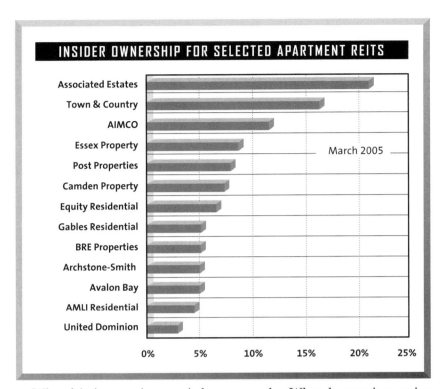

INSIDER OWNERSHIP FOR SELECTED APARTMENT REITS

Associated Estates
Town & Country
AIMCO
Essex Property
Post Properties
Camden Property
Equity Residential
Gables Residential
BRE Properties
Archstone-Smith
Avalon Bay
AMLI Residential
United Dominion

March 2005

0%   5%   10%   15%   20%   25%

SOURCE: GREEN STREET ADVISORS

Why this is true is certainly no puzzle. What better incentive for success can there be than for the operator of the company to be an owner? Managements that have a large equity stake in their company are more likely to align their personal interests with public shareholders' interests and look for long-term appreciation rather than the fast buck. They will sacrifice faster short-term FFO increases, if necessary, in order to reach a long-term goal. They will avoid "goosing" FFO by taking on too much short-term, variable-rate debt and will not buy properties with limited long-term growth prospects just to increase FFO in the current fiscal year. Furthermore, REIT managements with high insider ownership are likely to be more conservative about new development projects and less tempted when presented with a conflict of interests to take advantage of their insiders' position at the expense of the shareholders.

Fortunately for us, REITs have a much higher percentage of stock owned by their own managements than most other publicly traded companies. The 2003 Green Street Advisors report *REIT Pricing—An Update of Our Pricing Model* indicates that in February

2003, REITs' average insider ownership was 12.6 percent and the median was 8.3 percent—both figures significantly higher than in other public companies. The main reason for this is that a large number of REITs that went public during the last twelve years had been very successful private companies, and, as these companies became REITs, the insider owners continued to hold large stock positions in the public entity.

Needless to say, a high percentage of insider ownership will be an important criterion in determining which of the REITs can be considered blue chips. However, it's also important to realize that the percentage of insider ownership will continue to decrease over time as the number of outstanding REIT shares are diluted by additional stock offerings, as those within management diversify their own investment assets, and as younger professional managers are brought onboard. The chart on the previous page includes the percentages of outstanding stock held by insiders at the thirteen apartment REITs followed by Green Street Advisors, as of March 2005. Due primarily to the amount of consolidation within the apartment sector, the insider stock ownership is slightly lower than in other sectors, but is still respectable.

LOW PAYOUT RATIOS

A low dividend-payout ratio allows the REIT to retain some cash for external growth.

Another criterion for separating the wheat from the chaff is the REIT's payout ratio of dividends to FFO or adjusted funds from operations (AFFO). Since new equity capital is so expensive, the best-managed REITs prefer to retain as much of their operating income as possible for acquisitions, developments, and other opportunities that invariably arise from time to time; using their own retained capital is cheaper than borrowing or selling additional shares.

A low payout ratio is also good insurance against unexpected events that might cause a temporary downturn in FFO or AFFO. Although it would be nice if their earnings climbed higher every year, REITs operate in the real world and are subject to such surprises as recessions, higher vacancy rates, and tenant defaults; lower rents because of overbuilding or other supply/demand imbalances; or higher-than-anticipated operating expenses. If a REIT pays out too much of its AFFO in dividends, it may create investor concern about the possibility of a dividend cut and depress the stock price.

Traditionally, REIT investors have been attracted to REITs for their high and steady dividend yields. However, with the recent increase in REITs' popularity among institutional as well as individual investors, together with the increasing importance being placed upon FFO and AFFO growth, the importance of retained earnings and low payout ratios is now being recognized.

REITs with low payout ratios will normally have better growth potential, as well as better perceptions of safety, and, thus, higher stock prices.

Just what should we be looking for in payout ratios? Let's begin with the premise that AFFO is superior to FFO in determining a REIT's free cash flow. If a REIT claims to have earned $1.10 per share in FFO but uses $.15 of that for recurring capital expenditures each year, it really has only $.95 available for dividend distributions. Further, if it pays out the full $.95 in dividends, it will have retained absolutely nothing with which to expand the business or to offset the effects of occasional stormy weather. Accordingly, the wise investor will look at a REIT's ratio of dividends to AFFO, not FFO. If AFFO is $.95 and the dividend rate is $.85, the payout ratio would be $.85 ÷ $.95—or 89.5 percent. Sometimes the formula is reversed, with the $.95 AFFO divided by the $.85 dividend; this is known as the *coverage ratio*, in this example approximately 112 percent ($.95 ÷ $.85).

NAREIT regularly publishes the average payout ratios of REITs over time, using FFO rather than AFFO, as the former measure is calculated by each REIT on a quarterly basis. As of the end of 2003, the average payout ratio as a percentage of FFO was 81 percent. This figure is higher than the high 60 percent range in 1999–2001, due to weaknesses in cash flows resulting from the real estate recession, but is higher than in the 1994–95 time period, when the payout ratio was in the 85–89 percent range.

These are nice, tidy figures, but there are wide differences from REIT to REIT, with a number of companies, particularly in the apartment and office sectors, at the end of 2004 having payout ratios of 100 percent or higher. Ratios like these can limit growth and increase risk.

We should keep in mind, however, that high payout ratios do not necessarily mean dividend cuts. Most REITs will keep their dividends intact when they can anticipate a near-term recovery in their cash flows due to strengthening real estate markets. Furthermore, many REITs have been able to fund a significant portion of the shortfall out of property sales at substantial profits. This isn't a good formula for long-term growth derived from retained earnings, but does make sense at times, and each REIT's payout practice should be examined on its own merits.

A few last words about payout ratios. There may be times in the REIT sector's business cycle when acquisition or development just doesn't make sense. At such times, a higher payout ratio might be the most efficient use of the REIT's free cash flow. Also, there may be occasions when a REIT structured as an UPREIT or a DownREIT can acquire properties through the issuance of operating partnership (OP) units rather than the payment of cash. Home Properties has been particularly successful at this. In these cases, it will be less necessary to fund acquisitions out of retained earnings, and thus a low payout ratio will not be quite so important.

Finally, if your REIT investment goal is income rather than substantial long-term growth, you want the REIT to have a high payout ratio, subject to retaining enough cash flow to withstand the occasional decline in property market conditions. That's a different case entirely, and such investors should seek out REITs with high payout ratios, including bond-proxy REITs. Most blue-chip REITs, however, have low payout ratios, which are likely to contribute to faster long-term growth.

ABSENCE OF CONFLICTS

Conflicts of interest between management and shareholders are inevitable in any company. The shareholders, for instance, might benefit if the company is acquired, but such a takeover would probably put management on the unemployment line. In some cases, management shareholders or passive insider owners have the ability or even the right to prevent such a takeover, regardless of the public shareholders' wishes. Or, management might have a compensation plan that would motivate them to emphasize short-term profits over higher long-term growth that would better benefit shareholders. These are but a few possible conflicts of interest that might arise between management and public investors.

One of the worst kinds of conflict of interest was prevalent many years ago, when most REITs' charters did not prohibit officers or directors from selling to the REIT properties in which they themselves had a financial interest. The sale prices of some of these assets were later determined to have been vastly inflated—with dire consequences for the REIT. Today most REITs prohibit such transactions, but there are other types of conflicts unique to REITs that must be watched carefully.

Another type of conflict can arise when a REIT is externally administered and advised. Some years ago, when REITs had outside companies providing corporate services, property acquisitions, and property management, these outside advisers' fees were based not on the profitability of the REIT or its returns to shareholders, but on the dollar value of its assets. This gave the outside company an incentive to increase the amount of the REIT's assets simply as a basis for increasing the fees, but not necessarily for the long-term benefit of the REIT or its shareholders. Today, fortunately, the vast majority of REITs are internally administered and managed, and managements' interests are aligned much more closely with shareholders' interests. Of course, a high percentage of stock owned by management can also alleviate the concerns of shareholders.

Unclear management involvement of high-profile insiders can sometimes be a problem as well. Richard Rainwater, whose business acumen has always been very highly respected, organized Crescent Real Estate Equities, a diversified REIT, in the mid-1990s. While his knowledge, expertise, and reputation were instrumental in bringing the REIT public, some investors felt that he was not as involved in its management as they had been led to believe. When this REIT encountered problems in certain segments of its business some years ago, many investors blamed Mr. Rainwater for not having spent sufficient time personally monitoring the company's business. Investors should ask questions regarding management involvement when they see a high-profile investor lending his or her name to a REIT.

A relatively new area of concern is that of potential conflicts created by the UPREIT format. As discussed earlier, an UPREIT is merely a type of REIT corporate structure in which the REIT owns a major interest in a partnership that owns the REIT's properties, rather than owning them directly. Other partners in the operating partnership will often include the senior management. Sometimes one or more of the properties owned indirectly by the REIT has reached its full profit potential and might best be sold in order to use the equity elsewhere. Such a sale is not a tax problem for the shareholders, but since, in an UPREIT, the partners are carrying their interests in that property on their books at the same price as before the REIT was formed, a sale may trigger a significant capital gains tax to the partner-officers of the REIT.

Hotel REITs are subject to yet another type of conflict of interest. We discussed in an earlier chapter how, because of a REIT's statutory requirements, its income from non–property ownership sources is restricted. Because of this legal limitation, hotel REITs are particularly ripe for conflicts. Hotel REITs' properties must be managed by an outside company in order to fulfill the REIT requirements. Further, until the enactment of the REIT Modernization Act, REITs were required to lease their hotels to outside entities. Because hotel ownership is very management intensive and since the REIT's shareholders may want the properties managed by the founders or top management of the hotel REIT, the REIT's hotels are sometimes leased to and managed or supervised by an entity controlled by the REIT's senior management. This can create conflicts regarding how such management handles and accounts for operating expenses and is an arrangement investors need to be careful of.

Another area that REIT investors should watch for, applicable to non-REIT companies as well, is the issue of "management entrenchment." The public markets have witnessed many instances when an attractive buyout offer (for either a REIT or another public company) at a premium price is rejected by the board of directors, sometimes at the insistence of the CEO or a major insider shareholder. The motivation of the directors and management team might be to continue running the company for as long as possible, for monetary or even psychological reasons; on the other hand, the motivation of the public shareholders is often to obtain the best price possible for their stock, particularly if it's not been a good performer in the past and has uncertain prospects going forward. The conflict of interest is readily apparent in these situations.

REIT boards of directors seeking to ward off unwelcome suitors have one particular advantage over those of non-REITs. We learned earlier in this book that the law pertaining to REITs states that "five or fewer" individuals cannot own more than 50 percent of the value of a REIT's stock. This enables REIT organizations to insert in their charter documents a provision that no person may acquire more than, say, 10 percent of the stock of the REIT without prior approval of the REIT's board of directors. Accordingly, hostile offers to acquire a company are very rare in REITdom, and established management teams and their boards have been able to "just say no" to merger and acquisition offers.

This strategy may be bolstered by other defensive tactics such as "staggered" boards of directors, different classes of stock (each with different voting rights), poison pills, incorporation in states whose laws tend to favor incumbents, and super majority voting requirements. In these respects, REITs are no different from other public companies. The lesson here is that we want to see boards of directors and management teams create structures to protect, and to act in the best interests of, *all* the shareholders. Good corporate governance, like a lack of conflicts of interest, is a hallmark of the blue-chip REIT.

Suppose you discover a conflict of interest or less than ideal corporate governance in a REIT that otherwise seems like an attractive investment. Does that mean you don't want to own it? Not necessarily. Just because there is an opportunity for a decision that could adversely affect public shareholders doesn't mean that such a decision will in fact be made. But this is an area investors need to watch. The blue-chip REITs, as a group, tend to have fewer conflicts between management and shareholders, but, nevertheless, *caveat emptor*—buyer beware.

For most REIT investors, owning a portfolio consisting primarily of blue-chip REITs—those with above-average growth prospects, quality assets in desirable real estate markets, a strong balance sheet, and experienced and innovative management who have few or no conflicts of interest—will be most worry-free and the best route to long-term financial success.

SUMMARY

◆ The shares of growth REITs might appreciate quickly, but you can't expect substantial dividend income. Also, because of their aggressive business strategies and high shareholder expectations, there's more of an element of risk with them than with most other REITs.

◆ The value, or turnaround, REIT is the "junk bond" of the REIT world. The shares of such REITs usually bear high dividends and have a high-risk factor. Sometimes they do manage to turn themselves around and appreciate in value, but these REITs must be watched closely, as it's difficult to differentiate between an investment that has bottomed out and one that's still on the way down.

◆ Bond-proxy REITs provide high dividend yields—in the range of 6–7 percent—but they have less well-defined growth prospects compared with other REITs. It's a trade-off.

◆ Blue-chip REITs may not have a dividend yield as high as other REITs, but, when purchased at reasonable prices, they are usually the best long-term REIT investment for conservative investors.

◆ Qualities to look for in blue-chip REITs are outstanding proven management, access to capital when necessary to fund growth opportunities, balance sheet strength, sector focus and strong regional or local management, substantial insider stock ownership, a low dividend-payout ratio, and absence of conflicts of interest.

◆ The very best management teams perform well even when their tenants do not; difficult economic periods frequently bring opportunities to those who can take advantage of them.

◆ Access to capital—and the intelligent and profitable deployment of that capital—is a key factor in separating the blue-chip REITs from the rest.

◆ A REIT with a relatively low payout ratio has more capital available for growth and has better protection against economic downturns.

◆ Beware of conflicts of interest between management and shareholders; blue-chip REITs are subject to minimal conflict of interest.

◆ For most investors, owning a portfolio of mostly blue-chip REITs—those with above-average growth prospects, strong balance sheets, and experienced and innovative management—will be the best route to long-term and worry-free investment success.

CHAPTER 9

THE
Quest
FOR INVESTMENT
VALUE

S UCCESS IN REIT investing will be determined, at least over the short term, by the ability to buy REIT stocks at attractive prices. In this chapter we'll look at some yardsticks for determining the investment value of a REIT's stock. Sure, we want to buy high quality, moderate risk, and above-average growth, but only at prices that make sense.

THE INVESTOR'S DILEMMA: BUY AND HOLD VERSUS TRADING

One school of thought is that the key to investment success is to purchase shares of stock in the largest, most solid companies, or to buy index or mutual funds, and to hold those stocks or funds indefinitely. The only time to sell, say the buy-and-hold advocates, is when you need capital.

The other school of thought—a more hands-on approach—says that, with hard work and good judgment, an intelligent investor can beat the market or the broad-based averages—either by astute stock picking or by clever market timing. Some advocates of this approach, which rejects the theory that markets are "efficient," point to investors like Warren Buffett and Peter Lynch as examples of what a talented stock picker can accomplish, while others in this group believe that certain signs—technical or even astrological— can indicate when either the entire market or specific stocks will rise and fall.

Advice for the buy-and-hold crowd is simple: Assemble a portfolio of blue-chip REITs or buy a managed REIT mutual fund or an index fund. Then, if you've chosen solid stocks or performing funds, you can go off to Tahiti, collect the steadily rising dividends, and not worry about price fluctuations, beating the competition, or any other such irrelevancies. If history is any guide, such a strategy may be able to average 8–12 percent in total returns over a long time horizon.

Advice for the active trader or the REIT investor who desires to perform better than the REIT market is somewhat more complicated. First, you must have a way to determine when a REIT stock is overpriced or underpriced, given its quality, risk, underlying asset values, and growth prospects. Second, you must have a way to determine when REIT stocks as a group are cheap or expensive. Valuation of any stock is never easy, but there are guidelines and tools that can help determine approximate valuation.

Before examining REIT valuation methods in detail, let's take a closer look at the buy-and-hold strategy and the logistics of putting together a diversified portfolio of blue-chip REITs.

THE BUY-AND-HOLD STRATEGY

The buy-and-hold strategy has a number of advantages. Investors don't need to worry about fluctuations in rates of FFO growth, occupancy or rental rates, or even asset values.

Also, since these investors are not active traders, commission costs and capital gains taxes are much lower. Furthermore, if the efficient-market theory is correct, it's not possible to beat the market anyway. If not, an index-based, buy-and-hold REIT portfolio will slightly outperform a traded portfolio or an actively managed mutual fund.

However, buy and hold has some disadvantages. If mutual funds are used—whether indexed or actively managed—investors will pay an annual management fee and other expenses and, in some cases, a marketing or sales charge. Mutual funds often involve extensive record-keeping, especially when dividends and capital gains are reinvested. And, on occasion, entire property sectors may underperform for a number of years; buying and holding forever may not generate the best returns.

Investors who like the buy-and-hold approach to REIT investing but who don't want to go with a REIT mutual or index fund (or, as we'll review in Chapter 10, exchange-traded funds) should be careful to construct a portfolio consisting primarily of a broadly diversified group of blue-chip REITs. These REITs are likely to grow in value over time, notwithstanding occasionally difficult real estate markets, and to have managements that can be counted on to avoid serious blunders. They can be compared to blue-chip, non-REIT stocks such as Johnson & Johnson, Coca-Cola, General Electric, Intel, and Procter & Gamble. The blue-chip REIT of the type we discussed in the previous chapter isn't always large in size; there are a number of excellent smaller REITs, not specifically mentioned in this book, that qualify as blue chips. The investor may also want to include some "growth," "value," or "turnaround" REITs for additional diversification.

Of course, not all blue-chip REITs will deliver the expected returns, since individual companies are subject to management mistakes, changing economic conditions, overbuilt markets, declining demand for space, and a slew of other potentially negative developments. Furthermore, all stocks, including REITs, are subject to periodic bear markets, sometimes having little to do with how the company itself is performing.

REIT STOCK VALUATION

Active REIT investors will want to spend time analyzing and applying historical and current valuation methodologies to seek maximum investment performance for their portfolios.

Investors who are not content with the buy-and-hold strategy and who want to buy and sell REIT stocks more actively and take advantage of undervalued securities will need to know how to determine value. After all, it doesn't make sense to overpay, even if you're buying blue-chip REITs.

How can we determine what a REIT is worth relative to other REITs? And how can we decide whether REITs as a group are cheap or expensive? Professional REIT investors and analysts all have their own approach; there is no consensus as to which one works best. Thus, although there is no Holy Grail of REIT valuation, there are commonly used methods and formulas that can provide crucial insight into a REIT's relative investment strengths and weaknesses, bands of reasonable values for a REIT's stock price based on historical precedent, and even the fairness of pricing within the entire REIT industry.

REAL ESTATE ASSET VALUES

Until fairly recently, investment analysts have thought it important to look at a company's "book value," which is simply the net carrying value of a company's assets (after subtracting all its obligations and liabilities), as listed and recorded on the balance sheet. Whatever the merits of such an approach in prior years, investors today place more emphasis on a company's "going concern" value and growth prospects than upon tangible assets such as plant, equipment, and inventory. Furthermore, "intellectual capital" and "franchise value" are also deemed more important than the value of physical assets. Indeed, few stocks sell today at prices even close to book value.

Book value has always been a poor way to value real estate companies because offices, apartments, and other structures do not necessarily depreciate at a fixed rate each year, while land is carried at cost but tends to increase in value over time.

Although some analysts and investors like to examine "private-market" or liquidation values rather than book values, the majority today focus on a company's earning power rather than its breakup value. Nevertheless, while most of today's REITs are operating companies that focus on increasing FFO and dividends and will rarely be liquidated, they do own real estate with valuations that can be assessed and approximated through careful analysis. Furthermore, these assets are much easier to sell than, say, the fixed assets of a manufacturing company, a distribution network, or a brand name, and thus the market values of their assets are much easier to determine.

REITs are much more conducive than other companies to being valued on a net-asset-value (NAV) basis, and many experienced REIT investors and analysts consider a REIT's NAV to be very important in the valuation process, either alone or in conjunction with other valuation models.

One of the leading advocates of using NAV to help evaluate the true worth of a REIT organization is Green Street Advisors, an independent REIT research firm that has a well-deserved, excellent reputation in the REIT industry for its in-depth analysis of the larger REITs. Green Street's primary approach is first to determine a REIT's NAV. This is done by reviewing various segments of the REIT's properties, determining and applying an appropriate cap rate to groups of owned properties, and then subtracting its obligations as well as making other adjustments; undeveloped land and developments-in-process are valued separately, then added in. The

FINDING NET ASSET VALUE

UNFORTUNATELY, A REIT'S NAV is not an item of information that can be easily obtained. REITs themselves don't appraise the values of their properties, nor do they hire outside appraisers to do so, and very few provide an opinion as to their NAV. Net asset value is not a figure you will find in REITs' financial statements. However, research reports from brokerage firms often do include an estimate of NAV. Also, investors can estimate NAV on their own by carefully reviewing the financial statements, asking questions of investor relations personnel, and talking with commercial real estate brokers (or reviewing their websites) to ascertain appropriate cap rates.

current value of debt is also taken into account. Recognizing that REITs vary widely in quality, structure, and external growth capabilities, it then adjusts the REIT's valuation upward or downward to account for such factors as franchise value, sector and geographical focus, insider stock ownership, balance sheet strength, overhead expenses, share liquidity, and possible conflicts of interest between the REIT and its management or major shareholders.

The net result, under Green Street's methodology, is the price at which the REIT's shares should trade when fairly valued. The firm uses a *relative valuation* approach, weighing one REIT's attractiveness against another's. It does *not* attempt to decide when a particular REIT's stock is cheap or dear on an absolute basis, or to determine when REITs as a group are under- or overvalued.

Let's assume that, with this approach, "Montana Apartment Communities," a hypothetical apartment REIT, has an NAV of $20, and, because of good scores in the areas discussed above, the REIT's shares "should" trade for a 10 percent premium to NAV. Accordingly, Montana's shares would trade, if fairly priced, at $22. If they are trading significantly below that price, they would be considered undervalued and recommended as buys. Those trading at prices significantly in excess of this "warranted value" would be recommended for sale.

This approach to determining value in a REIT has a great deal of merit, notwithstanding its being difficult and imprecise. It combines an analysis of underlying real estate value with other factors that, over the long run, should affect the price investors would be willing to pay for the shares. Since REITs are rarely liquidated, investors should expect to pay less than 100 percent of NAV for a REIT's shares if the REIT carries excessive balance sheet risk, is managed poorly, is plagued with major conflicts of interest, or is merely unlikely to grow FFO even at the rate that could be achieved if the portfolio properties were owned directly, outside of the REIT. Why pay a premium if the management of the REIT is likely to mis-allocate capital or to otherwise destroy shareholder value? Indeed, a number of REIT shares deserve to trade at an NAV discount.

Conversely, investors should be willing to pay more than 100 percent of NAV for a REIT's shares if the strength of its organi-zation and its access to capital, coupled with a sound strategy for external growth, make it likely that it will increase its FFO, NAV, and dividends at a faster rate than a purely passive, buy-and-hold real estate strategy. This approach to valuation has worked well for Green Street and its clients, as the firm's track record of forecast-ing over- and underperformance of specific REIT stocks has been excellent.

At any particular time, the premiums or discounts to NAV at which a REIT's stock may sell can be significant. Kimco Realty, for example, since going public in late 1991, has been regarded as one of the highest-quality blue-chip REITs, and its shares have almost always traded at a premium to its estimated NAV. At the end of June 1996, for example, Kimco was trading at a premium of 35 percent to its estimated $20.75 NAV. Conversely, at the same time, an apartment REIT, Town & Country, was trading at a *discount* of almost 20 percent to its $15.50 NAV, because of concerns over its dividend coverage and its anemic growth rate. Eight years later, in June 2004, Kimco's shares were priced at a 27 percent premium to its estimated NAV of $35.75, but Town & Country's stock was trad-ing at a 15 percent *premium*. In this method of valuation, investors should develop their own criteria for determining an appropriate premium or discount to NAV, taking into account not only the rate at which the REIT can increase its NAV, FFO, or AFFO in relation-ship to the growth expected from a purely passive business strategy, but all the other blue-chip REIT characteristics we have discussed.

Perceived risk, of course, should play a key role in this process.

An advantage to this approach is that it keeps investors from getting carried away by periods of eye-popping, but unsustainable, FFO growth that occur from time to time. From 1992 to 1994, apartment REITs enjoyed incredible opportunities for FFO growth through attractive acquisitions, since capital was cheap and there was an abundance of good-quality apartments available for purchase at cap rates above 10 percent. Furthermore, occupancy rates were rising and rents were increasing, since in most parts of the country few new units had been built for many years. Since FFO was growing at surprisingly strong rates, analysts using valuation models based only on current FFO growth rates might have had investors buying these REITs aggressively when their prices were sky-high, reflecting potentially huge growth prospects for many years. But, as it happened, growth slowed substantially in 1995 and 1996 as apartment markets returned to equilibrium. Investors who bought stocks of apartment REITs trading at the then-prevailing high multiples of projected FFO never saw FFO growth live up to projections, and, consequently, saw little appreciation in their share prices for quite some time. A similar phenomenon occurred in 1998–99, when external growth slowed substantially for most REITs, and investors who bought in 1997 at very high NAV premiums suffered significant stock price declines.

Using an NAV model may also keep an investor from giving too much credit to a REIT whose fast growth is a result of excessive debt leverage; interest rates on debt are often lower than cap rates on real estate, making it easy for a REIT to "buy" FFO growth by taking on more debt, especially lower-cost variable-rate debt. If only price P/FFO models are used, such a REIT might be assigned a growth premium without taking into account that such growth was bought at the cost of an overleveraged balance sheet. Essentially, an NAV approach that focuses primarily on property values is a valid one and, if used carefully, can help the investor avoid overvalued REITs. We must, of course, remember to apply an appropriate premium or discount to NAV—*appropriate* being the significant word here—in order to give credit to the value-creating ability (or tendency to destroy value) of the REIT. At times, the ability of creative management to add substantial value and growth beyond what we'd expect from the properties themselves can significantly exceed the real estate values; a good example of this may be Vornado Realty, as well as Kimco Realty. Once assigned, these premiums and discounts will change from time to time in response to economic conditions applicable to the sector, to real estate in general, and to the unique situation of each REIT. For example, a larger NAV premium would be warranted during periods in which external growth opportunities are abundant, and vice versa. Most seasoned REIT investors believe that reasonable NAV premiums are warranted under the right circumstances, for example, 5–10 percent; the real debate is over their appropriate size at any particular time.

P/FFO MODELS

Some investors reject the NAV approach, considering it flawed because a REIT's true market value isn't based only on its property assets, and an NAV approach ignores the REIT's value as a business enterprise. These investors argue that, since REITs are rarely liquidated, their NAVs are not terribly relevant. If investors wanted to buy only properties, they argue, they would do so directly. These REIT investors are more like common stock investors, who want to judge how much is too much to pay for these active real estate enterprises. If we use P/E ratios to value and compare regular common stocks, the argument goes, we should use P/FFO or P/AFFO ratios to value and compare REIT stocks.

This argument has some appeal—much more now than it did many years ago—since today many more REITs are truly businesses and not just collections of real estate. Indeed, most brokerage firms today make extensive use of P/FFO ratios (and P/AFFO ratios) when discussing their REIT recommendations. Furthermore, a number of REIT managements, for example, John Bucksbaum at General Growth Properties, have expressed the opinion that their companies should be valued as operating businesses. Nevertheless, P/FFO ratio analysis has major defects that make it difficult to use as the sole valuation tool, in spite of their being somewhat helpful in comparing *relative* valuations among REITs. They are less helpful still as a measurement of *absolute* valuations.

Since the various valuation tools do not always agree, they should be used in conjunction with one another and only as a general indication of whether a REIT stock is cheap or expensive at a specific point in time.

The P/FFO ratio approach works something like this: If we estimate Sammydog Properties' FFO to be $2.50 for this year, and we think that it should trade at a P/FFO ratio of 12 times this year's estimated FFO, then its stock would be fairly valued at 12 times $2.50, or $30. If it trades lower than that, it's undervalued; if it trades higher than that, it's overvalued, right? Well, it's not that easy. How do we decide that Sammydog's P/FFO ratio *should* be 12, and not 10 or 14? Sammydog's price history should be our starting point. We need to look at Sammydog's past P/FFO ratios. Let's assume that between 1995 and 2005, the average P/FFO ratio for Sammydog Properties' REIT, based upon expected FFO for the following year, was 10.

Let's assume further that Sammydog's management, balance sheet, and business prospects have improved modestly and that the prospects for its sector are better than what they had been earlier. That might justify a P/FFO ratio of 12 rather than 10, but we need to do more. If we think that the market outlook for REIT stocks as a group is more or less attractive than it has been, we can use higher or lower multiples; and, of course, we need to look at the P/FFO ratios of its peer group REITs. We also need to factor in interest rates, which have historically affected the prices of all stocks. Perhaps a 1 percent increase or decrease in the yield on the 10-year Treasury note might equate to a similar adjustment in the ratio. But that's still not enough. We should adjust our warranted ratio in accordance with prevailing price levels in the broad stock market; if investors are willing to pay higher prices for each dollar of earnings for most other public companies, they should likewise be willing to pay a higher price for each dollar of a REIT's earnings, subject to growth rates and risk levels of REITs versus other equities.

We could go through this process with all the REITs we follow, assigning to each its own ratio, based on historical data, and making all the appropriate adjustments. Then we must compare the P/FFO ratio of each REIT against ratios of other REITs in the same sector and against the ratios of REITs in other sectors. Furthermore, we should take into account the cap rates of the REIT's properties; a REIT owning 6 percent cap-rate assets should trade at a higher P/FFO ratio than a REIT owning 9 percent cap-rate properties. We must take qualitative factors into account as well, including the balance sheet. A blue-chip REIT should trade at a higher P/FFO ratio than a weaker one, as risk is an important factor in determining any stock's valuation.

Finally, as we discussed, adjusted funds from operations, or AFFO, is a better indicator of a REIT's free cash flow than FFO, but, unfortunately, AFFO figures are not reported by most REITs. The investor has the choice of either digging through various disclosure documents filed with the Securities and Exchange Commission to construct a quarterly approximation of AFFO, or getting a brokerage report or REIT newsletter. Most brokerage firms that deal with REITs issue research reports on individual REITs, and industry publications such as those of SNL Securities are other good sources of current AFFO estimates.

After all adjustments have been factored into FFO or AFFO, the ratio valuation arrived at is, at best, still a subjective "guesstimate," because of the difficulty in determining what the appropriate ratio should be, even if we were able to predict FFO or AFFO to the penny. For example, to what extent are past ratios relevant in future investment landscapes? How relevant are cap-rate changes in the private commercial real estate markets? How important are long- or short-term interest rates in stock valuation, and how should they be figured in? In months and years to come, how will the individual and institutional investor perceive the value of REITs relative to other common stocks? Are all these attempts at fine-tuning "appropriate" P/FFO or P/AFFO ratios shrewd estimates or just wild guesses? These are just a few of the questions that arise when using P/FFO and P/AFFO models.

On October 31, 1997, the shares of Boston Properties, a widely respected office REIT, were trading at $32 (a P/AFFO multiple of 18.6 times the estimated 1997 AFFO of $1.72), perhaps in anticipation of continuing rapid AFFO growth. That multiple certainly seemed fair at the time for the stock of such a promising (and high-quality) REIT. Yet, although Boston Properties delivered outstanding AFFO growth over the next few years (AFFO rose to $2.96 in 2001), its growth rate would slow with the office market recession. When the P/AFFO ratio on its shares began to decline in 1998, the increased AFFO in future years was offset by a lower P/AFFO ratio, and the stock price stagnated, trading at $31.13 at the end of 1999. Investors who had bought at the high over two years earlier received nothing more than the dividends (though the dividend rate grew during that time period). Unfortunately, P/FFO and P/AFFO models can't really answer the key issue of the "correct" valuation of a REIT stock at any particular time, except in hindsight.

These problems and issues involving P/FFO or P/AFFO models shouldn't cause us to discard them entirely as useful tools, but we must understand their limitations. An existing multiple that appears "too high" may merely be reflective of improving asset values and rising cash flows—and vice versa. Furthermore, we need to avoid the practice of constantly boosting ratios (or target prices) higher as prices rise, and play the "greater-fool" game. These P/FFO or P/AFFO models are most helpful as *relative* valuation tools, for determining whether one REIT is a better investment value than another at any given time. If we believe one REIT has a stronger balance sheet, better management, more valuable properties, a less risky business strategy, and better growth prospects than another within its peer group, but the two trade at equal P/FFO or P/AFFO ratios, that's when the ratios can be helpful; they help us choose between the two. Concluding, however, that one is overvalued because it sells at 18 times estimated 2006 AFFO when our P/AFFO model says it should sell at only 16.2 times the 2006 estimated AFFO—well, don't bet the farm on that one. Another valuation tool is called for.

DISCOUNTED CASH FLOW AND DIVIDEND GROWTH MODELS

Another useful method of share valuation is to discount the sum of future free cash flows, or perhaps AFFOs, to arrive at a "net present value." If we start with current AFFO, estimate a REIT's AFFO growth over, say, thirty years, and discount the value of future AFFOs back to the present date on an appropriate interest-rate or discount-rate basis, we can obtain an approximate current value for all future earnings. This method of valuation can help determine a fair price for a REIT on an absolute basis; however, discounting AFFO this way somewhat overstates value, since investors don't receive *all* future AFFOs as early as implied by this method. Shareholders receive only the REIT's cash dividend, with the rest of the AFFO retained for the purpose of increasing future AFFO growth.

Several methods can be used to determine the assumed interest or discount rate by which the aggregate amount of future AFFOs is discounted back to the present. One way is to use the average cap rate of the properties contained in the REIT's portfolio, adjusted for the debt leverage used by the REIT. If the cap rate on a REIT's portfolio of properties averages 6 percent, and if the REIT uses no debt leverage at all, we apply a 6 percent discount rate. The use of debt, of course, would require us to increase the discount rate applied; the greater the debt leverage, the higher the discount rate. This method has the advantage of applying commercial-property market valuation parameters to companies that own commercial properties, and allows a drop or rise in cap rates to translate into a lower or higher current valuation for the REIT.

Perhaps a better method of ascertaining the appropriate discount rate is to evaluate the different degrees of risk inherent in each particular REIT stock and decide what kind of total return we demand from our investment dollars when adjusting for that risk. If, for instance, we feel that, in order to be compensated properly for the risk of owning a particular REIT, we need a 10 percent return, we'll

DISCOUNTED CASH FLOW MODEL	
YEARS	VALUE
1–5	$4.26
6–10	$3.54
11–15	$2.93
16–20	$2.43
21–25	$2.02
26–30	$1.97
TOTAL	$17.16

use 10 percent as the discount rate. A higher-risk REIT investment, such as some hotel REITs, or REITs with a risky or very aggressive business strategy, or those using large amounts of debt leverage, would dictate a higher total-return requirement. This method will produce more consistent valuation numbers, but it will be less sensitive to interest-rate and cap-rate fluctuations.

The discount rate we use will produce wildly varying results. For example, a REIT with an estimated first-year AFFO of $1.00 that is expected to increase by 5 percent a year over thirty years will have a net present value of $17.16, if we use a 9 percent discount rate. Applying a 12 percent discount rate will give us a net present value of only $12.35. Using a discount rate that approximates the expected or required total return for a REIT investment (for example, 10 percent) may provide a more realistic net present value approximation, in line with how REIT stocks have traditionally been valued.

Because of the peculiarities of compound interest, there is little point in trying to estimate growth rates beyond thirty years; indeed, the contribution to net present value from incremental future earnings begins to taper off substantially after even just five years. Fortunately, while earnings forecasting is difficult—and is as much art as it is science—it's somewhat less difficult to forecast earnings for the next five years than it is for the next thirty! A variation of this model might be to use only AFFO growth estimates for the next five years, and then to discount the expected value of the REIT's stock at that time at the same discount rate.

A variation of the discounted cash flow growth model is the discounted dividend growth model. It starts with the dividend rate over the last twelve months, rather than current FFO or AFFO, and projects the current value of all future dividends over, say, thirty years, based on an assigned discount rate and an assumed dividend growth rate. A problem with this approach is that it can penalize those REITs whose dividends are low in relation to FFO or AFFO, unless the lower payout ratio is reflected in a higher assumed dividend growth rate. Alternatively, a model can be created that assumes faster dividend growth in the early years. A positive aspect is that it values only cash flow expected to be received in the form of real money—dividend payments.

Both discounted cash flow and dividend growth models have

their limitations. The net-present-value estimate is only as good as the accuracy of future growth forecasts and the validity of our assigned discount rates. As to the former, if we forecast 6 percent growth and get only 4 percent, our entire valuation will have been incorrectly based and therefore will be much too high. Also, I believe it is appropriate, when using the discounted cash flow growth or dividend growth models, to take into account the *qualitative* differences among the various REITs. Fans of this method therefore may want to adjust for qualitative differences by adjusting the total return required and thus the discount rate to be applied (that is, a riskier REIT will bear a higher discount rate). And "risk," of course, will be a function of many variables, including track record, business strategy, balance sheet, conflicts of interest, and other factors.

VALUING REITS AS A GROUP

Now that we've seen how individual REITs can be valued based on NAVs, P/AFFO ratios, and discounted cash flow and dividend growth models, what about determining whether REITs, *as a group,* are cheap or expensive?

Investors who bought REITs in the fall of 1993 or the fall of 1997 learned, to their regret, that sometimes *all* REITs can be overvalued—at least with hindsight. If so, it may take a few years before REITs' FFOs and dividends grow into their stock prices. Although, fortunately, REITs pay dividends while we wait, it still isn't much fun to watch the stock prices languish—or even drop sharply—for a couple of years.

For example, in October 1997 Equity Residential, the largest apartment REIT, was trading at $50, or 13.6 times estimated FFO of $3.68 for 1997. Three years later, in October 2000, Equity Residential's stock was selling at $47, or 9.5 times its estimated FFO of $4.97 for 2000. FFO growth was significant, but the stock price stagnated. "Multiple compression" hurt those shareholders who bought REIT shares at prices that we know, with hindsight, were too high in 1997.

No matter what product you're buying, it doesn't pay to over-pay—even if you're buying blue-chip REITs.

THE RELEVANCY OF OLD STATISTICS

ALTHOUGH IT IS TRUE that before 1992, the beginning of what is referred to as "the modern REIT era," there were few institutional-quality REITs, statistics from pre-1992 still have relevance for investors. They provide an accurate picture of the returns available to most investors who bought shares in such widely available REITs as Federal Realty, New Plan Realty, United Dominion, Washington REIT, and Weingarten Realty, all of which have been public companies for many years. Furthermore, there's no reason to think that REITs' total returns should be lower after 1992. Indeed, due to the quality of many of the newer REITs, one could make the argument that the pre-1992 statistics understate the kinds of total returns that REIT investors might reasonably expect in the future. Much, however, depends upon the prices at which REIT shares are acquired.

If we use P/FFO ratios as our valuation method and a high-quality apartment REIT like Equity Residential (EQR) is selling at, say, 12 times expected FFO, and one of comparable quality, such as Archstone-Smith (ASN), is selling at 10 times expected FFO, we may conclude that ASN is *undervalued* relative to EQR. But this doesn't tell us whether they're *both* cheap or *both* expensive. Similarly, EQR may be trading at a premium of 15 percent and ASN may be trading at a premium of 5 percent over their respective NAVs, but this tells us nothing about what premiums over NAVs these REITs *should* sell for. Is there any way out of this dilemma? Is there a way to determine how the entire REIT industry ought to be valued?

The use of a well-constructed, discounted AFFO growth or dividend growth model may be of some help here. When the REIT market is cheap, the current market prices of most REITs will be significantly lower than the "appropriate" prices indicated by such a model, assuming our projected growth rates and our discount rates are reasonable. For example, if sixty of the seventy REITs that we follow come out of the "black box" of our discounted AFFO or dividend growth models as significantly undervalued, this is likely to mean that REIT stocks, as a group, are being undervalued by the market. Of course, these valuation models need to reflect what's going on in the real world. It may be that these models have failed to take into account fundamental negative changes in real estate or the economy that will cause future AFFO or dividend growth rates to be significantly lower than we've projected in our models. If we believe that this is the case, we must revise our models, since it may be that REITs, as a group, are not undervalued at all when the new and more pessimistic assumptions are put into the equation.

How, then, do we get our bearings? Is there some lodestar by which we can determine the prices at which REIT stocks should sell? Unfortunately, no. As no one can predict the future with certainty, determining intrinsic values for any equity (or group of equities) will be merely an educated guess, at best. Yet all is not lost—we do have history as a guide, imperfect though it might be. If we know that REITs have historically provided earnings yields (as defined below) modestly above that of a benchmark such as a bond index, we have at least one useful tool by which to measure current REIT valuations. It would also be useful to know whether REITs have historically traded at prices above or below their NAVs and by how much, and what has subsequently happened to REIT prices when they were trading at a large premium or discount to NAV. A third method would be to compare REITs' current average P/AFFO ratios to their historical P/AFFO ratios, and to look for reasons for variances.

REITS' AFFO YIELD SPREADS
GreenStreet Advisors has been publishing monthly graphs comparing REITs' average forward-looking AFFO yield to a representative bond yield, such as the Baa-rated long-term bond. REIT "AFFO yields" or "earnings yields" are merely the inverse of the forward-looking P/AFFO multiple, that is, if the multiple is 16×, the earnings yield is $\frac{1}{16}$, or 6.25 percent.

The graph on the following page shows a fair degree of correlation between the two yields during most time periods. For example, between January 1993 and late 1994, both REITs' AFFO yield and the Baa bond yield rose, both then falling until 1997–98. Then, although REIT AFFO yields began to rise earlier, they again rose together (although at different rates) until topping out in early 2000, when they again descended through 2004.

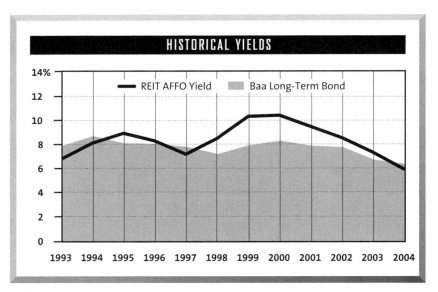

To make use of this data, we need to take a look at a concept called "AFFO yield spread." This is merely the difference between the average REIT AFFO yield and the Baa-rated long-term bond yield at any particular time. For example, if the average REIT AFFO yield is 7 percent and the Baa bond yield is 6 percent, the AFFO yield spread would be the difference between 7 percent and 6 percent, or 1 percent, which is sometimes expressed as "100 basis points." It is interesting to note that between January 1993 and December 2004, the average AFFO yield spread, according to Green Street's calculations, was 51 basis points (about one-half of 1 percent), but the AFFO yield spread got as high as 338 basis points in early 2000, and as low as *negative* 120 basis points in mid–1997. Now let's consider whether these AFFO yield spreads can tell us, with hindsight, whether REIT shares were unusually expensive or cheap during these periods.

The graph above shows that the lowest AFFO yield spread within the past ten years was in 1997, when the spread was –120 basis points. And that was a year in which REIT stock prices peaked; a bear market began in the fall of 1997 and continued throughout 1999. A similar event occurred in 1993, when the REIT AFFO spread was negative all year, ranging from –200 basis points at the beginning of the year to just slightly negative by the end of that year; this period was followed by weak performance in 1994, when REIT stocks turned in a

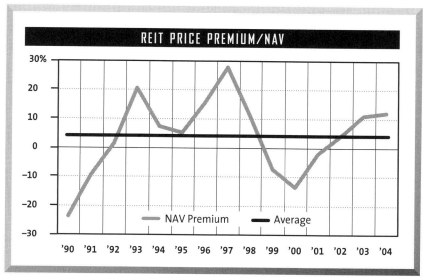

disappointing 3.2 percent total return. Conversely, the *highest* AFFO yield spread during the period covered by the graph was at the end of 1999, when it reached 338 basis points. A month later, REITs' great 2000–2004 bull market had begun. This phenomenon could be a coincidence, as it's difficult to draw firm conclusions from limited data. Nevertheless, this is information that shouldn't be ignored.

The conclusions we can reach from this admittedly cursory exercise is that REITs' AFFO yield spreads can provide us with a very rough guide as to whether REIT stocks are expensive or cheap at any particular time, that is, when the spreads turn negative, REIT stocks appear to be expensive, and when they are positive by more than 100 basis points, they are likely to be cheap. However, this tool should be used as only one of several by which we can determine the reasonableness of REIT stock valuations, as relying exclusively on past relationships can be dangerous for investors. For example, a negative AFFO REIT spread could indicate above-average growth prospects over the coming two to three years. But now let's look at another tool.

THE NAV PREMIUM

Consider the Green Street graph above, which charts the average REIT's stock price in relation to Green Street's estimate of its NAV. Between January 1990 and the end of 2004, the typical REIT (using averages for an entire year) traded at prices as low as 24 percent *below* NAV (in 1990) and as high as 27.4 percent *above* NAV (in 1997); the average has been an NAV premium of just over 7 percent. Following the late 1990 period, when the discount was unusually large, REITs' stocks mounted a furious rally, as indicated by their 1991 total return of 35.7 percent. Conversely, 1998 (the year following the year in which REIT stocks reached a 27.4 percent premium to NAV) was very disappointing; in that year the equity REITs suffered a negative 17.5 percent total return. Also, in 1994, the year after REITs had traded at an NAV premium which averaged 20 percent, they managed a total return of only 3.2 percent. More recently, the NAV discount became substantial in 1999 and into 2000, which led to a very strong period in 2000 and 2001, when REITs' total returns were 26.4 percent and 13.9 percent respectively.

What can we learn from this NAV approach to REIT industry valuation? Can this indicator tell us something despite its relatively modest 15-year sampling period? One simple observation is that when REIT shares traded at a significant discount to NAV (as they did near the end of 1990 and again in early 2000), they appear to have been very cheap, as suggested by their strong performance during the following twelve months, and when they traded at an NAV premium of more than 20 percent, such as in 1993 and in the latter half of 1997, they were probably expensive (as indicated by their poor market performances in 1994 and in 1998–99). However, a high premium over NAV doesn't always presage an immediate decline in REIT stock prices: REIT stocks traded at a 30 percent NAV premium in December 1996, but they still managed to perform well in the succeeding year (+20.3 percent on a total return basis in 1997). Furthermore, despite selling at double-digit NAV premiums throughout most of 1993 and 1994, REIT stocks delivered outstanding total returns in those years. These apparent anomalies may merely have meant that NAV estimates were much too conservative in those periods, and REIT investors were aware of that, discounting a continuing increase in property values; or, possibly, it was a repetition of an old rule on Wall Street: An expensive stock can become yet more expensive before "reverting to the mean."

The foregoing observations should, on balance, make REIT investors cautious when the average NAV premium is well into double-digit territory. Certainly a handful of REITs, based upon their excellent track records and consistent ability to create substantial values for shareholders beyond the growth implied by their portfolio properties, can justify such heady NAV premiums—assuming that such past performance can be projected well into the future. REITs such as Kimco, Vornado, and CenterPoint might fit into that rarefied group. However, during periods in which real estate markets are in relative equilibrium—and thus do not provide an abundance of unusual opportunities to create extraordinary value for shareholders via either acquisitions or developments—it would seem that few REIT organizations would be "entitled" to see their stocks trade at 15–20 percent NAV premiums. REIT pricing history during the last few years has not been lost on investors, and it would be surprising to see the typical REIT stock trade at a sizeable NAV premium as has happened in the past, absent a discounting of unusually strong real estate markets, real estate pricing, or unusually large value-creation opportunities over the following eighteen to twenty-four months.

P/AFFO RATIOS

Let's take yet another look at historical versus current valuations, this time from the perspective of P/AFFO ratios. Merrill Lynch & Co., which has followed REIT stocks for many years, keeps a substantial database on REITs and REIT share pricing. Its *Comparative Valuation REIT Weekly* includes data on REIT AFFO multiples on a twelve-month forward basis going back to 1993, when the size of the REIT industry expanded significantly. The average REIT P/AFFO multiple for the period from 1993 through March 2005 was 11.7×, and ranged from a high of 18.7× at the end of 2004 to a low of 8.2× in March 2000.

From 1993 to 2003, the band of P/AFFO ratios was fairly narrow (8.2× at its low and 14.7× at its high), and low ratios tended to be predictive of good REIT stock values and higher prices ahead, while high ratios suggested overvaluation and poor near-term stock price performance. Thus, the highest P/AFFO ratios from 1993 through late 2003 were in December 1993 (12.9×) and December 1997 (13.1×), and both peaks in the ratios were followed by weak REIT stock performance the following year (in 1994, REITs' average total return was a subpar 3.2 percent and in 1998 REITs' average total return was miserable, at –17.8 percent). Conversely, the low P/AFFO ratio of 8.2× in March 2000 was followed by a strong REIT bull market lasting through 2004.

Beginning in 2004, however, REIT P/AFFO ratios roared into territory never seen by REIT investors. Merrill data show that REIT stock prices traded consistently at P/AFFO multiples ranging from 16× to 18× throughout 2004. One logical inference from this is that REIT stocks would turn in a subpar performance in 2005, but as this book went to press REIT stocks were on course to deliver a reasonably decent year of performance.

However, it is extremely important to note that P/AFFO ratios for REITs, like P/E ratios for other equities, are dependent upon many variables, including growth prospects, perceived risk, and interest rates. Real estate was at a cyclical low with respect to property cash flows in 2004, and was in the process of bottoming—providing solid evidence that cash flow growth would soon accelerate and that risk levels were declining. Furthermore, long-term interest rates remained very low throughout 2004 (the 10-year Treasury note ended the year at a 4.25 percent yield). So it's fair to question whether REITs' high P/AFFO multiple at the end of 2004 was proof that the stocks were "too expensive."

The conclusion we may draw from this discussion is that, like NAV premiums, P/AFFO ratios can be a good indicator of REIT values (or lack thereof), but should not be applied mechanically, and not without looking at other valuation metrics. Many factors will affect REITs' P/AFFO ratios—not only growth prospects, risk perceptions, and interest rates, but also prevailing values and cap rates in the vast private real estate markets. REIT investors should expect their stocks to trade at higher multiples during periods of low interest rates, low cap rates, and above-average growth prospects, and vice versa.

The point to remember in applying all these yardsticks is that a healthy dose of skepticism and caution is warranted: REITs' AFFO yield spreads, NAV premiums and discounts, and P/AFFO comparisons may certainly be used as guides or indicators, but more in-depth review will be necessary to determine whether the observed spreads, premiums, or multiples, no matter how high or low, are sending us accurate messages about the future. There will never be any substitute for detailed factual investigation and thoughtful analysis, both on a quantitative and qualitative basis, and history is but a guide. While it's rarely, if ever, "different this time," we also don't want to drive forward by looking exclusively through the rearview mirror.

SUMMARY

◆ Buy-and-hold investors should have relatively less concern regarding quarter-to-quarter data such as FFO growth rates, occupancy and rental rates, or even asset values.

◆ Active REIT investors will need to spend a fair amount of time analyzing and applying historical and prospective valuation methodologies to achieve maximum investment performance for their portfolios.

◆ There are a number of tools to help us evaluate REIT stocks. These include NAV-based models, P/FFO or P/AFFO models, and discounted cash flow (AFFO) and dividend growth models—all of which have their strengths and weaknesses.

◆ REITs are more conducive than other companies to being valued on a net-asset-value basis, and many experienced REIT investors and analysts consider a REIT's NAV to be very important in the valuation process, either alone or in conjunction with other valuation models.

◆ Since the various valuation tools do not always agree, they are best used in conjunction with one another and only as a general indication of whether the shares of a REIT are cheap or expensive at a specific point in time.

◆ Similar tools can help to determine whether REITs, as a group, are cheap or expensive on a current basis. These include REITs' AFFO yields in relation to an appropriate high-grade bond benchmark, the premiums at which they trade versus their NAVs, and their current P/AFFO ratio versus REITs' historical P/AFFO ratios.

◆ History is often a useful tool in stock valuation, but must be tempered with careful inquiry regarding future growth prospects, perceived risks, and the relative attractiveness of other asset classes.

CHAPTER

10

Building a
REIT PORTFOLIO

I F YOU'VE READ this far, you're definitely interested in REITs. You may already have some idea which sectors you like and whether you want to go for total return or pursue high yields, but, before you call your broker, let's get a little perspective on REITs as investments.

HOW MUCH OF A GOOD THING DO YOU WANT?

Almost every book on investing talks about asset allocation: how much of your portfolio should be in stocks (both domestic and international, large cap and small cap, growth and value), how much in bonds, how much in real estate, and how much in cash. Some experts say that as you get older you should shift more into bonds and have less in stocks in order to reduce risk, while others recommend that your asset allocation be adjusted according to the investment environment or one's tolerance for risk and volatility. Who's right?

The only right answer is that the proper asset mix depends on one's financial objectives, ability to absorb losses in portfolio value, and tolerance for risk, and the same answer applies to how much you should be investing in REITs. One of the most important factors to consider is how long you can wait before you'll need to begin selling off assets to generate cash to fund retirement needs. But much also depends upon your investment goals. Are you a newly-wed who's saving to buy a house? Perhaps you have a five-year-old who's just starting school, and you think you need to start thinking about college tuition. Or maybe you're a baby boomer who is finally starting to think about retirement.

Before you make any decision on precisely what to invest in, you need to determine why you're investing—you need to define your investment goals.

If you're going to need those liquid assets in the next year or two, just sitting on them is probably the best thing to do. Put your cash in the bank, maybe in a CD, where you know you'll have it when you need it. Investing—whether in stocks, bonds, or REITs—is still an uncertain venture. It should be no surprise that the market is affected by such variables as interest rates, inflation, corporate profits, the strength of the dollar, world geopolitics and terrorist activities, trade and budget surpluses or deficits—even whether or not Alan Greenspan smiles at reporters on the way into the Congressional Committee hearing—or some other event you can't even conceive of right now. And, of course, investment styles shift constantly; if your particular stocks are out of favor, perhaps nothing will get them to perform well even over time periods as long as two to three years.

Nevertheless, let's assume you have $20,000 or $100,000 that you don't think you'll need for many years, and you already have something set aside for a rainy day. The way you should divide the pie depends on your answers to questions such as these:

1 How aggressive an investor are you?
2 How comfortable are you with market volatility?
3 How depressed would you feel if you were holding a number of stocks that declined substantially?
4 How much do you need to withdraw annually from your portfolio investments to supplement your salary, pension, or Social Security payments?
5 How important is a steady stream of dividend income?

AGGRESSIVE INVESTORS SHOULD HAVE MODEST EXPOSURE TO REITS

Aggressive investors seeking very large returns over a short period should not put a high percentage of their assets into REITs.

While it's true that, on a long-term, total-return basis, REITs have been competitive with the S&P 500 index, in the short term, REITs are a singles-hitter's game. Very few REIT investments will enable an investor to score a 50 percent gain in one year or rack up a "ten-bagger," to use Peter Lynch's expression, within just a few years. Some have called REITs the ultimate "un-tech" investment, and their correlation with the Nasdaq Composite Index during the period from January 1995 through January 2005 is only 0.17. Despite what many people believe, real estate ownership, as long as one avoids excessive debt leverage, is a low-risk, modest-reward venture. Shareholders of even the fastest-growing REITs organizations should not expect average annual total returns exceeding 10–14 percent, at most. While these are outstanding returns indeed, some investors want more. Investors looking to double their net worth in eighteen months had better look elsewhere.

VERY MODEST RISK OF MAJOR PRICE DECLINES

One nice thing about REITs is that even those that turn out to be turkeys don't often decline quickly. From time to time, usually because of overleveraging or management incompetence, there have been some big declines among REIT stocks, but the declines have usually been gradual, giving investors a chance to react. The more sudden drops have mostly been because of significantly reduced dividends, but, even then, there are clues. For one thing, beware of an exceptionally high dividend, particularly in relation to the company's free cash flows. If it's too good to be true, it won't be true for long. In general, if you watch FFO or AFFO closely and compare it with a REIT's regular dividend, you will often know when a dividend cut is a real possibility and act accordingly. Other common stocks are far more sensitive to negative news, as we've seen often, particularly during the last few years. Furthermore, among such stocks, it's not at all unusual for an earnings shortfall, lower revenue "guidance," a product liability claim, a rejected new drug application, or a new competing technology to decimate the price of a stock overnight.

WHEN STABILITY IS WHAT YOU'RE LOOKING FOR . . .

"I DO BELIEVE REITS are unique," says Geoff Dohrmann, CEO of *Institutional Real Estate*. "No other sector of the stock market enjoys cash flow based on a diversified portfolio of relatively stable, predictable, contractual revenues (rents) that in most cases are essential components in the ability of the customer (tenants) to continue to do business. Consequently, even though as subject to the business cycle as any other corporation, REIT cash flows will tend to be more defensive than most other cash flows. REITs, therefore, offer relatively high, stable yields that—because of their stock market effect—adjust well to inflation, but that also tend to be defensive on the downside."

Of course, as we learned in 1998, REIT stocks can decline substantially if REITs as an asset class become disliked by, or fall out of favor with, investors. But that is far different from a 15–20 percent decline overnight due to a sharply reduced profit estimate for next year.

REITS PROVIDE A HIGH CURRENT INCOME LEVEL

Some financial planners advocate a large common stock weighting even for people near or in retirement. They argue that bonds don't protect retirees from inflation, and, over any significant period of time, common stocks have provided more appreciation than almost any other kind of investment.

It's hard to criticize the wisdom of investing in common stocks, but the problem with many investment theories is that they're based on recent stock market history. The years up through 1999 were excellent years for most equities, but the markets have been far less predictable and satisfying since then. Bear markets arrive when we least expect them. Many investors at or near retirement must live off their investments; selling off a piece of their portfolios is not something they will enjoy doing in a bear market. Owning REIT stocks provides a high level of current income, with dividend yields only modestly lower than yields on bonds, but it also provides long-term price appreciation prospects. The higher yield makes the investor less dependent upon ever-increasing stock prices to fund living expenses.

LOOKING FOR THE "HOLY GRAIL": THE PERFECT REIT ALLOCATION

There are two parts to the question of allocation. First, there is the weighting of REITs as an asset class or market sector relative to other investments such as non-REIT equities, international stocks, bonds, and cash. Your answers to the above five questions will help you work out the optimal allocation of REITs in your portfolio, as they help define the risk levels with which you are comfortable. Unfortunately, there are just too many variables to suggest any rigid formulas.

REIT allocation within a broadly diversified investment portfolio must necessarily be different for each investor, depending on the investor's financial goals, age, risk tolerance, and desire for current income.

Even if, because of all their unique qualities, you absolutely love REIT stocks, you still shouldn't put the vast majority of your portfolio in them. The most fundamental principle of investing is that, over time, diversification is the key to stability of performance and preservation of capital. You *might* have outstanding results if you put a huge portion of your assets in REITs, but nobody can foretell the future. Occasionally even Warren Buffett has zigged when he should have zagged, and real estate has, in the past, been a very cyclical investment.

Thus, investors must do what is appropriate with regard to their specific needs and investment goals. However, I can suggest some general guidelines to use as a barometer. If you're a fairly conservative investor looking for steady returns with a modest degree of risk and volatility, where capital appreciation is only a secondary consideration, a REIT allocation of somewhere between 20 and 25 percent of your portfolio should suit you. If the stock market seems overpriced, you might feel comfortable moving up toward 25 percent— and down toward 20 percent if the opposite market conditions exist. But if you are more aggressive and looking for higher returns, and are psychologically suited to handle more risk and volatility, then perhaps a modest 5–10 percent allocation to REITs would be appropriate. Of course, these are only very general guidelines—in investing, it's rare that "one size fits all." As noted in Chapter 1, adding a REIT component of 20 percent to a diversified investment portfolio, as noted by Ibbotson Associates, can increase investment returns by 0.6 percent annually, while reducing risk by a like amount.

DIVERSIFICATION AMONG REITS

All right, you've decided what percentage of your portfolio should be allocated to REITs. Now comes the second part of the allocation question. Within your REIT allocation, what would be an appropriate allocation for the different property sectors, investment characteristics, and geographical locations that REITs offer?

BASIC DIVERSIFICATION

Much depends, of course, on the absolute level of cash you have to invest. One way to diversify is through REIT mutual funds and even "exchange-traded funds" (ETFs), which we'll discuss later in this chapter. But now, let's look at ways to diversify when buying individual REITs.

For most investors, an absolute minimum of six REITs is necessary to achieve a bare-bones level of diversity of sector and location.

The problem is that, at some asset level—perhaps below $30,000—you just can't get enough diversification without getting clobbered by commissions. Suppose, for example, you have $6,000 to invest in REITs. If you invest $1,000 each in six different REITs and your brokerage firm has a minimum commission of $50 per trade, your 5 percent commission would cost you virtually all of your first year's dividend. On the other hand, with $30,000 to invest in REITs, six trades would amount to $5,000 each, and the $50 commission would be only 1 percent of the purchase price on each trade.

Six different REITs would provide an acceptable level of sector diversification, but ten REITs would be preferable. If you're in a position to buy ten different REITs, a good allocation would be two each in apartments, retail, and office (the major sectors), and one each in industrial, health care, self-storage, and hotels. With more available investment funds, you might seek to add additional sectors such as manufactured home communities, or a triple-net lease REIT. Or you may also want to widen your geographical diversification within each sector, adding an apartment REIT on the West Coast, for example, if you already own one in the Southeast, or one that's national in scope. The same approach can be applied in other sectors, such as neighborhood shopping centers or office/industrial properties. A well-managed, diversified REIT that owns

REIT DIVERSIFICATION

WITH SIX REITS, a reasonable diversification would call for one REIT in six of the following eight sectors: apartments, retail, office, industrial, hotel, health care, self-storage, and manufactured-housing communities. Office and industrial might be combined in one REIT (e.g., Duke Realty or Liberty Property).

DIVERSIFICATION WITH REITS

ACCORDING TO Roger C. Gibson, CFA, CFP, a nationally recognized expert in asset allocation and investment portfolio design, "The investment diversification achievable with REITs is of particular value to investors. Unlike the case with direct real estate ownership, a REIT investor can easily diversify a relatively small sum of money both geographically and across different types of real estate investments, such as shopping centers, office buildings, and residential apartment complexes."

---

several different types of properties within a fairly narrow geographical location—such as Washington REIT, Vornado Realty, Colonial Properties, or Cousins Properties—may be considered, but there are very few from which to choose.

OVERWEIGHTING AND UNDERWEIGHTING

One of the key issues involving diversification is the weighting of REIT holdings for particular property sectors. There are differing opinions on this topic, even among institutional REIT investors. Some REIT asset managers don't try to adjust their portfolios in accordance with how much they like or dislike a sector or geographical area but simply use "market weightings." For example, if mall REITs make up 10 percent of all equity REITs, such investors, using a market weighting, will make sure that mall REITs comprise 10 percent of their REIT portfolio. The theory here is similar to what many investors do in the wider world of equities; they try to add value by owning the best stocks, without making large sector bets. Advocates of this approach would argue that all stocks, including REITs, are usually efficiently priced, and it's unrealistic to assume that anyone can forecast with any accuracy and consistency which property sectors will do better than others.

Other investors, frequently those oriented toward maximum short-term performance, think that they *can* figure out the best sectors or property locations to be in at any particular time. They will closely examine the fundamentals within the entire national real estate markets—and overweight or underweight their portfo-

AUTHOR'S CHOICE

THE INVESTMENT STYLE I prefer is to put most of my REIT investment dollars in blue chips, add some that seem underpriced and misunderstood—perhaps with higher yields and less well-defined growth prospects—and then add a few more that look as if they'll enjoy rapid growth. I'm wary of mortgage REITs since they've often been badly hurt by rising interest rates and other gyrations pertaining to the credit markets. Fortunately, the REIT industry is now so vast that the choice is very wide. More thoughts on REIT portfolio management are contained in Appendix E.

lios accordingly. They will seek those sectors and markets where demand for space exceeds the supply, where rents and occupancy rates are rising fastest, where profitable acquisition or development opportunities abound, or where some other factor seems to make the outlook particularly favorable. Or they might merely emphasize those REIT sectors where REIT prices look the cheapest. Kenneth Heebner, a well-known fund manager, seems to have used this approach at CGM Realty Fund, and many others use a similar strategy.

Unless investors believe that they can determine which sectors will do appreciably better than others over the next couple of years, a portfolio allocated somewhere near market weighting makes the most sense.

Overweighting what you perceive to be the "right sectors" is tricky, since, if other investors have the same perceptions, that will already be factored into the stock prices, and you won't have gained anything.

DIVERSIFICATION BY INVESTMENT CHARACTERISTICS

Another approach to diversification is not to pay much attention to sectors or property locations, but instead to own a package of REITs with different investment characteristics. This diversification-by-investment-style approach would have the investor assemble one group of REITs with high-quality assets, led by widely respected real estate executives, that offer very predictable and steady growth with little regard to sector or location; another group of "value" REITs with low valuations based on a substantial discount to estimated net asset value (NAV) or a low P/AFFO multiple; a group of higher-growth REITs; and, to round out the portfolio, a few bond proxies, with high yields and price stability but very modest growth prospects. Such an approach may help to insulate the portfolio from major price gyrations as institutional investors shift their REIT funds from one style of REIT investing to another.

TOWARD A WELL-BALANCED PORTFOLIO

Which approach toward diversification is best? By property type? By geography? By investment characteristics? Or by all of the above? There isn't any definitive statistical evidence that one approach is better than another. The significant expansion in size of the REIT industry has been so recent that there's not enough history to guide us, nor are there any academic studies regarding this issue. And few REIT mutual funds are willing to place themselves in a particular style box. While there's no agreement on *how* to diversify, there is almost universal agreement on the *need* to diversify.

Although REIT investors shouldn't ignore the concerns expressed by industry observers with respect to particular sectors, neither should they take them too seriously, particularly when investing in the blue chips; REIT investing is a long-term strategy, and the prospects for any particular sector can change rapidly and without prior notice. REIT investors thus needn't become terribly concerned if they find themselves temporarily overweighted in an unpopular sector, as long as the quality is there. Real estate, like stock, always seems to revert to the mean.

Unlike most sectors, geographic diversification isn't a major issue with respect to mall and outlet REITs, health care REITs, and self-storage REITs, since most of these REITs are widely diversified by property location, and detailed knowledge of the conditions and opportunities peculiar to local markets isn't nearly as important in these sectors.

The table on pages 244–245 is just a sample of the kind of diversification that can be obtained within certain major sectors. Areas of major geographical focus are included. The table includes many of the largest REITs as of the end of 2004.

HOW TO GET STARTED

As an investor, you can choose from three very different approaches in building a REIT portfolio: You can do the research yourself; you can rely on a professional, such as a stockbroker, financial planner, or investment adviser; or you can buy a REIT mutual fund or "exchange-traded" fund (ETF). Let's examine what's involved in each approach.

DOING IT YOURSELF

The tools required to build and monitor your own REIT portfolio are (1) a willingness to spend at least a few hours a week following the REIT industry and your REIT portfolio, and (2) a subscription to a REIT newsletter and/or access to REIT research reports.

The do-it-yourself approach is the most difficult and time-consuming method, but many investors find it the most rewarding. There are several ways to stay informed of what's happening in the world of REITs. For example, SNL Securities covers the entire REIT industry thoroughly, providing vital REIT data, dividends, and earnings estimates. *Realty Stock Review* has also been a valuable resource for REIT investors over the years. Most retail brokerage firms will also provide research reports on individual REITs. More information than ever before can be obtained online, and most individual REITs, as well as the National Association of Real Estate Investment Trusts (NAREIT), have established their own websites. The Motley Fool and others also provide REIT and real estate message boards.

Since REITs are not complicated and their business prospects do not change quickly, they are less data- and research-intensive than most other common stock investments. With access to a database such as that provided by *Realty Stock Review* or SNL Securities, a willingness to listen in on quarterly conference calls (or replays), and the discipline to review the information publicly available—such as annual reports, 10-Qs, and various other filings with the Securities and Exchange Commission—most investors can do a good job managing their own REIT portfolios. The table on pages 248–249

PROPERTY TYPES, REITS, AND PRIMARY LOCATIONS

REIT	PRINCIPAL LOCATIONS
APARTMENTS	
Archstone-Smith	California; Washington, D.C.; Chicago; Boston; Florida
Apartment Investment and Management	Nationwide
Avalon Bay	West Coast, Northeast, Mid-Atlantic
BRE Properties, Essex	California, Western U.S.
Camden Properties	Sunbelt
Equity Residential Properties Trust	Nationwide
Gables Residential	Southeast, Texas
Post Properties	Southeast, Texas, Washington, D.C.
United Dominion Realty	Nationwide
RETAIL: NEIGHBORHOOD SHOPPING CENTERS AND OUTLET CENTERS	
Developers Diversified	Nationwide
Federal Realty	Northeast, Mid-Atlantic, West Coast
Kimco Realty	Nationwide
New Plan Excel	Eastern U.S.
Regency Realty	Southeast, California, Texas
Tanger Outlet Centers	Nationwide
Weingarten Realty	Southwest, Sunbelt
RETAIL: MALLS	
CBL & Associates	Southeast
General Growth Properties	Nationwide
Macerich	California, Arizona, New York
Mills Corporation	Nationwide
Simon Property Group	Nationwide
Taubman Centers	Nationwide
HEALTH CARE	
Health Care Properties	Nationwide
Health Care REIT	Nationwide
Healthcare Realty	Nationwide
Nationwide Health	Nationwide
OFFICE	
Alexandria Real Estate	East and West Coasts (office/lab space)
Arden Realty	Southern California

REIT	PRINCIPAL LOCATIONS
Boston Properties	New York; Washington, D.C.; Boston; San Francisco
Carr America Realty	Selected markets nationwide
Duke Realty	Midwest, Southeast
Equity Office	Nationwide
Highwoods Properties	Southeast, Midwest
Kilroy Realty	Southern California
Mack-Cali Realty	Northeast
Prentiss Properties	Selected markets nationwide
Reckson Associates	New York, New Jersey, Connecticut
SL Green Realty	New York City

INDUSTRIAL

AMB Property	Major "hub" cities nationwide
CenterPoint Properties	Greater Chicago
First Industrial Realty	Nationwide
Liberty Property	Mid-Atlantic, Southeast, Midwest
ProLogis Trust	Nationwide, International

SELF-STORAGE

Public Storage	Nationwide
Shurgard Storage Centers	Nationwide, Europe

HOTELS

FelCor Lodging Trust	Nationwide
Hospitality Properties	Nationwide
Host Marriott Corporation	Nationwide
Sunstone Hotel Investors	Nationwide

MANUFACTURED HOMES

Equity Lifestyle Communities	Nationwide
Sun Communities	Midwest, Southeast

DIVERSIFIED REITS

Colonial Properties	South
Cousins Properties	Southeast, Texas, California
Crescent Real Estate	Southwest, Denver, Miami
Vornado Realty	New York City; Washington, D.C.
Washington REIT	Greater Washington, D.C. area

provides a general description of some very good sources of information for REIT investors; note, however, that Web addresses tend to change from time to time. If you go through all of these and are still hungry for more, just do a Web search on the word *REIT*.

The do-it-yourself approach has several advantages. First, it saves on management fees and brokerage commissions, since, without the need for outside advice, you can use a discount broker for at least some of your trades. Second, the realization of capital gains and losses can be tailored to your own personal tax-planning requirements. Third, a significant portion of many REITs' dividends is treated as a "return of capital," and is not immediately taxable to the shareholder. Owning REIT stocks directly allows you to take direct advantage of this tax benefit. Finally, the knowledge and experience gained from managing your own portfolio may well lead to good investment results and a great deal of personal satisfaction.

USING A STOCKBROKER

For investors who don't enjoy poring over annual reports and calculating NAVs and AFFOs, one good solution is to find a stockbroker who is very familiar with REITs and who has access to the research reports published by his or her brokerage firm.

Most investors would rather not spend their spare time managing their own portfolios when they could be playing golf, taking the kids to a baseball game, or gardening. Not too many years ago, however, individual investors had no alternative, since it was difficult to find a broker who knew much about REITs. Today, such brokers are easy to find. REITs are continuing to grow in popularity. Now you read about them in personal finance magazines and the business section of major newspapers, and most major brokerages employ one or more good REIT analysts. You should have no problem finding at least one REIT-knowledgeable registered representative in any good-sized brokerage office.

Assuming that you find a good broker, the advantages of this approach are lots of personal attention, the ability to decide when you want to take capital gains or losses, and the relief of not having to research and worry about such issues as AFFO, rental rates, and other REIT essentials. The brokerage commissions will be higher than for the do-it-yourself investor, but, if you're careful to avoid excessive trading and you buy only those REITs consistent with your investment objectives, higher commissions may be a small price to pay for the service provided.

FINANCIAL PLANNERS AND INVESTMENT ADVISERS

Today, as the average age of the population increases, there are more people concerned about investing for a longer life expectancy and a retirement free of financial worry.

Financial planners can act in different capacities. Some manage and invest their clients' funds directly in specific stocks and bonds; others invest such funds in well-researched mutual funds. Still others refer the client to an investment adviser. Some are paid on the basis of commissions from insurance or other investments, while others charge on a fee basis only.

Investment advisers, on the other hand, generally do little or no financial planning and specialize in investing client funds in stocks, bonds, and other securities. Generally their only compensation is a commission of between 1 and 2 percent of the assets they manage. Thus, as the portfolio grows, so does the adviser's fee. Some advisory firms provide a great deal of personal attention and hand-holding, while others do not. Some take great care to individualize a portfolio, taking into account their clients' personal tax situations before making buy-and-sell decisions, and others buy and sell solely on the basis of maximizing their clients' investment gains.

Many investors find that using a financial planner or investment adviser has its advantages: the lack of conflicts of interest between the firm and its clients, the personal attention given to clients, and the customizing of clients' portfolios based on their tax situations and financial objectives. For someone who is interested in REITs, however, the advantages are not so clear. It can be difficult to find a financial planner or investment adviser who is experienced in REIT investing, and fees will continue to be paid whether or not any trades are made in the account. Also, many financial-planning firms do not have good REIT research services available. Some of these issues should diminish over time, of course, as REITs become better understood.

SOURCES FOR THE DO-IT-YOURSELFER	WHERE TO FIND IT
Barron's	Weekly magazine (subscription or on newsstand)
Green Street Advisors	http://www.greenstreetadvisors.com
Institutional Real Estate	http://www.irei.com/default.html
Korpacz Real Estate	https://www.pwcreval.com/home.asp
Major Brokerage Firms	Contact your registered representative at a major or regional firm
Motley Fool REIT Board	http://boards.fool.com/Boards.asp?fid=10098&bid=114416
NAREIT	www.nareit.com
National RE Index	http://www.graglobal.com/index.php?section=products&page=aboutNREI
REIT Zone Publications	http://www.reitzone.com
ReitNet	http://www.reitnet.com/
SNL REIT Weekly	http://www.snl.com/products/real_estate/rpr.asp?PID=RPR
Websites and Home pages	Available from NAREIT and various REIT organizations

REIT MUTUAL FUNDS

As recently as fifteen years ago, only about five mutual funds were devoted to investing in real estate–related securities such as REITs. Today there are more than seventy such funds. Most of them are modest in size, but there were three giants, including Cohen & Steers Realty Shares ($2.3 billion at March 2005), Fidelity Real Estate ($4.6 billion), and Vanguard REIT Index Fund ($5.7 billion). A great deal of information is available regarding REIT and real estate mutual funds through Morningstar (www.morningstar.com). While some may scoff at the modest size of most of these funds, they have generally done well during their relatively short histories. The Vanguard Group, which has a market niche in index funds, operates the Vanguard REIT Index Fund, a REIT mutual fund indexed to the MSCI US REIT Index (successor to the Morgan Stanley REIT Index), launched at the end of 1994. The MSCI US REIT Index, it should be noted, excludes mortgage REITs and health care REITs, as well as REITs below a minimum size. These exclusions mean that this index could modestly outperform or underperform a broader REIT index, such as any of the NAREIT indices.

REIT mutual funds provide an excellent way for individuals to obtain sufficient REIT diversification.

To take a purely arbitrary number, if we assume that the REIT investor wants to put 20 percent of a $50,000 investment portfolio into REIT stocks, the total REIT investment would be just $10,000. It will be difficult to obtain satisfactory diversification with that relatively modest amount. In contrast, with the same or even a smaller REIT budget, you can get much more diversification through a REIT mutual fund, since most such funds own at least thirty different REITs.

What is perhaps even more important, however, is that, in a REIT mutual fund, the investor gets the benefit of professionals who, when they make their investment decisions, have access to REITs' top managements as well as extensive research materials and sophisticated valuation models. Even active investors might want to invest a minimum amount in some of these funds in order to benchmark their personal REIT investment track records against the results of the professional fund managers.

Despite their significant strong points, REIT mutual funds are not without disadvantages. Although no brokerage commissions are payable when investing in no-load funds, management fees can be sizable, typically ranging from 1–1.5 percent of total assets. Fund investors do not receive individual attention, nor do they have the ability to align purchases or sales with tax needs. A fund that actively trades REIT stocks may present its investors with a large capital gains tax bill following a REIT bull market, as all the gains or losses realized by the fund during the year are simply passed on to the individual investor. Finally, investors who reinvest dividends and capital gain distributions in additional fund shares and who trade in and out of the same fund may find it difficult to keep current and accurate records of their cost basis and tax gain or loss information.

REIT investors who decide to go with a mutual fund have a wide array of choices today. Most funds are actively managed, and each utilizes a somewhat different investment strategy. Some focus almost exclusively on the large REITs, while others look for the smaller names. High current yields are important to some, but total returns drive the decisions of others. Investing in non-REIT real estate companies is done in some funds, not others. Fund A will keep real estate sectors roughly in line with the benchmarks, but Fund B will ignore these market weightings. If you have read this far in the book, you have enough knowledge to analyze a wide variety of real estate funds to determine their broad strategies and to pick one or a few that best coincide with your investment preferences.

As noted earlier, investors can also invest in an indexed REIT fund that is designed to perform in line with a REIT index. The most popular of these, by far, has been the Vanguard REIT Index fund (symbol: VGSIX), which is indexed to, and will closely track, the MSCI US REIT Index, less a relatively small management fee.

A MUTUAL FUND ALTERNATIVE: ETFS

Another type of indexed fund that is fairly new on the investment scene and which seems to be gaining investment popularity is the "exchange-traded fund" (ETF), which is essentially an indirect ownership interest in a basket of stocks put together by a sponsoring organization and which is traded as a single stock on a major stock exchange. These ETFs seek to track a specific index or basket of stocks, and thus lack an active portfolio manager; they want to replicate the performance of the targeted group of stocks, but not beat it. These ETFs, because they are traded as stocks, can be bought and sold during the trading day, even on margin, and one of their key advantages is that the management expense ratios tend to be very low; for example, the streetTRACKS (as described below) had an expense ratio (in early 2005) of just 0.26 percent.

There are presently four such ETFs that specialize in REIT stocks. The largest, the Dow Jones U.S. Real Estate iShares (symbol: IYR), tracks the price and yield performance (prior to expenses) of the Dow Jones U.S. Real Estate index. Others include iShares Cohen & Steers Realty Majors Index Fund (symbol: ICF), which tracks the "Cohen & Steers Majors" index; streetTRACKS Wilshire REIT Index Fund (symbol: RWR), which obviously tracks the Wilshire REIT index; and the newest of the group, Vanguard REIT VIPERs Index Fund (symbol: VNQ), which tracks the MSCI US REIT Index. These are all good choices for a low-cost, index-oriented approach to REIT investing.

Another type of fund that has drawn REIT investor interest in recent years is the closed-end REIT fund, which may own only REITs, or REITs along with other income-oriented stocks such as utilities—and, in some cases, preferred stocks. There are many types of these closed-end funds, each with different capital structures and investment strategies, but two characteristics they have in common are that they trade as stocks and do not, unlike conventional "open-ended" mutual funds, allow for shareholder redemptions or reinvestment. These features allow the shares of these funds to be bought and sold quickly, and shareholders won't need to worry about their fund having to liquidate lots of assets in a bear market when less patient fellow shareholders bail out. (Cynics will note, however, that these funds never go away, and they generate income for their sponsors even when they perform poorly.)

Investors need to be careful with these closed-end funds, as many of them use leverage, by issuing preferred stock or borrowing in the credit markets, to boost investment returns. However, leverage is a two-way street. While returns will be enhanced in strong markets, they will suffer much worse in down markets. Thus, leverage will increase both the investment risk and the share volatility of the closed-end fund that uses it. And, as higher interest rates will have a greater impact upon a closed-end fund that uses leverage, its shares may perform poorly indeed in bear (and rising interest rate) markets. Investors also need to be aware of the amount of leverage being used, how it is structured, and whether or not the preferred coupon or the amounts borrowed are at fixed—or variable—rates of interest. The latter, of course, creates yet more risk for investors in these funds, particularly if exposure to rising interest rates is not hedged.

For investors who don't want to invest on their own or don't have the resources to diversify REIT holdings adequately, do the advantages of a fund, an ETF, or closed-end fund outweigh their disadvantages? Clearly they do—especially if the investor refrains from doing a lot of trading in and out of these shares. REIT funds are especially good for IRAs, where neither tax gains and losses nor cost bases are relevant.

SUMMARY

◆ Before you make any decision on precisely what to invest in, you need to determine why you're investing—you need to define your investment goals and risk tolerances.
◆ The aggressive investor seeking very large returns over short periods should not put a high percentage of assets into REITs.
◆ Allocations to REIT investments will be different for each investor, depending on the investor's financial goals, age, portfolio characteristics, risk tolerance, and desire for current income, but the author believes that a 15–20 percent allocation to REITs is appropriate for most investors.

◆ An absolute minimum of six REITs is necessary to achieve a bare-bones level of diversity of sector and location.

◆ Unless an investor is very confident about which sectors will do best over the next couple of years, a portfolio allocated according to market weighting makes the most sense.

◆ Investors who want to be somewhat involved but who don't want to worry about frequent monitoring of their investments can use the assistance provided by the services of a knowledgeable stockbroker, financial planner, or investment adviser.

◆ Investors who prefer not to do any individual research can invest passively through REIT mutual funds or even a REIT ETF. Both provide an excellent way for individuals to obtain sufficient REIT diversification and with minimal expenditure of time.

RISKS AND
Future
Prospects

PART

IV

CHAPTER

11

What Can
GO WRONG

NOW THAT YOU know the beauties and benefits of REITs and REIT investing, it's time that you also understand what can go wrong. Alas, no investment is risk free (except perhaps T-bills, which don't provide anything except a safe yield). In general, the risks of REIT investing fall into two broad categories: those that might affect *all* REITs, and those that might affect *individual* REITs. There is also a third category, which is related to REITs' investment popularity at various times. First we'll address the broad issues.

ISSUES AFFECTING ALL REITS

All REITs are subject to two principal potential hazards: an excess supply of available rental space and rising interest rates.

A supply/demand imbalance, with the excess on the supply side, is often referred to as a "renters' market," because, in such a market, tenants are in the driver's seat and can extract very favorable rental rates and lease terms from property owners. Excess supply can be a result of more new construction than can be readily absorbed, or of a major falloff in demand for space, but there's an old saying that it doesn't matter whether you get killed by the ax or by the handle. Either way, excess supply, at least in the short term, spells difficulties for property owners.

Rising interest rates can also have a dampening effect upon property owners' profits. When interest rates skyrocket, borrowing costs increase, which can eventually reduce growth in REITs' FFO. But there is another implication here. Those rising interest rates can slow the economy, which in turn may reduce demand for rental space. Furthermore, rising interest rates can have implications for REIT stock pricing. As investors chase higher yields which may be available elsewhere—perhaps in the bond market—they may decide to sell off their REIT shares, thus depressing prices, at least in the short term.

Although excess supply and rising interest rates aren't the only problems that can vex the REIT industry, they are easily the two most critical; let's talk about them in more detail.

EXCESS SUPPLY AND OVERBUILDING: THE BANE OF
REAL ESTATE MARKETS

Earlier we discussed how real estate investment returns can change through the various phases of a typical real estate cycle. Rising rents and real estate prices eventually result in significant increases in new development activity. We also discussed how overbuilding in a property type or geographical area can influence and exacerbate the real estate cycle by causing occupancy rates and rents to decline, which in turn may cause property prices to fall. Over time, of course, demand catches up with supply, and the market ultimately recovers.

Whereas a recessionary economy sometimes results in a temporary decline in demand for space, the excess supply that is brought on by overbuilding will sometimes be a larger and longer-lasting problem.

Overbuilding can occur locally, regionally, or even nationally; it means that substantially more real estate is developed and offered for rent than can be readily absorbed by tenant demand, and, if an overbuilt situation exists for a number of months, it puts negative pressure on rents, occupancy rates, and "same-store" operating income. Overbuilding will discourage real estate buyers and can cause cap rates in the affected sector or region to increase, thus reducing the values of REITs' properties—and, perhaps, their stock prices. To the extent that a REIT owns properties in an area or sector affected by overbuilding, the REIT's shareholders often sell their shares in anticipation of declining FFO growth and reductions in net asset values, which, in turn, drives down the share price of the affected REIT. The share prices of most office REITs lagged the REIT market in the early years of the current decade, due in large part to rising vacancy rates and falling market rents for office properties. This resulted not from overbuilding but rather from softening demand and an increased amount of sub-lease space tossed onto the market by busted dot-coms and other shrinking businesses. In extreme cases, the reduced prospects for a REIT may cause lenders to shy away from renewing credit lines, preventing a REIT from obtaining new debt or equity financing, perhaps even forcing a dividend cut. Not a pretty picture.

Of course, problems caused by excess supply vary in degree. Sometimes the problem is only slight, creating minor concerns in just a few markets. Sometimes the problem is devastating, wreaking havoc for years in many sectors throughout the United States. We saw the effects of severe overbuilding in the late 1980s and early 1990s in office buildings, apartments, industrial properties, self-storage facilities, and hotels. The problem for most real estate owners from 2001 to 2004 was not due so much to overbuilding, but to a significant weakening in demand for space. Either way, when supply greatly exceeds demand, real estate owners suffer. A mild oversupply condition, whether due to excessive new development or a slowdown in demand for space, will work itself out quickly, especially where job growth is not severely curtailed. Then, absorption of space alleviates the oversupply problem before the damage spreads very far. In these situations, investors may overreact, dumping REIT shares at unduly depressed prices and creating great values for investors with longer time horizons.

Investors must try to distinguish between a mild and temporary condition of excess supply and one that is much more serious and protracted, in which case a REIT's share price may decline and stay depressed for several years.

Overbuilding, as opposed to a scarcity in demand for existing space, can be blamed on a number of factors. Sometimes overheated markets are the problem. When operating profits from real estate are very strong because of rising occupancy and rents, property prices seem to rise almost daily. Everybody "sees the green" and wants a piece of it. REITs themselves could be a significant source of overbuilding, responding to investors' demands for ever-increasing FFO growth by continuing to build even in the face of declining absorption rates or unhealthy levels of construction starts. Today there are many more REITs than ever before that have the expertise and access to capital to develop new properties, and those that do business in hot markets will normally be able to flex their financial muscles and put up new buildings.

In the past, new legislation has sometimes been a major cause of overbuilding. In 1981, when Congress enacted the Economic

TOO MANY "BIG BOXES"?

"BIG-BOX" DISCOUNT RETAILERS, such as Wal-Mart, Target, and Costco, have been doing well for a number of years, and investors have thrown a lot of money at them in order to encourage continued expansion. Today some observers fear that big-box space is rapidly becoming excessive. On a smaller scale, this had been the case with large bookstores such as Crown, Borders, and Barnes & Noble; Crown filed for bankruptcy in 1998. The number of bankruptcy filings by movie theater owners in 2000 suggests that too many theaters had been built in the latter part of the 1990s. Can America support all of the big-box discount retailers?

Recovery Act, depreciation of real property for tax purposes was accelerated. The tax savings alone justified new projects. As we discussed in previous chapters, investors did not even require buildings to have a positive cash flow, so long as they provided a generous tax shelter. The merchandise was tax shelters, not real estate, and tax shelters were a very hot product. This situation was a major contributing factor to the overbuilt markets of the late 1980s. Similar legislation does not seem to be a danger today, but because REITs pay no taxes on their net income at the corporate level, some may argue that Congress is "subsidizing" and "encouraging" real estate ownership.

While participation of investment bankers is essential in helping REITs raise extra capital that can generate above-normal growth rates, these same firms can sometimes be another source of trouble. When a particular real estate sector becomes very popular, Wall Street is always ready to satisfy investors' voracious appetites. But do investment bankers know when to stop? Too many investment dollars were raised for new factory outlet center REITs a number of years ago, and it's quite likely that office REITs raised an excessive amount of capital in 1997–98. Much of this new capital found its way into new developments that ultimately contributed to an excess of supply.

Strangely, even when it has become obvious that we are in an overbuilding cycle, the building may continue. As early as 1984 it was apparent to many observers of the office sector that the amount of new construction was becoming excessive; nevertheless, builders and developers could not seem to stop themselves, and they continued to build new offices well into the early 1990s. Similarly, an inordinate amount of office building was done in the late 1990s, particularly in "high-tech" markets, even after many observers and lenders realized that the pace of absorption was unsustainable. Although some would explain this by the long lead time necessary to complete an office project once begun, it's more likely that there were some big egos at work among developers—each believing that *his* project would become fully leased—and that too many lenders were too myopic to detect the problem early enough. Just as dogs will bark, developers will develop—if provided with the needed financing.

Today, however, excessive new development is not a significant issue, and one may dare to hope that perhaps major real estate developers and their lenders have become more intelligent and careful. The tax laws no longer subsidize development for its own sake. Lenders, pension plans, and other sources of development capital that were "once burned" are now "twice shy," and very circumspect with respect to development loans for largely unleased projects.

Further, there is much more discipline in real estate markets today. The savings and loans, a major culprit of the 1980s' overbuilding, are no longer the dominant real estate lenders. The banks, which often funded 100 and sometimes 110 percent of the cost of new, "spec" development during that decade, have "gotten religion" and subsequently adopted much more stringent lending standards, which are still in effect today, often limiting construction loans to just 60–70 percent of the cost of the project. They require significant equity participation from the developer—a factor, like insider stock ownership, that generally increases the success rate. Lenders are also looking at prospective cash flows much more carefully, relying less on property appraisals and requiring a prescribed minimum level of pre-leasing before funding a new office development.

REITs may eventually become the dominant developers within particular sectors or geographical areas, as is largely true today in the mall sector. Should this happen, new building in a sector or an area may be limited by investors' willingness to provide REITs with additional equity capital. This may be one reason for the stable supply/demand conditions we've seen in the mall sector in recent years. Perhaps even more important, in view of the fact that managements normally have a significant ownership interest in their REITs' shares, they will have no desire to shoot themselves in the foot by creating an oversupply. Of course, it's important to emphasize that none of this prevents the occasional supply/demand imbalance that's created when demand for space cools because of a slowing economy and weak or negative job growth.

WHITHER INTEREST RATES?

When investors talk about a particular stock or a group of stocks' being interest-rate sensitive, they usually mean that the price of the stock is heavily influenced by interest-rate movements. Stocks with high yields are interest-rate sensitive since, in a rising interest-rate environment, many owners of such stocks will be lured into safer T-bills or money markets when yields on them become competitive with high-yielding stocks, adjusted for the latter's higher risk. Of course, a substantial number of shareholders will continue to hold out for the higher long-term returns offered by REIT shares, but selling *will* occur—driving down REIT share prices (and the prices of virtually all bonds and equities).

A sector of stocks might also be interest-rate sensitive for reasons other than their dividend yields. Homebuilders are but one example, as they rely upon the availability of reasonably low mortgage rates to their customers. Also, the profitability of a business might be very dependent on the cost of borrowed funds. In that case, in a rising interest-rate environment, the cost of doing business would go up, since the interest rates on borrowed funds would go up. If increased borrowing costs cannot immediately be passed on to consumers, profit margins shrink, causing investors to sell the stocks.

Whether their perception is correct or incorrect, if investors *perceive* that rising interest rates will negatively affect a company's profits, then the stock's price will vary inversely with interest rates—rising when interest rates drop, and dropping when interest rates rise.

How, then, are REIT shares perceived by investors? Are they interest-rate sensitive stocks? Is a significant risk in owning REITs that their shares will take a major tumble during periods when rates are rising briskly? Before we try to answer these questions, let's take a quick look at why REIT shares are bought and owned by investors, and how rising interest rates affect REITs' expected profitability.

Traditionally, REIT shares have been bought by investors who are looking for attractive total returns with modest risk. "Total return" is the total of what an investor would receive from the combination of dividends received plus stock price appreciation. Yields have traditionally made up about one-half to two-thirds of REITs' total returns. For example, a 5.5 percent yield and 4.5 percent annual price appreciation (perhaps resulting from 4.5 percent annual FFO growth and assuming a stable price P/FFO ratio) results in a 10 percent total annual return. Because the dividend component of the expected return is so substantial, REITs must compete in the marketplace, to some extent, with such income-producing investments as bonds, preferreds, and even utility stocks.

For example, let's assume that in January "long bonds" (with maturities of up to thirty years) yield 6 percent and the average REIT stock yields 6 percent as well. If the long bond drops in price in response to rising interest rates and inflationary pressures, causing it then to yield 7 percent, the average REIT's price may also drop, causing its yield to rise to 7 percent. This kind of "price action" would preserve the same yield relationship then in effect between bonds and REITs. However, it's important to note that in the real world of stock markets, REIT prices don't always correlate well with bond prices (in 1996, for example, there was no correlation whatsoever, and, according to NAREIT, REIT stocks' correlation with a domestic high-yield corporate bond index for the period January 1995 through January 2005 was just 0.32).

Nevertheless, the reality remains that a large segment of REIT stock owners invest in them for their substantial yields, and the rest rely upon dividend yields for a significant part of their expected total returns; some of these investors may shift their assets into bonds and other high-yielding securities when the yields on them become competitive with the yields offered by REIT shares. Furthermore, some large investors will sell, or even short, REIT stocks before interest rates rise if they believe that rates will increase in the near future. As a result, REIT investors should assume that

REIT prices, like the prices for almost any investment, will weaken in response to higher rates.

A second, related, and very important question is whether a rise in interest rates might cause significant problems for REIT investors by causing FFO growth to decelerate, weakening balance sheets, diminishing their asset values, or otherwise affecting REITs' merits as investments. This is a multifaceted issue, and of course it also depends upon the individual REIT, its sector, its properties' locations, and its management, but let's consider the possibilities.

Higher interest rates are generally not good for any business, since they soak up purchasing power from the consumer and can eventually lead to recession.

Apartment REITs, then, or retail REITs, which cater to individual consumers directly or indirectly, may be adversely affected by higher interest rates if rising rates slow the economy and reduce available consumer buying power. However, even REITs that lease properties to businesses, such as office and industrial-property REITs, will also be adversely affected, since businesses will also be influenced by rising interest rates and a slowing economy. In general, property sectors that enjoy longer-term leases (such as offices and industrial properties, as well as some retail properties) will see their cash flows less affected by a slowing economy, since their lease payments will be more stable. However, if the slowdown becomes severe, they, too, will suffer from occupancy declines and prospective rent roll-downs as leases expire. For apartment owners, rising rates are a mixed blessing. They will slow the migration of tenants to single-family residences (a big problem for apartment owners in 2001–2004), but if rising interest rates slow the economy enough to cause job losses, that will obviously impact their business prospects.

Interest is usually a significant cost for a REIT, since, like other property owners, REITs normally use debt leverage to increase their investment returns and will frequently borrow to fund a portion of property acquisition and development investments. The concept of variable-rate debt is that it allows the lender to adjust the rate according to the interest-rate environment. In a rising interest-rate environment, then, the lender's rates will rise; the higher the amount of variable-rate debt a REIT is carrying, the greater will be the impact on its profit margins and FFO. But, even with fixed-rate debt, REITs must be concerned with interest rates—when they are rolling over a portion of their debt and when they are taking on new debt. New developments, too, will often be funded with short-term variable-rate debt, then permanently financed upon completion with long-term fixed-rate debt. Rising interest rates can significantly impact the investment returns from these new developments.

Even when a REIT chooses to raise capital through equity offerings rather than debt financing, higher interest rates can have an adverse effect if rising interest rates depress REIT share prices; this will raise a REIT's nominal cost of equity capital.

Another negative aspect of rising interest rates relates to the value of a REIT's assets. Although real estate cap rates are influenced by many factors, it's almost intuitive that a major increase in interest rates will exert upward pressure on cap rates. All things being equal, property buyers will insist on higher real estate returns when interest rates have moved up; correspondingly, property values will tend to decline, which affects the asset values of the properties owned by REITs. Asset values are very important in determining a REIT's intrinsic value, as we've seen in Chapter 9, and thus falling asset values will often have an impact on REIT share pricing.

Any significant decline in the value of its underlying real estate properties could affect the share price of a REIT.

The foregoing discussion shows how rising interest rates can negatively affect a REIT's operating results, balance sheet, asset value, and stock price. However, we might also note that in one important respect REITs may actually be *helped* by rising interest rates. This relates to the overbuilding threat. New, competing projects, whether apartments, office buildings, hotels, or any other type of property, must be financed. Clearly, higher interest rates will increase borrowing costs and make developing new projects more costly or, in some cases, *too* expensive. Higher rates may also affect the "hurdle rate" demanded by the developer's financial partners, again causing many projects to be shelved or canceled. Obviously, the fewer new competing projects that get built, the less existing properties will feel competitive pressure. Threats of overbuilding can rapidly fade when interest rates are rising briskly.

We should keep in mind, of course, that we are speaking in generalities here, and the extent to which rising interest rates will affect a particular REIT's business, profitability, asset values, and financial condition must be analyzed individually. On balance, however, rising interest rates are generally not favorable for most REITs. Combined with the tendency of all companies' shares, including REITs', to decline in response to rising interest rates, REIT investors need to be very much aware of the interest-rate environment and to expect some stock price weakness when interest rates look as though they will be moving higher.

HOSTILE CAPITAL-RAISING ENVIRONMENTS

REITs must pay their shareholders at least 90 percent of their taxable income, but most pay out more than that because net income is calculated after a depreciation expense, most of which does not require the immediate outlay of cash. As a result, REITs are unable to retain much cash for new acquisitions and development and are, therefore, dependent to a substantial extent on the capital markets if they want to grow their FFOs at rates higher than what can be achieved from real estate NOI growth. Their FFO growth, without new acquisitions and development, will therefore depend only on how much REITs can improve the bottom-line income from *existing* properties.

As a result of this inherent legal limitation, investors must be mindful that even the most highly regarded REIT may not, during most economic and real estate climates, be able to grow its FFO at a pace beyond a mid–single digit rate unless it has access to additional equity capital. There will always be another bear market and, when it comes, many REITs will find it difficult to sell new shares to raise funds for new investments. The equity market for REITs slammed shut in early 1998 and re-opened only in 2001. Such recurring events will tend to retard FFO growth until such time as the markets return to "normalcy."

However, bear markets are not the only circumstance in which REITs could find their flow of capital shut off. There is also the great specter of overbuilding that can only be beaten back but never

A BUBBLE? OR JUST HOT AIR?

EVER SINCE THE 2000–2001 crash of technology and dot-com stocks rattled investors, we've seen the word "bubble" used often in the financial press. But the term isn't a new one; indeed, many of us may recall discussions in history or economics classes of the "South Sea Bubble," describing an "irrationally exuberant" period of investing back in the early eighteenth century. More recently, some self-proclaimed pundits have been depicting real estate markets as "bubbles."

Just what is a "bubble?" According to Dictionary.com, a "bubble" is something "insubstantial, groundless, or ephemeral" or, more applicable to the financial world, "a speculative scheme that comes to nothing." Alternatively, according to Life Style Extra's glossary of financial definitions, a "bubble" is "an explosive upward movement in financial security prices not based on fundamentally rational factors, followed by a crash." Real estate prices, particularly for homes in California and some cities on the East Coast, including Florida, have been rising rapidly in the early years of the twenty-first century. It has been estimated by the California Association of Realtors that the median home price in California jumped 17 percent in 2003 and another 22 percent in 2004. And prices for many high-quality commercial real estate assets have also been rising, even though 2001–2004 was a very difficult period for owners with respect to vacancies and rental rates.

So, is real estate in a "bubble" mode, making a substantial drop in prices likely? If so, how would this affect REIT stocks? Unfortunately, investment bubbles are labeled as such only with hindsight. However, as we are in the "Risks" section of the book, I'll climb out onto the proverbial limb with some observations.

Residential real estate, that is, single-family homes and condos, does, in some locations, exhibit some aspects of the typical investment bubble. Prices have risen dramatically in many coastal markets, despite modest growth in personal incomes and job growth. Many baby boomers appear to have decided that the stock market won't provide them with sufficient assets with which to retire, and have taken advantage of "hot" real estate markets and low (e.g., 5 percent) down payments to speculate in residential real estate. The number of homes bought for investment jumped 50 percent during the four-year period ending in 2004, according to the San Francisco research firm LoanPerformance.

In many neighborhoods, a home bought at today's prices cannot be rented out for anywhere near what it would cost to service the mortgage. Furthermore, risks are increasing. The percentage of homes priced above $359,650 financed with adjustable-rate mortgage loans (vs. fixed-rate loans), according to Freddie Mac, has risen to about two-thirds as of March 2005. LoanPerformance has calculated that California homes bought with interest-only loans rose from 2 percent in 2001 to 48 percent in 2004. If interest rates should rise significantly, or if buyers' ardor cools, residential real estate prices in a number of markets are likely to weaken considerably.

Equity REITs, fortunately, don't own residences or condos; they own commercial real estate. And while commercial real estate prices have been strong, in response to demand for these assets from institutions and even smaller investment groups, they don't appear to be out of touch with reality. Real estate cap rates hovered in the 5–7 percent range for most quality assets in mid-2005; while these rates are lower than the 9 percent considered "normal" throughout much of the latter part of the twentieth century, they are not out of line against the backdrop of 4.25 percent yields that prevailed on the 10-year Treasury note and intermediate-grade corporate bonds yielding 5.5–6.0 percent in effect during that time period.

Further, many seasoned investors and noted academics have been forecasting a lower rate of investment return for stocks compared with their historic averages over the last fifty to seventy years. Thus, in a period of low return expectations for stock and bonds, a real estate cap rate of 5–7 percent is not out of line; this is particularly so when real estate fundamentals are stable and improving. Was it crazy for Regency and Macquarie to pay a 6.25 percent cap rate for the Calpers/First Washington neighborhood shopping center

---

A BUBBLE? OR JUST HOT AIR? (CONT'D.)

portfolio of 101 high-quality properties that has historically been growing net operating income at close to 3 percent annually? Or for Macerich to pay a 6 percent cap rate for the Wilmorite portfolio, a group of shopping malls considered by many to contain some of America's most productive malls? I think not.

So, while some residential assets in some coastal markets may very well be in danger of suffering from "bubble" pricing, it would be difficult to sustain that claim for commercial real estate generally. Is it possible that some commercial real estate prices will be proven, with hindsight, to have been frothy in 2005? Perhaps so—particularly if interest rates move substantially higher. But it would be wrong to apply the "bubble" label across the board to all commercial real estate as of mid-2005.

---

eliminated entirely. In mid-1995, when a few apartment REITs owning properties in the Southeast tried to raise new equity capital by selling additional shares, there were few takers. This was due to perceptions that these markets were rapidly becoming overbuilt.

Individual REITs with lackluster growth prospects, excessive debt, or conflicts of interest will also have problems attracting potential investors, as will REITs that are perceived as being unable to earn returns on new investments that exceed the REIT's cost of capital. Although some REITs, due to new "asset recycling" and joint venture strategies, have been able to substantially reduce their dependency upon fresh equity offerings, attracting new capital remains a very important tool for most growing REIT organizations. External and even internal events over which management may have little or no control may cut a REIT off from this essential new capital and thus affect its rate of FFO growth, which in turn affects investor sentiment and the REIT's stock price. This is one reason investors will pay a premium for those REITs whose track record of successfully deploying capital, strong balance sheet management, and growth prospects are perceived as being most likely to attract additional equity capital, as needed, on favorable terms, or which have reduced their dependency upon external capital raising.

LEGISLATION

If the cynic's view that "no man's life, liberty, or property is safe when Congress is in session" is correct, we must recognize that Congress giveth, but Congress also taketh away. But it is highly unlikely that Congress would enact legislation to rescind REITs' tax deduction for the dividends paid to their shareholders, thus subjecting REITs' net income to taxation at the corporate level.

There are several public policy reasons for this. First, because of REITs' high dividend payments to their shareholders, they probably generate at least as much income for the federal government as they would if they were conventional real estate corporations that could shelter a substantial amount of otherwise taxable income by increasing debt and deducting their greater interest payments. (It's just that the taxes are paid by the individual shareholders rather than the corporation.) Second, property held in a REIT most likely provides more tax revenues than if it were held, as it historically has been, in a partnership. Finally, REITs have shown that real estate ownership and management can generate excellent returns without using excessive debt leverage, which, if not for the REIT format, would be the way real estate would probably be universally held. Excessive debt can be a very destabilizing force in the U.S. economy, and it's unlikely that Congress would want to contribute to that.

Encouraging greater debt financing of real estate could substantially exacerbate the swings in the normal business and real estate cycles, harming the economy over the long term.

In early 1998, the Clinton administration proposed legislation as part of its fiscal 1999 budget that would affect certain REITs. One of the proposals, since enacted into law, targeted those REITs that had the ability to engage in certain non–real estate activities (such as hotel and golf course management) through a sister corporation ("paired-share" REITs). This law directly affected four REITs by preventing them from operating businesses that generate income that doesn't qualify under the REIT laws, but only with respect to new properties or businesses acquired. While this new law had a major impact on the "paired-share" REITs, it had no effect on the rest of the REIT industry.

THE BEAUTY CONTEST

AS WE HAVE learned by now, REIT stocks have enough investment peculiarities that they may fairly be regarded as a separate and distinct asset class. Furthermore, despite their stable and predictable cash flows and steady dividends, REIT stocks have, at times, been very unpopular with investors. In 1998 and 1999, despite rising cash flows and strong real estate markets, investors didn't seem to want any part of them (although valuation issues and excessive stock offerings may have played a large role in the bear market of those years). That difficult cycle for REITs was followed by another in which REIT stocks could do no wrong—despite very weak real estate markets almost everywhere.

This conundrum should teach us REIT investors an important lesson: We need to be prepared for periods in which REIT stocks are simply unpopular and won't perform well even when all the stars are properly aligned. This means that one additional risk in owning REIT shares is that these investments may decline in value for reasons having nothing to do with their intrinsic valuations or growth prospects.

How can we protect ourselves from this risk? Simply put, we cannot. However, our best defense is a simple one: We must think of REIT stocks as long-term investments and, aside from those who desire to be stock traders, own them over long time horizons as a permanent part of our investment portfolio, secure in the knowledge that over all meaningful time frames REIT stocks have delivered outstanding returns in line with our expectations.

Another proposal would have tightened the restrictions on the ability of a REIT to own controlling interests in non-REIT corporations; the rules at that time were designed to prevent a REIT from indirectly generating impermissible non–real estate income through controlled subsidiaries. However, this proposal was modified significantly and was ultimately incorporated into the REIT Modernization Act (RMA) (discussed earlier in this book). Indeed, the RMA contains many benefits and flexibilities for the REIT industry, as well as acceptable limitations.

So far, Congress has deemed it important to encourage a regular flow of funds into the real estate sector of the economy and has enabled individuals as well as institutions to own real estate through the REIT vehicle. Over the years, thanks in large part to both the efforts of NAREIT and simple common sense, Congress has, if anything, liberalized the laws to expand the scope of REITs' authorized business activities. Thus, the risk of adverse legislation, while always present, isn't large enough to keep REIT investors awake all night worrying.

PROBLEMS AFFECTING INDIVIDUAL REITS

Sometimes one REIT in a sector has a problem and all the other REITs in its sector suffer from guilt by association. The following is a good illustration: In early 1995, two of the newly created factory outlet center REITs, McArthur/Glen and Factory Stores of America, got into trouble—the former by being unable to deliver the new and profitable developments it promised Wall Street, the latter by expanding too aggressively and taking on too much debt. The market, often prone to shooting first and asking questions later, assumed that the illness was sectorwide and destroyed the stock prices of such steady performers as Chelsea and Tanger, as well as the two problem-plagued outlet REITs. However, by the end of 1995, Chelsea's stock was back near its all-time high, and Tanger's stock was in the process of recovering as well. Investors who dumped their Chelsea stock at very depressed prices because of their inability to distinguish between a major, sectorwide problem and problems with a couple of individual REITs had to swallow a bitter pill but learned a valuable lesson.

LOCAL RECESSIONS

We discussed recessions earlier in the context of problems that may affect the entire REIT industry. But there are also local recessions that can impact specific REITs. An economic recession can hurt real estate owners even when supply and demand for space in a particular market was previously in equilibrium—or even unusually strong. A retail property, for example, located in a healthy property market may be 95 percent leased, but its tenants' sales might decline in response to a severe local recession. This will result in lower "overage" rentals (additional rental income based on sales exceeding a preset minimum), lower occupancy rates, and even tenant bankruptcies. Apartment units, especially newly built ones, may be slow to lease, perhaps because of declining job growth in specific local markets. Generally speaking, during recessionary conditions, both consumers and businesses will cut back on their spending patterns. In this situation, rents cannot be raised without jeopardizing occupancy rates.

We've mentioned that focusing on a specific geographical area is something that REIT owners like to see, due to focused local expertise, but the downside is that local or regional recessions can be more damaging for a geographically focused REIT. Despite national recessions that take place from time to time, such as the one beginning in 2001, we've learned that economic conditions in the United States aren't always the same in every geographical area, and local recessions are not uncommon. We can have an oil-industry depression in the Southwest, while the rest of the country is doing fine. Or the Northeast can be in the dumps, while Florida's economy is humming along. More recently, the problems in the technology sector have hit some markets particularly hard, such as the San Francisco Bay Area and Seattle. This has had a temporary negative impact on the shares of REITs with heavy concentrations in those markets, such as Avalon Bay and Essex. Local or regional economic declines often result in disappointing FFO growth, shareholder nervousness, and declines in the affected REIT's stock price.

CHANGING CONSUMER AND BUSINESS PREFERENCES

Investors must also watch for trends and changes in consumer and business preferences that can reduce renters' demands for a property type, causing existing supply to exceed demand and reducing owners' profits.

Today, for example, because of our increasingly mobile population, self-storage facilities are popular. Will they always be so? Will the increased popularity of owning a home or a condo, rather than renting an apartment, accelerate, or has this been just a short-term phenomenon? Will Americans travel a lot more, thus stoking demand for hotel rooms, or will they become more stationary? Will businesses continue to lease the types of industrial properties they've always found necessary, or will some new form of business practice render many of the current facilities obsolete? Will companies continue to absorb space in large office buildings as they have in the past, or will telecommuting stage a revival and make a major dent in the demand for traditional office space? And will businesses seek out locations in major cities, or look more favorably on suburban locations? What effect will Internet shopping have on traditional retailers? Will malls lose their allure as a fun destination? How much competition will "lifestyle" centers provide? These are questions about basic trends in how we live, how we play, and how we work. No one can answer them now with absolute certainty, but if REIT investors ignore signs of changing trends, their investment returns from some REIT stocks may prove disappointing.

CREDIBILITY ISSUES

Probably the most common type of REIT-specific problem that can cause investor headaches is the error in judgment that raises significant management-credibility questions.

Here, for example, are just some of the unpleasant situations that have occurred in past years:

◆ Overpaying for acquired properties and later having to sell them at a loss (e.g., American Health Properties)

◆ Expanding too quickly and taking on too much debt in the process (e.g., Patriot American Hospitality and Factory Stores of America)

◆ Underestimating the difficulty of assimilating a major acquisition (e.g., New Plan Excel)

◆ Expanding into entirely new property sectors, especially without adequate research and preparation (e.g., Meditrust)

◆ Providing investors with unreliable information by, for example, underestimating overhead expenses (e.g., Holly Residential Properties)

◆ Overestimating future FFO growth prospects (e.g., Crown American Realty)

◆ Being unable to generate expected returns on newly developed properties (e.g., Horizon Group)

◆ Setting a dividend rate, upon going public, that exceeds reasonable expectations of FFO levels, thus raising concerns about the adequacy of dividend coverage (e.g., Alexander Haagen)

◆ Engaging in aggressive hedging techniques such as forward equity transactions (e.g., Patriot American Hospitality)

◆ Proposing a merger that makes little strategic sense (e.g., Mack-Cali and
   Prentiss Properties)
◆ Failure to entertain a reasonable buy-out offer (e.g., Burnham Pacific
   Properties)
◆ Investing in new technologies or Internet initiatives and having to write
   them off (too many to mention)

The common denominator in most of these situations is the perception among investors that management has lost control of its
business, that it lacks discipline, or that it is otherwise taking undue
risks with the shareholders' capital.

Yet another kind of credibility issue arises when there is a material
conflict of interest between management and shareholders. REITs
that are externally managed are always subject to such conflicts, but
even those that are managed internally can sometimes exhibit conflicts. The most serious of these are when a REIT's executive officer
sells his or her own properties to the REIT, or when an executive
officer is allowed to compete with the REIT for potential acquisitions. Excessive executive compensation for mediocre operating
results, on the other hand, while annoying to shareholders, is not
usually as damaging as the other types of conflicts mentioned.

Many investors are wary of the UPREIT format, which poses
knotty conflict-of-interest issues. UPREITs, as you may recall from
an earlier chapter, are those whose assets are held by a limited partnership in which the REIT owns a controlling interest and in which
REIT "insiders" may own a substantial interest. Since these insiders
may own few shares in the REIT itself, the low tax basis of their partnership interests creates a conflict of interest should the REIT be
subject to a takeover offer, or in the event it receives an attractive
offer for some of its properties.

Most problems like these can be remedied by a REIT's management if it is forthright with investors, quickly recognizes any mistakes
it has made, and promptly takes action to rectify the situation.

In September 1999, Duke Realty sold $150 million of new com-
mon stock to ABP Investments, a large Dutch pension fund, at a price
below what most analysts determined to be Duke's per share net asset
value (NAV). REIT investors never like seeing their REITs sell equity
at prices that are dilutive to NAV and, indeed, many investors are

willing to pay price premiums for REITs that are able to consistently increase their NAVs by various value-creative deals. Thus they were not happy that Duke, a highly regarded office and industrial REIT, would decide to sell new shares at a dilutive price, and they pushed the price of Duke's stock down by 15 percent shortly after the secondary offering. Some wondered about management's ability to make sound capital market decisions. Management reacted promptly, however, and soon explained that it was going to a "self-funding" strategy, whereby its development pipeline would be funded by retained earnings and asset sales and that it did not contemplate additional equity offerings. Duke's stock price then recovered nicely over the next few months.

The key issue in these situations is management's loss of credibility with investors. When a REIT has disappointed investors as a result of poor judgment, it can be very hard to regain investors' confidence; in extreme cases, the only alternatives for such a REIT are to become acquired or to obtain new management. It was just such a loss in credibility that caused Chateau Communities, a manufactured-home community REIT, to sell off its assets and liquidate a few years ago.

 Loss of management credibility can be crippling to a REIT.

There is obviously no way for REIT investors to avoid such problems altogether; human nature is such that no executive is immune to the occasional lapse in judgment; furthermore, some of these problems become apparent only with hindsight. The most conservative strategy is to invest only in those blue-chip REITs that have demonstrated solid property performance, good capital allocation discipline, and excellent balance sheets over many years (and preferably over entire real estate cycles). Of course, this policy of going only for pristine quality will often mean investors will have to pay significant price premiums and will miss out on lesser-known REITs or those REITs that are primed for a rebound.

Another conservative strategy is to avoid REITs that have been public companies for only a short time, since most of these management credibility issues seem to have arisen in "unseasoned" REITs. Again, this approach could mean missing out on some very promising newcomers. The "right" investment strategy depends, in large part, upon the individual investor's risk tolerance, as well as his or her total return requirements. There is rarely a "free lunch" in the investment world.

BALANCE SHEET WOES

Debt will always be a potential problem, as well as an opportunity—for people, for nations, and, no less, for REITs. If management overburdens the REIT's balance sheet with debt, investors must be particularly careful. High debt levels often go hand in hand with impressive FFO growth and high dividend yields, but investors need to be wary of such apparent benefits when they have been subsidized by excessive debt. Too much debt, particularly short-term debt, can virtually destroy a REIT, a fact to which shareholders of Patriot American Hospitality and Factory Stores of America can certainly attest. Earlier we discussed the importance of a strong balance sheet in recognizing a blue-chip REIT. The importance of a strong balance sheet cannot be overemphasized, because those REITs that are overloaded with debt will not only be looked upon with suspicion by investors but may, if their property markets deteriorate, have to be sold to a stronger company at a fire-sale price or, worse, be dismembered.

A balance sheet can be judged "weak" from a number of different perspectives: high debt levels in relation to the REIT's market capitalization or net asset value (NAV), a low coverage of interest expense from property cash flows, excessive variable-rate debt, or a large amount of short-term debt that will soon come due. A weak balance sheet can seriously restrict the REIT's ability to expand through acquisitions or developments, and excessive debt leverage will magnify the effects of any decline in net operating income (NOI). Further, a weak balance sheet can make equity financing expensive (new investors will have the greatest bargaining power); and it also creates the danger that lenders will not roll over existing debt at maturity, that covenants in credit agreements will not be complied with, and that, should interest rates rise substantially, the REIT will be exposed to a rapid deterioration in cash flows.

The market has usually factored potential problems like these into the stock price before the REIT actually feels their effects. A REIT, therefore, that is perceived to be overleveraged or to have too much short-term (or even variable-rate) debt will see its shares trade at a low P/FFO ratio in relation to its peers and to other REITs. In short, the risk perception is rapidly incorporated into the stock price.

SMALL MARKET VALUATIONS

REIT investors need to be aware that despite REITs' forty-five year history, very few are large companies compared to many major U.S. corporations. Let's take Hewlett-Packard (HP) as an example. On March 23, 2005, HP had 2.9 billion shares outstanding; at its market price of $19.65 per share, HP's total outstanding shares had a market value of $56.9 billion. Procter & Gamble, at the same time, had shares outstanding worth approximately $133.7 billion. Moving away from the real giants, let's look at Costco, a large discount retailer. In March 2005, its outstanding common stock had a market value of $20.7 billion.

Compare these market caps to some major REITs' market caps. Simon Properties, the largest mall REIT in early 2005, had, as of

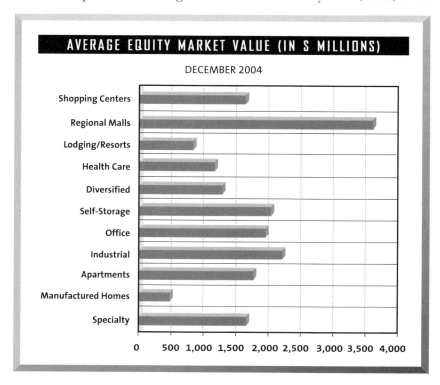

AVERAGE EQUITY MARKET VALUE (IN $ MILLIONS)

DECEMBER 2004

SOURCE: GREEN STREET ADVISORS

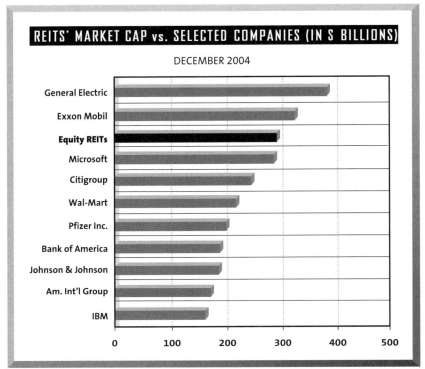

REITS' MARKET CAP vs. SELECTED COMPANIES (IN $ BILLIONS)

DECEMBER 2004

SOURCE: COMPUSTAT

March 1, 2005, an equity market cap of $13.7 billion. Simon was followed very closely by Equity Office Properties, at $12.2 billion. While General Growth's equity market cap has expanded substantially since its acquisition of Rouse and is now among the largest, other very large REITs such as Archstone-Smith, Boston Properties, Equity Residential, Kimco, Plum Creek Timber, ProLogis, Public Storage, and Vornado all had market caps in early 2005 of below $10 billion. Indeed, according to NAREIT, only twenty-three REITs had equity market caps in excess of $3 billion as of March 1, 2005.

The market cap of the entire REIT industry, as well as many of the individual REITs within it, has been growing rapidly in recent years. According to NAREIT, by March 2005 the total equity market capitalization for just the equity REITs amounted to $265 billion. This compares with only $11 billion at the end of 1992, $50 billion at the end of 1995, and $147 billion at the end of 2001.

Nonetheless, while the "typical" REIT is by no means a tiny company, it is hardly a major U.S. corporation. As of March 2005, the equity market cap of the entire equity REIT industry, at $265 billion, was smaller than the equity market cap, at that time, of either Exxon Mobil ($384 billion) or General Electric ($376 billion); it did, however, recently surpass Microsoft ($264 billion) and Citigroup ($232 billion).

There are several potential problems that can result from small size: A REIT with a small market cap, perhaps $500 million or less, may not be able to obtain the public awareness and sponsorship necessary to enable it to raise equity capital. Further, although increasing pension and institutional ownership of REITs could be a new trend fostering the growth of the entire REIT industry, a small market cap is likely to discourage such entities from investing in a REIT due to its stock's lack of market liquidity. Also, costs of compliance with Sarbanes-Oxley will be proportionately greater for smaller REITs. Finally, a minor misjudgment on the part of management of a small REIT (see "Credibility Issues," above) could have a significant impact on the REIT's future business prospects, FFO growth, and reputation with investors. It would seem that a small company must do everything right if it wants to attract a greater number of investors.

DEPTH OF MANAGEMENT AND MANAGEMENT SUCCESSION ISSUES

Perhaps a more serious potential problem related to the relatively small size of many REITs is the issue of management depth and succession. Smaller companies, whether REITs or other businesses, because of their limited financial resources, are often unable to develop the type of extensive organization found in a major corporation such as McGraw-Hill or Kroger, let alone Wal-Mart or General Electric. We must ask ourselves whether the REIT might be at a competitive disadvantage if, perhaps, it cannot afford to hire a staff of employees of the highest caliber or obtain the very best market information concerning supply and demand for properties in its market area. Other questions might relate to the depth and experience of the REIT's property acquisition team or property management department, or perhaps the sophistication and strength of the REIT's financial reporting, budgeting, and forecasting systems. There are certain efficiencies that can be enjoyed by companies of substantial size, among them, greater bargaining power with suppliers and tenants. These are issues that must be addressed separately for each REIT, but small size can limit any company's ability to attract high-quality executives, particularly at the middle-management level, and small size can affect a REIT's ability to remain a strong competitor in its markets.

Even if we, as investors, are comfortable with a small REIT's management capabilities, modest size often means we must rely on the management of a few brilliant people to produce superior long-term results with the least risk. Let's face it, while we occasionally see "superstar" management in large corporations (e.g., Warren Buffett at Berkshire Hathaway, Sandy Weill at Citicorp, or Jack Welch at General Electric), we often see more "high-profile" management in smaller companies such as REITs.

Knowledgeable investors are attracted to such REITs as Kimco Realty, Equity Office Properties, Simon Property Group, and Vornado Realty Trust, to name a few, because they are led by such well-known real estate investors and managers as Milton Cooper, Sam Zell, the Simon family, and Steven Roth, respectively.

WHAT HIGH-PROFILE MANAGEMENT CAN MEAN

In late 1996, Vornado Realty hired well-known real estate executive Mike Fascitelli away from a major investment banking firm. While his compensation package was the talk of the REIT world for a couple of weeks, investors gave Steven Roth a vote of confidence by boosting Vornado's share price substantially in the days immediately following the announcement. They knew that a strong successor would be in place should Mr. Roth decide to retire.

The challenge for REIT investors is to determine whether their superstar managers have developed a strong business organization, with highly capable individuals to succeed them when they no longer run the company. Outstanding business leaders, like Jack Welch, create strong and deep organizations because there are always events (retirement, death, disability)—expected and unexpected—that necessitate a backup plan in the event a company loses its superstar. It's never good for an organization to be dependent upon the efforts of one individual, no matter how talented.

Related to the superstar problem is determining how much the REIT's stock price reflects the "star" status of its top management. For example, if Steve Roth or Milton Cooper were to decide next week to retire, what would happen to the share price of Vornado or Kimco? A REIT's stock price is less likely to tumble with the departure of a key executive if senior management has added depth to the organization and created a sound succession plan.

Management succession is a sensitive issue that is, for obvious reasons, difficult for both investors and REIT managements to discuss, but it is of vital concern to investors. Genius is tough to replace in any organization, but it's particularly tough to replace in small and mid-cap companies like REITs. An older generation of smart, entrepreneurial managers will eventually retire, and REIT investors need to assess the capabilities of those who will be replacing them. However, as important as the succession issue is today, it is only a part of the larger issue of how successful a particular REIT has been in building a strong, deep, and motivated management team.

SUMMARY

◆ REIT investors are subject to such potential hazards as an excess supply of available rental space and rising interest rates, as well as changes in investor sentiment.

◆ While a recessionary economy sometimes results in a temporary decline in demand for space, the excess supply that is brought on by overbuilding can be a much larger and longer-lasting problem.

◆ High interest rates are generally not good for any company since they soak up purchasing power from consumers as well as businesses and can cause recession; they also can affect REIT stock prices and asset values.

◆ Overleveraged balance sheets and conflicts of interest by management can create problems for specific REITs—and their stock prices.

◆ Financial or business disasters have been very rare among REITs, while major share price collapse has been infrequent.

◆ Despite outstanding long-term investment returns and other favorable attributes, investors have, at times, shunned REITs as investments—which can affect short-term investment results.

◆ Investors should be careful of credibility issues that haunt some management teams, as well as "broken" balance sheets.

◆ The small size of some REITs can be a competitive disadvantage.

◆ Succession planning is important for all corporations, but particularly for smaller companies such as many REIT organizations.

CHAPTER

12

Tea Leaves:
WHERE WILL REITs GO FROM HERE?

NVESTORS' LOVE AFFAIR with REIT stocks seems to wax and wane every few years; meanwhile, however, the REIT organizations themselves quietly do their job of increasing FFOs, net asset values, and dividend payments to their shareholders.

REIT stocks have yet again become popular, as stable cash flows and high yields are "in" and speculation is "out." Does this mean the REIT industry will never again be banished to the murky backwaters of the investment world? Will the ongoing securitization of real estate continue to attract billions of investment dollars from institutions and individuals? Will the "graying" of America mean that more and more investors will seek high current yields along with moderate growth, and look to REITs to fill that need? Let's break out the crystal ball and look at some of the issues that could affect the size and landscape of the REIT industry over the next several years.

Before we start forecasting the future, though, let's look at the past and the present. The total equity market cap of equity REITs did not reach $1 billion until 1982, twenty years after the first REIT was organized, and as recently as 1992 it was still just $11 billion. However, equity REITs' market cap reached $275 billion by the end of 2004. Thus, it's clear that most of this growth occurred within the last dozen years, driven by the IPO boom of 1993–94 and the massive wave of secondary offerings in 1997–98, as well as the steady appreciation in the value of most REIT stocks, particularly from 2000 through 2004. There were only twelve publicly traded equity REITs at the end of 1971. By the end of 2004, nearly thirty-three years later, there were 160.

Despite this impressive growth, as we discussed briefly in the last chapter, the REIT industry remains small in comparison with both the broader stock market and the total value of commercial real estate in the United States. Equity REITs owned approximately $338 billion in net real estate investments as of the third quarter of 2004 (per NAREIT), or just under 10 percent of the total value of all institutional quality commercial real estate in the United States (which has been estimated at close to $4 trillion).

REITs' property ownership percentage is low, not only on an absolute basis, but also in relation to that of other countries. NAREIT has estimated that in the United Kingdom, for example, approximately 50 percent of the market value of that country's commercial real estate has been securitized and is publicly traded. Should securitization become as prevalent here as in the United Kingdom, the total market cap of the U.S. REIT industry would expand dramatically, to something like $2 trillion. Can this happen? Will it happen? In order to hazard a guess, we will need to consider two key questions: (a) Will a significant number of private real estate owners want either to become REITs or to sell their properties to REITs, and (b) Will investors want to own substantially more REITs in their portfolios?

SUPPLY SIDE: MORE REAL ESTATE COMPANIES WILL WANT TO "REITIZE"

A successful and growing real estate organization could list several reasons why it might choose to go public as a REIT. Some of these have to do with the pricing of real estate on "Wall Street" compared with its pricing on "Main Street," while others have to do with the advantages of the REIT format.

ARBITRAGE

A trend much in evidence over the past twelve to fifteen years is that a larger number of real estate companies are inclined to go public and become REITs when REIT stocks are trading at prices significantly above their estimated net asset values. Such private organizations are thus motivated to capture the "spread," or "arbitrage," between the pricing of real estate assets in private markets versus public markets. Conversely, there is much less motivation to become a public company when REIT shares are trading at prices that are below underlying real estate values. Indeed, if NAV discounts become very large, many REITs may decide to capture that "reverse arbitrage" by either going private or selling out at a premium to the depressed market price—this occurred in several instances in late 1999 and early 2000.

We saw in an earlier chapter that when REIT stocks were priced at significant NAV premiums, for example, from the end of 1992 through mid-1994, a major REIT-IPO boom was launched. Another sizable wave of real estate companies went public as REITs from 1997 through mid-1998, during which time the average REIT stock traded at a substantial NAV premium. And yet another, albeit smaller, wave of IPOs crested in 2003–2004. Thus, the pace at which the REIT industry expands beyond its present size—or even contracts—may be significantly affected by how REIT shares are priced in public markets. If there is a prolonged period in which the shares trade at NAV premiums, we can expect to see more real estate organizations go public in the form of REITs, the only issue being size and number.

But there are also reasons beyond arbitrage for a strong real estate company to go public as a REIT. These include tax advantages, greater access to capital, the ability to strengthen and motivate the organization, and liquidity and estate planning. Kimco Realty had been very successful as a private company for twenty-five years and completed its initial public offering in November 1991 when REIT shares were still relatively unknown. Kimco did not go public to capture the arbitrage, but rather for these other (and more permanent) reasons.

TAX ADVANTAGES

Perhaps one of the most obvious reasons a corporation might choose to become a REIT is that, unlike most corporations, REITs rarely pay corporate income taxes; rather, their shareholders pay taxes on the earnings in the form of dividends received. This enables REITs and their shareholders to avoid double taxation.

Although many property-owning companies can avoid taxation entirely by taking on a large amount of debt and writing off the interest expense (as well as a real estate depreciation expense), the REIT format allows the real estate owner to do business with less debt leverage and thus less risk. This is no small advantage in an increasingly uncertain and more competitive world economy.

Finally, it's possible that a significant number of publicly traded, non-REIT, real estate–owning corporations might elect to become REITs in order to take advantage of the lack of double taxation. For example, in 1997, the Rouse Company (since acquired by General Growth Properties) became a REIT—notwithstanding many years of successful operation as a regular C corporation. Host Marriott, which owns a large number of upscale and luxury hotels, also elected REIThood a few years ago. Catellus Development Corp., a successful real estate developer for many years, became a REIT in 2004 before being acquired by another REIT, ProLogis. Also, timber companies Plum Creek Timber, L.P. and Rayonier Inc. recently became REITs, adding a new sector to REIT world. Conversely, Starwood Hotels & Resorts, which has a substantial hotel management business (an activity not allowed to REITs), elected to de-REIT several years ago despite the adverse tax consequences.

That REITs generally pay no taxes at the corporate level is a factor that will, for a long time to come, motivate many real estate companies to join the trend to REITize.

ACCESS TO CAPITAL

A primary inducement for going public is the greater access to capital and financing flexibility that publicly traded companies enjoy. Successful and growing real estate organizations constantly need additional capital for building and buying real estate, for improving and upgrading individual properties, and to otherwise take advantage of opportunities. As we discussed earlier, successfully accessing the capital markets provides the REIT with the opportunity to grow FFO at above-average rates, but, as Kimco CEO Milton Cooper has reminded us, lenders have been manic-depressive over the years when it comes to lending to real estate owners, developers, and operators. During some periods they seem almost to be throwing money at these enterprises, while at other times they are absolute skinflints. It's difficult to finance and manage a growing business under such stop-and-go conditions, particularly when the best opportunities seem to be available when financing is the most scarce.

This is not to say that the traditional sources of financing will be discarded when a REIT is formed. Successful REITs normally obtain traditional short-term financing and mortgage loans from banks and other lenders, as well as longer-term, private financing from various lenders—such as insurance companies—in the same way that they did earlier as private companies. These financing sources are particularly important at times when public markets are reluctant to provide equity or debt capital. REITs can also enter into joint venture deals with financial partners, whether public or private; they may sell assets to these joint ventures and use the proceeds for higher-profit opportunities, while continuing to manage these assets and retain client relationships.

Access to the public markets provides flexibility and financial resources to REITs and allows managements to have access to reasonably priced capital to plan for the long term and to prevent being at the mercy of private lenders.

The issuance of common stock, while expensive, provides the most permanent type of financing since there is no obligation to repay it. Furthermore, common stock issuance allows the REIT to leverage this additional capital by adding debt to it. Before a borrower becomes eligible for certain types of loans, most lenders insist on a substantial cushion of shareholders' equity, as well as a certain minimum "coverage" of interest payment obligations. Thus, selling common stock provides permanent capital and allows the REIT to add a debt component to the total capital raised, reducing the total cost of the new capital.

The sale of preferred stock is another avenue normally open only to publicly traded companies. Although preferred stock adds financial leverage to REITs' balance sheets and investors should therefore treat it as debt in analyzing a REIT's financial strength, it is not recorded as debt on the company's balance sheet and is generally not treated as such by lenders. Furthermore, nonconvertible preferred stock does not dilute common shareholders' equity interest in the REIT.

A significant number of REITs have been able to raise capital by the issuance and public sale of unsecured notes and debentures, all of which enable the REIT to access the public debt markets and diversify away from a reliance on banks and other private lenders, while providing them with more flexibility in asset recycling strategies. The broad mix of available financing options is of significant value to a real estate company. It is likely that at various times the public markets will be closed to a REIT as a result of depressed market conditions or for some other reason; private financing may then be readily available. Conversely, at other times private lenders may be exceedingly tightfisted, while the public markets extend an open hand.

Finally, becoming an UPREIT or a DownREIT gives the real estate organization a significant advantage in the acquisition of properties from sellers who, by accepting operating partnership (OP) units, can defer capital gains taxes. This approach to financing real estate acquisitions has become popular over the last few years and gives REITs a competitive edge.

Expanded access to capital via common stock, preferred stock, and debt securities, as well as through the issuance of OP units, is a key reason why more well-run and growing real estate companies will become REITs in the years ahead.

ABILITY TO STRENGTHEN AND MOTIVATE THE ORGANIZATION

Today, more than ever before, owning and operating commercial real estate successfully is a *business*—no matter whether the real estate be apartments, office buildings, retail properties, or any other type. For a business, a strong organization is essential to success; competition is fierce everywhere, and strong real estate organizations can often operate at lower costs and are likely to have a significant competitive edge.

Although private companies, even large ones, can build solid organizations and motivate employees and management, it is easier to accomplish these objectives if the company is publicly held. Stock options, restricted stock, and stock bonuses are good motivational tools for employees—from the most recently hired all the way to top management, and only public companies provide ample liquidity for equity holdings.

Today, stock options, restricted stock, and stock purchase plans (allowing employees to buy their company stock at a discount) are strong employee incentives for public companies, including REITs.

Disciplined decision-making and adequate financial controls are becoming increasingly important to managements in their efforts to stay a step ahead of the competition. Many public companies find that the corporate governance requirements imposed upon them, while often nettlesome and costly, strengthen the organization in the long run. These requirements include having a board of several outside directors with whom business plans and projects must be discussed and justified; having to answer to the shareholders with respect to expense control, compensation programs, and other shareholder concerns; and implementing strong financial systems and controls.

These factors, by strengthening the organization and its financial discipline, allow public REITs to become more efficient owners and managers of real estate. As such, they should be able to continue to take tenants and market share from many smaller, less capitalized and less disciplined real estate owners.

LIQUIDITY AND ESTATE PLANNING

Another factor likely to induce well-run real estate companies to go public is the ability of the public markets to provide liquidity for the ownership interests of management and employees. In all businesses—real estate, manufacturing, or service providing—management changes from time to time, and individuals who have devoted years to a successful operation may want to cash out for retirement or for some other reason. Even key personnel who stay with the company need to convert some of their capital to cash from time to time, perhaps to buy a house or to pay their children's college tuition. The public market provides the liquidity necessary for selling their shares, since transfers of privately held shares or partnership interests are costly, time-consuming, or simply not available.

Estate-planning concerns may also induce successful real estate companies to "REITize." Uncle Sam takes a big bite out of substantial estates, and even the recent legislation that may ultimately repeal the estate tax will self-destruct if not extended or renewed by Congress. This is not to say that an entrepreneur who goes public will be able to avoid estate taxes, but going public may keep heirs from being forced to sell all or part of the business or dumping real estate assets to pay estate taxes. Public shares can be sold in the public markets, which will allow the business itself to remain undisturbed.

And yet, there are some reasons for a company *not* to go public: Management will have to operate in a fishbowl. Almost every major decision must be explained to the analysts and shareholders, who will be constantly looking over management's shoulder and second-guessing them. The recent Sarbanes-Oxley legislation imposes severe penalties upon careless management teams, and its compliance costs are substantial. Independent directors will need to be selected, and consulted on all major projects. There will be significant pressure to perform, often on a very short-term basis. The costs of running a public company will be large, including premiums for directors' and officers' insurance, expensive audit fees, costs of maintaining an investor relations department, transfer agent fees, and legal and accounting costs for SEC and federal law compliance. And as mentioned earlier, the prospect that REIT shares may trade at discounts to estimated net asset values can discourage some private real estate companies from going public as a REIT.

These drawbacks notwithstanding, the benefits of being a public company as a REIT organization substantially outweigh the drawbacks for long-term success. In 1997–98, forty-three companies went public as REITs. IPO activity shut down in subsequent years, due to the REIT bear market of 1998–99, while few REITs traded at NAV premiums until 2001. From 2001 through 2004, another thirty-nine companies went public via IPOs. It seems quite likely that, particularly if REIT share pricing remains firm, with the vast majority of REIT shares trading above estimated net asset values, many of the "best and brightest" real estate entrepreneurs will also want their companies to become public REITs in the years ahead.

It is fair to question, however, whether the REIT industry will expand substantially in size purely from a large additional number of high-profile REIT IPOs. Some knowledgeable REIT observers have noted that most of the large real estate organizations in the United States have already gone public as REITs, and those who are still private have had lots of opportunities to take their companies public—but have elected not to do so. One example may be the Shorenstein Company LLC, which has been a major real estate owner, acquirer, developer, and manager in the San Francisco Bay Area for many years; since 1992 it has used closed-end investment funds to acquire over $3.7 billion in investment properties. The Shorenstein Company seems perfectly content to remain private, particularly as it appears to have had no difficulty raising funds for whatever acquisitions and developments it deems attractive.

Many of these companies may decide that they just don't need the annoyances that "come with the territory" of being a public company. If the Shorensteins of the real estate world continue along their present path, the continuing expansion of the REIT industry will be driven by additional smaller IPOs, property acquisitions, and developments—including joint ventures with institutional real estate owners—by existing REITs and a gradual increase in the values of REIT assets—and the values of their shares—perhaps helped along by the occasional non-REIT real estate organization electing to become a REIT.

DEMAND SIDE: MORE INVESTORS WILL WANT TO OWN REITS

It obviously won't matter how many successful real estate companies want to become REITs if there is insufficient investor demand for REIT shares. Following the end of the IPO boom of 1993–94, many well-run and experienced real estate organizations were told that investor enthusiasm for REITs had chilled and that the IPO window had slammed shut. That situation was reversed in 1996–97, when not only individual investors began buying REITs as they never had before, but institutional investors, money managers, and pension funds also started moving into REITs in a big way. This favorable development reversed course during the bear market of 1998–99, but subsequently REIT investing again became popular. Will investment interest in REITs continue to be large enough in the future to allow for more IPOs and the secondary offerings that will enable REITs to resume their portfolio expansions?

INDIVIDUAL INVESTORS

A perceptive observer once noted that the baby boomer generation is like a rather large rat that has just been swallowed by a snake—it greatly changes the form of the snake as it wends its way through the snake's long torso. The baby boomers created overcrowded classes when they started school and spiraling tuition rates as they pursued higher education; they stoked demand for houses, BMWs, and Brie as they got jobs and began climbing the corporate ladder. More recently, they inspired an awesome explosion in the growth of mutual funds and 401(k) plans as they began to contemplate retirement. These boomers have become very serious indeed about investing.

FROM AN INVESTOR'S STANDPOINT

THE JUSTIFICATION FOR investing in REITs is clear: REITs have, over many years, delivered total returns to their investors that approximate those of the S&P 500 index; they have low correlations, which means that the REIT sector of one's portfolio won't move in lockstep with price movements of other asset classes; and they have shown themselves to be, during most market cycles, less volatile. They provide substantial dividend yields—well in excess of most other common stocks—and they respond to a different set of economic and market conditions from other common stocks and asset classes.

Although these new investors have channeled billions of dollars into mutual funds, they are also exploring other alternatives. Many are investing on their own, and both the full-service and discount brokerage firms, virtually all of which now provide for online trading, have benefited from their business; other new investors are turning to financial planners and investment advisers.

According to data compiled by Realty Stock Review, the number of mutual funds devoted primarily to REITs and real estate grew in number from six to more than seventy (not including multiple classes of essentially the same mutual fund) from December 1992 to December 2004. According to AMG Data Services, total assets under management in real estate open-end mutual funds at March 16, 2005, amounted to $43.7 billion.

More than $4.8 billion poured into REITs and real estate mutual funds in 1997 alone, but enthusiasm for real estate stocks waned in subsequent years as "growth" became the mantra of most new investors. Recently REIT investing, providing stable and predictable cash flows and high dividend yields, has enjoyed a new burst of popularity. But how much of the aggregate amount of the new investment funds that will be deployed into the first few decades of the twenty-first century will REITs be able to capture?

The signs point to a significant amount. New investors start with small investments, and mutual funds are one obvious beneficiary;

a mutual fund is a cost-effective way for new investors to get into a regular investment program. It is not necessary to become a financial analyst or even to follow specific stocks.

Popular 401(k) plans also encourage employees to invest through mutual funds. Although the number of 401(k) plans that offer REIT options is still in the minority, this will change over time—perhaps driven by readers of this book who will ask their plan administrator to create one. The availability of REIT choices in 401(k) plans will be driven, in large part, by plan participants.

Over time, investors' needs will grow, and may become more complex. Some investors will want to get more personally involved. For tax reasons, they will want to time their financial transactions. They will use individual stockbrokers to help them review specific investments. They will seek the help of professional financial planners and investment advisers. They will want to diversify their investments among different asset classes to minimize the adverse effects of the occasional crash or bear market within a particular asset class. The major debacle in tech stocks which began in 2000 has taught many new investors the value of diversification. And therein lies a golden opportunity for REITs to attract new investors.

As the years go by, REITs will continue to be an attractive method of diversification for these serious, new investors. As we saw earlier, REIT stocks' correlations with other asset classes are low, while their historical total returns have been impressive. Even if they don't make up the lion's share of these new investment dollars, a 10–20 percent asset allocation would result in huge additional demand for REIT shares. As investors' assets become larger and the investors themselves become more knowledgeable about the investment world, they will want to diversify into REIT investments.

In 1997, Bernard Winograd, CEO of Prudential Real Estate Investors, observed that "the kind and quality of the offerings and the players are beginning to improve, and the REIT business is shifting from being a cottage industry to a mainstream investment choice." He adds that as more large real estate companies go public, the growing liquidity will draw still more investors to the sector.

Despite the setback caused by REITs' 1998–99 bear market, Mr. Winograd's observation remains valid. Financial publications catering to individual investors are again discussing the benefits of REIT investing, while individual investors are beginning to appreciate the virtues of predictable earnings growth as well as the beauty of significant dividend income.

Brokerage firms, too, are expanding their coverage of REIT investments and today virtually all of the big brokerage firms now have REIT analysts, something that would have been unheard of several years ago. Additionally, NAREIT has a program to educate financial planners about REIT investing as an excellent form of diversification for their clients' assets, and is helping to expand the number of REIT options in the all-important 401(k) market. More investment advisers than ever before are looking at REITs as a strong alternative to often high-risk utility stocks. And, once again, there are the ever-present baby boomers. As they get longer in the tooth and closer to retirement age, the high, steady, and growing dividend income provided by REITs will become more and more attractive to them.

INSTITUTIONAL INVESTORS

Earlier we noted that institutions and pension funds were originally slow to embrace REITs, but, for many reasons, that is changing— perhaps not as quickly as the REIT industry would like, but changing nonetheless. First of all, REIT stocks were, until very recently, limited to a small number of property sectors. No more. Virtually all real estate types can be found among the assets of REIT organizations. Until 1993–94, the REIT industry was dismissed as insignificant, and many desirable types of properties, such as offices, malls, hotels, and self-storage facilities that dominate the REIT industry today, weren't even represented or were available only in very small quantities.

Objections were raised with respect to the small market caps of REITs, which made it difficult to buy and sell REIT shares in large blocks without affecting their market price. If an institution found a REIT in which it would like to invest, it couldn't buy a significant position without finding itself owning practically a controlling position in the REIT. Liquidity is still an issue for many REITs, but this has not prevented institutional investors from significantly increasing their ownership of REIT shares in the aggregate, as the market caps of many have grown dramatically.

INSTITUTIONAL OWNERSHIP OF REITS

SINCE INSTITUTIONAL INVESTORS historically have elected to own real
estate as one asset class within their broadly diversified portfolios, it
is easy to see why they would choose REITs as a supplement to their
direct ownership of real estate:

1 REITs provide much greater liquidity than ever before.
2 Institutions can now choose from an increasing number of high-
quality organizations with good management depth.
3 The number of REIT sectors has expanded geometrically.

The bottom line is that investing in REITs is a sound long-term
strategy for institutional investors.

Many institutions have "put their toes in the water" by forming
joint ventures with solid REIT organizations. Eventually, as their
comfort level rises, these institutions may, to some extent, increase
their commitments via direct purchase of REIT shares.

REITS' QUALITY

From the time that the REIT industry was born in the early 1960s
until about fifteen years ago, most REITs were managed in a passive
way by small real estate staffs. Those days are gone, and internal
management is now the order of the day. To have called these old-
style REITs "organizations" would have been a euphemism. Insider
stock ownership was nil, conflicts of interest were numerous, and
most REITs had limited access to capital. Institutional investors
would have found investing in such REITs almost laughable.

Today a large number of the sophisticated real estate companies
that had operated successfully for many years as private companies
have become REITs and, despite the inevitable hiccups along the
way, have earned solid reputations—no less as public REITs than
as private companies. Some of these include: among mall REITs,
General Growth Properties, Macerich, Simon Property Group, and
Taubman Centers; among neighborhood shopping centers, Developers Diversified, Kimco Realty, and Regency Realty; among apartments, Avalon Bay Communities, Post Properties, and Summit

Properties (the latter recently acquired by Camden Property); and, in the office and industrial sector, AMB Property, Boston Properties, CenterPoint Properties, Cousins Properties, Duke Realty, and Reckson Associates. Yes, there were some outstanding organizations operating under the REIT format before 1991, such as Federal, New Plan, United Dominion, Washington REIT, and Weingarten, but they were few in number. Investors' choices among quality REIT organizations are greater than ever today.

EARNINGS GROWTH

Another factor that has contributed to, and will continue to increase, the amount of institutional funds flowing into REIT investments is that investors are now recognizing the strength of many REITs' past and prospective growth rates. In the late 1980s and early 1990s, institutions learned to their great sorrow that management can be as important as location as a determinant of success for a portfolio of properties. Most REITs today can boast outstanding property management skills. Furthermore, because of managements' extensive tenant contacts, strong financial resources, in-house research capabilities, and, in some cases, an ability to issue OP units allowing property sellers to defer capital gains taxes, many REITs are often able to acquire quality properties at discount prices. These capabilities can create steady and impressive earnings growth, which is not going unrecognized by institutions, since they are likely, in the author's opinion, to generate better investment returns over time by buying REIT shares than by buying and owning properties directly. Although the larger pension funds and other institutions will never replace all their direct real estate investments with REIT shares, it is probable that REIT shares will find their way into many more institutional portfolios over time. Indeed, the trend has been moving in that direction, particularly in recent years.

INCREASED MARKET CAPS AND SHARE LIQUIDITY

If small market caps were a factor in keeping institutional fund managers away from REIT shares in the past, they must have been gratified to see REIT market caps increasing, thus providing increased liquidity for REIT shares. Before the 1993–94 IPO boom, not a single REIT could boast an equity market cap of as much as $1 billion. According to NAREIT, by the end of 1997, a total of forty-seven REITs had passed that milestone, and there were eighty-two of them by March 2005. Most REITs have continued to expand their property holdings over time, although expansion moderated beginning in 1999 due to the cutback in equity capital resulting from the 1998–99 bear market and REITs' increasing emphasis on capital recycling strategies. But, REITs will continue to issue equity from time to time; and although new equity offerings have the effect of reducing the ownership interests of the existing shareholders, they also increase REITs' equity market cap and the public "float" of available shares. Furthermore, property acquisitions are often made through the issuance of stock and OP units convertible into shares. Finally, to the extent that REIT shares trade at sufficiently high prices so that they may be used as "currency" to acquire private real estate companies, the REIT industry will see a larger number of REIT organizations with very substantial market caps.

The trading volume of many REITs today matches that of many mid-cap and larger non-REIT companies, and such volumes will increase with their increasing market caps. According to NAREIT, the average daily dollar trading volume of the shares comprising the NAREIT Composite Index rose from approximately $100 million in 1995 to more than $400 million by the end of 2000 and to approximately $1.4 billion by March 2005. The institutions, if patient, should be able to establish sizable positions without creating excessively large percentage holdings in a single REIT and without significantly affecting the current market price. Further, as institutions become more comfortable with REITs, they might find it less important to be able to dump hundreds of thousands of shares within twenty minutes.

One experienced REIT observer, William Campbell, has suggested several other advantages for pension funds and other institutions to own REITs rather than specific real estate. Some of these include the use of leverage in real estate investing (which is often not legally permitted in direct investments by pension funds); the greater ability of REITs to assemble multiple properties in a single geographical area, which can increase operating efficiency and bargaining power with tenants and thus generate better real estate returns; the ability of most institutional owners to obtain greater real estate diversification with respect to management style, geography, and property sector; and the ease with which the investment can be liquidated should it prove disappointing.

In what form will institutions continue to invest in REITs? There are several. They can, of course, simply buy REIT shares in the open market. They can negotiate private placements directly with a REIT, either through common stock or through a special issue of convertible preferred stock, and they can buy shares in "spot offerings" that are completed within a single trading day. They can form joint ventures with a REIT, putting up the funds for the acquisition of significant property portfolios or for the development of one or more new properties; some of these joint venture interests might eventually be converted into REIT shares. Or they can swap properties they already own for REIT shares. This institutional interest will continue to augment the credibility of REIT stocks as real estate–related investments, provide REITs with needed capital at reduced costs, and enable many more privately held, successful real estate companies to become REITs.

It is not important *how* institutions and pension funds choose to invest in REITs; it is important only that they are choosing REITs as a strong supplement to direct ownership of real estate and that they continue to increase their investment in them.

Institutional interest in the REIT industry continues to increase —on an absolute, if not a percentage, basis. Ohio Public Employees Retirement System, for example, has been investing in REIT stocks since 1997, and increased its allocation to REITs in 2004. ABP Investments, a large Dutch pension plan, is one of the largest institutional holders of REIT shares, with approximately 4 percent of the market, and continues to make investments in U.S. REITs. Matt Gilman, senior portfolio manager at ABP Investments, has stated that REIT liquidity is "infinitely better" than buying or selling individual buildings. Also, he notes, REIT investing makes it much easier to obtain the required diversification.

And many new institutional investors are beginning to invest in REITs. The University of California decided to invest in REITs for the first time in 2004, with a $50 million commitment; the Employees Retirement System of Texas committed, in 2005, to allocate 1 percent of its assets ($200 million) to REITs; the Alaska State Pension Investment Board recently allocated $100 million to REIT investing; and the City of Clearwater (Florida) is asking its citizens to approve a change in its employee pension fund rules that would allow an allocation to REITs (their intent is a 10 percent REIT allocation, or approximately $50 million). And these are merely but a few recent examples.

A recent study published by Deutsche Bank ("REIT Ownership Profile," February 2005), concluded that general equity investors, including institutions, owned approximately 40 percent of all outstanding REIT shares at September 2004; while this is down from 44 percent in 2003, the absolute number has increased. (The percentage of REITs owned by dedicated real estate funds is now up to 33 percent of the outstanding shares, according to the Deutsche Bank study.) While there hasn't been a flood of new institutional funds pouring into REIT shares, interest has been increasing steadily. According to Institutional Real Estate's Jennifer Babcock, "most pension funds see REITs as a permanent part of their core holdings."

Perhaps a major issue for institutions is the question of whether REITs are to be considered "real estate." As we've discussed in this book, REITs are a unique blend of both real estate and equities, and any attempts to assign them a single label will be doomed to failure. A study published in 2003, in *The Journal of Portfolio Management,* authored by Joseph Pagliari, Kevin Scherer, and Richard Monopoli, compared REIT stock price performance, based on the NAREIT index, to the performance of private real estate, as represented by the NCREIF Property Index. After adjusting to make the NAREIT and NCREIF indices more comparable, the authors concluded that "public and private [real estate investment] vehicles ought to be viewed somewhat interchangeably …, offering investors a risk-return continuum of real estate investment opportunities." If this is so, then REITs are *both* real estate *and* equities. In any event, it's quite likely that the modest pace with which institutions have increased their investments in REIT stocks has been due to this "equity versus real estate" conundrum, as well as the REITs' 1998–

99 bear market, which saw REIT stock prices decline significantly despite strong real estate markets across the United States. Eventually, however, institutional investors will most likely conclude that while REIT stocks are subject to the fashions and vagaries of the equities markets in the short term, they will deliver real estate–like returns in the long run—and, perhaps, do a lot better than that. Of course, as we've seen in Chapter 8, the quality of REITs' management teams—and how they perform over time—will be essential in attracting new institutional, as well as individual, REIT investors.

CHANGES IN THE NATURE OF REITS

A crucial point concerning the nature of today's REITs is that, until the IPO boom of 1993–94, most REITs were fairly small companies with limited capabilities. They acquired real estate, and most were able to manage their holdings quite well. Many were able to upgrade their properties and thus increase their enterprise value and FFO at a faster pace than if they had employed a purely passive buy-and-hold strategy, but very few were able to *develop* properties. In 1993 and 1994, however, this all changed when a large number of new REITs with well-established development capabilities went public. There are times in various real estate cycles when it is simply not going to be profitable, at least on a risk-adjusted basis, to develop new properties, such as when existing rental rates are insufficient to justify the costs of land acquisition, property entitlement, and construction, when interest and financing costs are excessive, or when tenant demand for space is falling. At other times, however, new development is clearly warranted and can generate strong investment returns. REITs capable of such development clearly have an advantage, since they will be able to avail themselves of opportunities when conditions are appropriate, and thus gain an edge by their ability to increase their FFO and NAV faster than those not so well situated.

It is likely that REIT investors will continue to have many investment choices. Many will choose to invest in the smaller REITs, some of which pay higher dividends and do not make growth a major focus of their business strategy. But it's also likely that even more investors, particularly the institutional type, will focus on those real estate organizations that can create the most additional value for their shareholders. These companies will have the acquisition skills to know when to buy properties and to find them at bargain prices, the research abilities to determine where growth will be strongest, the staff necessary to manage existing properties in the most creative and efficient manner, the size necessary to become the low-cost space provider and to negotiate the best deals with suppliers and tenants in their markets, the capability of developing the kinds of properties most in demand and in the best locations, and the foresight to create highly incentivized management teams and well-thought-out succession plans. Such real estate organizations, through their ability to attract new capital at appropriate times during most market cycles, will become significantly larger than most of today's REITs and will attract increasing institutional followings.

And yet, despite the promise and potential of these larger REIT organizations of the future, it is yet uncertain whether REIT investors want their REITs to become significantly larger if they must issue huge amounts of equity to buy assets or acquire other REITs to accomplish their growth plans. Some question the value to shareholders of becoming a "national REIT" with assets in far-flung locations, while others wonder whether REITs have paid excessive prices—in cash or in stock—to attain greater mass. A proposed merger of Prentiss Properties and Mack-Cali Realty a number of years ago was given the Bronx Cheer by investors, and was subsequently abandoned when investors could detect no value creation from such a business combination. And many question even Sam Zell for causing his REITs to make large numbers of acquisitions. Investors are becoming smarter and more discriminating, and they will give their approval only to those growth strategies that are likely to create substantial long-term values for REIT shareholders. Large REITs will certainly be strong competitors in real estate markets in the twenty-first century but, as Alexandria, CenterPoint, Cousins, SL Green, and others have shown, large size and huge footprints are not prerequisites for success in the REIT industry.

Until recently, many believed that the REIT of the future would be national in scope. Although many REITs specializing in malls, self-storage properties, health care facilities, and hotels have owned assets across the United States for many years, in the mid-1990s many apartment, office, and industrial REITs also greatly expanded their markets nationally, including, to name just a few, Apartment Investment and Management, Camden, Carr America, Equity Office, Equity Residential, and Prentiss Properties. Bay Apartment Communities and Avalon Properties tied the marriage knot, combining apartment assets on both coasts of America, while Security Capital Pacific and Security Capital Atlantic also merged to become Archstone Communities, a REIT focused on specific high-barrier-to-entry markets.

Although many REITs will continue to seek a presence in promising new markets (e.g., Archstone agreed in 2001 to merge with Charles Smith Residential and, in 2005, Camden Property acquired Summit Properties), they are, even at the same time, exiting markets and shedding assets, focusing more intensely on markets in which they are strongest or where they see the best long-term potential growth. Archstone-Smith is, perhaps, a prime example of a REIT that is investing in attractive new markets while departing others. Thus, many REITs are realizing that "local sharpshooters"—as CenterPoint has become in Chicago and as SL Green has long been in Manhattan—may create the most value for shareholders.

Although a large REIT may become a local sharpshooter in a number of markets, it has been very difficult, historically, for an apartment, office, industrial, or neighborhood shopping center REIT to be an effective competitor in more than eight or ten of them, particularly if their assets are scattered across the United States. A few have done so, such as Developers Diversified, Equity Residential, Kimco, Regency, ProLogis, and Weingarten, but it is not an easy task.

In any event, we have today a mixture of large, geographically diversified REIT organizations (e.g., Apartment Investment and Management, Equity Office, Equity Residential, Kimco, and United Dominion), REITs with a heavy emphasis on selected markets nationally (e.g., AMB Property, Archstone-Smith, Avalon Bay, Boston Properties, and Carr America), and yet others that remain very focused regionally (e.g., Essex, First Potomac, Reckson, SL Green, and Vornado). There are advantages and disadvantages to each business strategy, and the REIT investor should determine whether the REIT has the financial strength, the infrastructure, and the management expertise that fit the chosen strategy. What might make lots of sense for one REIT to pursue may be folly for another. Geographical diversification is not a sufficient reason for moving into new locations; we REIT investors can diversify on our own by buying a package of REITs.

CONSOLIDATION WITHIN THE INDUSTRY: IS BIGGER REALLY BETTER?

Despite the likelihood that more well-run, privately held real estate companies will become REITs in the years ahead, a countertrend has begun to manifest itself. Starting in 1995, there has been a persistent volume of merger activity among REITs. As far back as 1996, Barry Vinocur, editor and publisher of *Realty Stock Review*, noted: "There's been more merger activity in REIT land … [during the twelve months from March 1995 to March 1996] than in the prior five or ten years combined." Major acquisition activity during that period included Wellsford's acquisition of Holly Residential, McArthur/Glen's acquisition by Horizon Group, the merger of REIT of California with BRE Properties, the buyout of Tucker Properties by Bradley Realty, and Highwoods's purchase of Crocker Realty Trust. The pace picked up in late 1996 and early 1997 when South West Property Trust was merged into United Dominion Realty, Camden Property agreed to acquire Paragon Group, and Equity Residential and Wellsford Residential merged. The largest 1996 deal was the merger between DeBartolo Realty and Simon Property Group, which created the largest retail real estate organization in the United States.

REIT merger activity continued at a rapid pace well into 1997 and 1998. Noteworthy deals in the apartment sector included Equity Residential's acquisition of Evans Withycombe, Post's combination with Columbus, and Camden's agreement to buy Oasis. In the retail area, Price agreed in early 1998 to merge with Kimco, and Prime Retail made a deal to buy Horizon Group. Chateau and ROC Communities completed their long-contested merger in the manufactured-home community sector, and Meditrust acquired the Santa Anita Companies to become a paired-share REIT. In early 1998, Bay Apartment Communities agreed to join forces with Avalon Properties in a merger of equals, with the purpose of becoming a REIT specializing in upscale apartment communities in high-barrier-to-entry areas across the United States. Security Capital Pacific and Security Capital Atlantic likewise agreed to merge, becoming Archstone Communities. The largest merger in that time frame was the acquisition of Beacon Properties by Equity Office in a $4 billion deal, creating the largest REIT ever at that time, at an $11 billion total market cap.

In the early years of the twenty-first century, Felcor acquired Bristol Hotels, New Plan Realty acquired Excel Realty, and Bradley Realty bought Mid-America Properties, before itself selling out to Heritage Property Trust, a private REIT (which went public soon thereafter). Equity Residential bought Merry Land, and Reckson Associates and Tower Realty combined. ProLogis Trust bought the assets of Meridian Industrial Trust, Duke Realty and Weeks Corp. merged, as did Health Care Property and American Health Properties. Pan Pacific Retail bought neighborhood shopping center Western Investment, and Archstone acquired Charles Smith Residential, combining two strong apartment REITs. Finally, not content with an acquisition of Cornerstone Properties, Equity Office struck again—this time acquiring the highly regarded West Coast office REIT, Spieker Properties, in a deal valued at approximately $7.2 billion and boosting Equity Office's equity market cap to $14.2 billion.

Merger and acquisition activity continued apace in more recent years, although most of this activity was focused in the retail sector. The largest deal was concluded in November 2004 when mall REIT General Growth Properties acquired mall owner Rouse Company in a $13.4 billion deal. Just a little over two years previously, General Growth acquired JP Realty, a smaller mall REIT. Another fairly large recent transaction was Simon Property Group's $5 billion acquisition of premier outlet center owner, Chelsea Property Group, in 2004. This deal should give Simon the opportunity to cross-sell space to both traditional mall and outlet center tenants.

Two additional but smaller retail deals included Pennsylvania REIT's acquisition of fellow mall REIT Crown America, and Equity One's purchase of IRT Property, another neighborhood shopping center REIT. Macerich Company, a large mall REIT, didn't acquire other REITs, but did buy two large mall portfolios, Westcor (2002) and Wilmorite (2005).

Two companies left REITville to become part of the General Electric empire. Franchise Finance Corporation of America, a lender to restaurant owners and others, was sold to GE Capital in 2001, and Storage USA agreed to be acquired by Security Capital Group at the end of 2001, which in turn agreed to merge into GE Capital Real Estate in 2002. And, in the apartment sector, in early 2005 Camden Property completed its pending acquisition of apartment owner Summit Properties.

What seems to be driving these deals is the perception by some, at least in the REIT industry, that "bigger is better."

Is a larger REIT truly better—or, at least, a stronger competitor that will generate higher-than-average rewards for its shareholders over time? The proponents of large size make the following points: (a) the purchaser, due to economies of scale, can easily improve the profitability of acquired assets; (b) mergers deliver "synergies" in the form of overhead and other cost reductions; (c) larger companies have stronger bargaining positions with their suppliers and can obtain substantial price concessions; (d) larger companies also have more bargaining clout with tenants, particularly in the retail sector; (e) larger companies can offer more services to tenants, thus increasing retention rates; (f) larger size reduces the cost of capital—both debt and equity; and (g) investors appreciate—and will pay a premium for—the greater liquidity that large public real estate companies provide.

And yet, there are contrary arguments. Those who are not enamored with the strategy of a REIT buying other REIT organizations (or even large real estate portfolios) argue: (a) operating cost savings are minimal, particularly when a well-run REIT or property portfolio is acquired, and any cost savings are invariably paid to the shareholders of the acquired company up front in the form of a premium over the previous market price; (b) most REITs are not bloated with overhead, so any corporate general and administrative expense savings are minimal; (c) it is always very difficult to blend corporate cultures, and many valuable and experienced executives will depart, thus affecting the long-term value of any such mergers; (d) the "synergy gap" that's created when a premium price is paid for a company that substantially exceeds the cost savings may take years, if ever, to recover, and thus destroys value for the acquiring company's shareholders; (e) REIT organizations don't always have attractive "currency," in the form of expensive stock, that can be easily used in acquisitions; and (f) becoming ever larger makes it much more difficult for that splendid "one-off" acquisition or unique development to create a meaningful amount of incremental value for shareholders.

In 2000 many of the larger, more aggressive REITs enjoyed substantial appreciation in their share prices, while the stocks of the smaller and quieter REITs languished. This situation gave rise to the thought that consolidation in the REIT industry would accelerate, following the "year of separation," as the larger REITs with strong share "currencies" (trading at NAV premiums) would be able to acquire many of the smaller REITs at bargain prices. This did not happen, as many of the large-cap REIT stocks that did so well in 2000 gave up much of their performance edge to the smaller, higher-yielding REITs in 2001, as investors' on-again, off-again love affair with high yields turned steamy that year and benefited the smaller, higher-yielding REITs.

The net result of these countervailing influences is that we will quite likely see additional mergers and acquisitions in REITville, but a major wave of large deals isn't likely. So, speculating on the "next" buy-out candidate won't be very productive for REIT investors. Although the costs and aggravations of compliance with Sarbanes-Oxley may drive some smaller REITs to seek a merger partner, we cannot know in advance which ones they will be.

It is still too soon to know if mergers, on balance, bring benefits to acquisitive REITs. Although the advantages of becoming large can indeed be real, so, too, are shareholders' concerns.

REITs, of course, can grow their real estate portfolios in ways other than buying entire companies, such as the two Macerich acquisitions noted above, and Regency's $2.7 billion 2005 acquisition, along with Macquarie Countrywide (an Australian property trust), of a Calpers–First Washington portfolio of shopping centers. Transactions that are well conceived, priced attractively, and offer many of the potential advantages discussed earlier, while minimizing the problems and concerns also noted, will be greeted with

REITS IN THE S&P 500 INDEX

FOR SEVERAL YEARS the REIT industry had been seeking to have one or more of its members included within the Standard & Poor's major U.S. indices, including the S&P 500, the S&P MidCap 400, and the S&P SmallCap 600, and it redoubled its efforts in 2001 (the S&P established a *separate* index for REIT shares prior to 2001). The principal argument for inclusion was that modern REITs have evolved over a period of forty years from being relatively small ($10–$50 million) passive pools of investment properties with outside advisers and external property management into fully integrated, self-managed companies, many having market capitalizations larger than some companies already included in the S&P 500. Thus, the contention has been that REITs should be as entitled to membership in such an index as any other company if the S&P selection criteria are met.

The S&P decision-makers were finally convinced, as it was announced on October 3, 2001 that the S&P now regards REITs as eligible for inclusion in their U.S. indices. Indeed, at that time, S&P announced that Equity Office Properties, the largest REIT, had been selected to replace Texaco (which merged with Chevron) in the S&P 500, and several other REITs were then designated for inclusion in the S&P MidCap 400 Index and in the S&P SmallCap 600 Index. S&P stated that it had "conducted a broad review of Real Estate Investment Trusts (REITs), their role in investment portfolios, treatment by accounting and tax authorities, and how they are viewed by investors," and that "Standard & Poor's believes that REITs have become operating companies subject to the same economic and financial factors as other publicly traded U.S. companies listed on major American stock exchanges."

The long-term consequences of S&P's decision appear to be substantial. According to Green Street Advisors, index funds benchmarked to the S&P 500 amount to over $1 trillion. The first REIT included in the S&P 500, Equity Office Properties, initially represented approximately 0.1 percent of the S&P 500, or about $1 billion of new investment. Later in 2001, the largest apartment REIT, Equity Residential, was also added to the S&P 500. These REITs were followed by Plum Creek Timber and Simon Property Group (2002), Aimco and ProLogis (2003), and Archstone-Smith (2004). Two additional REITs were added to the S&P 500 in 2005 (as of August 11), including Vornado Realty and Public Storage. Regardless of any short-term "pop" in the shares selected for inclusion (these effects for the chosen REITs were mild), the long-term benefit of REITs' inclusion should be a major boost to REITs' credibility as solid, long-term equity investments. Many fund managers who currently do not own REIT shares—even those who focus on "equity-income" investments—are now taking a serious look at them.

A number of industry leaders have suggested that REIT organizations ought to be viewed as mainstream equity investments and should compete with all other equities for the attention of investors. This is one reason why some REIT organizations and investment analysts have been putting more emphasis on earnings per share in financial reporting and guidance; they believe that continuing to focus on FFO or AFFO keeps REITs out of the investment mainstream and justifies "benign neglect" on the part of many investors. Said Douglas Crocker, at the time the CEO of Equity Residential, "Our goal has always been to be valued as an operating company, not just an owner of real estate assets. Therefore, it is important to provide operating results to the investment community that are consistent with all other publicly traded companies."

There's an old saying, however: "Be careful what you wish for, as your wish may come true." A substantial part of the appeal of REIT stocks is that many investors regard them as a separate asset class, like bonds or international stocks, and that the inclusion of such a separate asset class within a broadly diversified investment portfolio has many advantages, particularly in view of their low correlations with other asset classes. If REIT shares become viewed simply as equities, like tech stocks or health care stocks, will this advantage be lost?

Perhaps—but not necessarily. It should not matter what label is placed upon a group of stocks if owning them as part of a diversified portfolio continues to provide the investor with significant advantages. If their investment characteristics are favorable, that is, modest risk, low correlations, and strong total returns, should investors care whether financial advisers call REIT shares a separate "asset class" or merely an "industry group"? Furthermore, the incipient movement to focus on earnings per share (as apposed to FFO or AFFO) seems to have lost momentum. In any event, inclusion of a number of REIT stocks within the S&P 500 has become a watershed event for the REIT industry.

enthusiasm and will benefit the shareholders of both the acquiring and the acquired companies. Others, less well-conceived or poorly executed, will leave many sad shareholders licking their wounds. The REIT industry will certainly expand over time, but, with the possible exception of shopping malls, where 85 percent of the top 400 malls in the United States are owned by REIT organizations, it's unclear whether commercial real estate will be dominated by a few huge companies.

ADDITIONAL NEW TRENDS

In Chapter 6, some recent new trends in the REIT industry were noted, including asset recycling strategies (in which existing assets are sold to fund higher growth opportunities such as development), stock repurchases, and joint ventures. Investors have also seen several other recent trends in the REIT world, many of which may be of significance to REIT valuations and growth rates.

Reporting and disclosure by REIT organizations have become much more comprehensive, and it's now easy, by going to a REIT's website, for the individual investor to obtain access to financial and other information that was previously available only to analysts and institutional investors.

Just one example of many is Avalon Bay's website (www.avalon bay.com), which provides quarterly financial information and numerous attachments and supplements, describing, among other matters, the status of the company's development pipeline, acquisitions and sales, and submarket profiles. Greatly encouraged by SEC disclosure rule Regulation FD, most public companies, including REIT organizations, are broadening their dissemination of important business and financial information, and a large number of quarterly earnings conferences are now available to all investors, either by phone or by webcast.

And disclosure itself is improving. Although REIT investors continue to be troubled by, among other things, the fact that different companies within a single sector sometimes calculate FFO differently—despite continual efforts by NAREIT to refine and improve the definition—progress is steadily being made toward more uniform disclosure and accounting practices, as well as the disclosure of more information. Investors are demanding ever more precise and meaningful financial information, and REIT organizations are increasingly complying with their wishes.

REITs have traditionally avoided investing in real estate abroad—and for good reason. The laws, customs, and economics of owning and managing real estate can be very different outside of the United States; real estate everywhere tends to be a very specialized business, demanding a strong local presence and employees who understand governmental regulation, tenant requirements, supply and demand trends, and land and building values, among many other things. But recently we have seen exceptions, as a few of the more aggressive REITs have been making real estate investments in foreign countries. Chelsea Property Group, acquired by Simon Property Group in 2004, has formed joint ventures with two major Japan-based corporations to build and manage outlet centers in Japan, and the results to date have been excellent. And Simon itself has been investing in Europe, including a new retail project in Warsaw, Poland. It is even putting its toe in the water in China. ProLogis Trust and more recently, AMB Property, have been acquiring and developing distribution properties in Europe, Mexico, and Japan, very often using local partners with specific local real estate knowledge, contacts, and experience. ProLogis is entering Chinese markets, and retail REIT Mills Corp. is building a large retail venue in Madrid, Spain. And these pioneers will be followed by other U.S. real estate companies.

Investing in foreign real estate certainly introduces significant risks (e.g., foreign currency losses and depreciation, issues involving relationships with foreign partners, unique regulatory and tax issues, etc.). However, a judicious amount of such investment can also be very profitable to the REIT and its shareholders if planned and executed with care and foresight, particularly if these business plans can take advantage of a combination of the expertise—and perhaps tenant relationships—of both the REIT and the foreign partner. But a merely passive investment by a REIT in a foreign country would seem to offer little advantage to the REIT's shareholders. The devil is, indeed, in the details, and some REITs will succeed in these endeavors while others will fail.

But let's now go beyond U.S. REITs investing in foreign countries for the benefit of us shareholders, and consider whether we might be able to invest in such foreign real estate directly. Diversification is an investment concept that has been widely embraced in recent years, and is one of the primary drivers for REITs' increased popularity. But if diversification is important, why stop at just U.S. REITs? Why not invest in real estate in Australia, France, Japan, and Singapore? If U.S. real estate can become securitized through REIT equities, why can't we buy shares in foreign REITs as well, or perhaps mutual funds that invest in foreign real estate companies?

Until recently the U.S. was the only country providing a REIT structure, and investing in foreign real estate companies was very difficult. However, in recent years a number of foreign countries have adopted REIT-type structures, including Australia, Canada, Belgium, France, Japan, the Netherlands, and Singapore, and several others, including Germany and the U.K., are considering it.

Today it is relatively easy for the individual investor to diversify into foreign real estate by virtue of the recent emergence of several global real estate funds that invest in both foreign REITs and real estate companies. Alpine International Real Estate Equity fund has a long and successful track record of investing in real estate outside the U.S. Newer global real estate funds include ING Global Real Estate Fund and Fidelity International Real Estate Fund. As this book went to press, others were waiting in the wings. This trend has been facilitated by the recent creation of the FTSI/EPRA/NAREIT Global Real Estate Index, which included, at December 2004, 243 real estate companies throughout the world, with a total market cap of $504.4 billion, including 122 companies in North America, 52 in Europe, and 69 in Europe. Mutual funds and other global investors now have a benchmark against which to measure their performance.

Of course, the dividend yields, capital appreciation prospects, and risk profiles of real estate stocks will differ by country, but, as real estate performs differently in each such country (as well as in every region and locality), real estate stock returns have shown low correlations across various countries. Thus, a good argument can be made that allocating a portion of one's "real estate" assets to global real estate stocks (or a global real estate fund) can provide further diversification benefits within an investment portfolio. As this book went to press, even the creation of one or more global real estate ETFs was being considered.

Whether global real estate investing is a good choice depends upon the individual investor's desire or need for further diversification and low correlations of performance, as well as his or her risk tolerance levels. And it is almost impossible to predict whether foreign real estate will perform better than U.S. real estate over the next five or ten years—but that's why diversification makes sense for most investors.

A 2001 development—that could eventually be of substantial importance to the REIT industry—was the issuance of Revenue Ruling 2001-29. This ruling, by determining that REIT organizations are engaged in "an active trade or business," makes it possible, if other criteria are satisfied, for corporations to spin off to their shareholders stock in a new REIT organization that would own the real estate previously owned by the corporation. Upon the issuance of this revenue ruling, investors immediately focused upon fast-food giant McDonald's Corp., wondering whether it might put all its real estate into a new REIT (McREIT?) that would lease these assets back to the corporation. The advantage to McDonald's and others in doing this could be significant tax savings, but it would also diminish the corporation's control over its locations. Of course, a REIT that leases all of its assets to a single tenant, no matter how strong, will encounter resistance from investors, who generally prefer their REIT to be diversified by tenant mix. However, the new REIT could also lease properties to others. The only spin-off transaction completed as a result of the new revenue ruling was the merger of Plum Creek Timber with a new REIT formed by a spin-off of Georgia Pacific's timber assets. Indeed, this proposed transaction was the reason the revenue ruling was requested. There are a number of large retailers who own their own stores, and given the very competitive retail environment, one may speculate whether some of those assets may be spun out in a REIT format.

The discussion of the REIT Modernization Act of 1999 in Chapter 3 noted that, under such law, REITs could organize taxable REIT subsidiaries (TRS) to engage in business activities for which they were not previously authorized. Many REITs are now implementing new business ventures outside of the traditional REIT business of acquiring and holding (or developing and holding) commercial real estate, quite often through a TRS. Kimco Realty, CenterPoint Properties, Duke Realty, ProLogis, and others are all developing new properties for clients and, with the assistance of a TRS, will have the flexibility of selling them upon completion—hopefully reaping a substantial development profit (even after taxes) and deploying it into other traditional or nontraditional investments.

Archstone-Smith, through its Ameriton TRS, is managing properties for others and even developing and trading properties. Equity Residential has been developing condominiums to take advantage of strong demand for such properties rather than selling apartment units to condo converters. Kimco Realty has been providing venture capital equity financing to retailers. A number of REIT organizations have made investments in real estate technology, such as broadband, cable, and Internet access, including the wiring of offices, industrial buildings, and retail properties, while others have even organized their own start-up technology, e-commerce, or telecommunications ventures.

The report card on these ventures has been mixed. Most of them outside of the technology sector have performed quite well, but they seemed to have flunked "Technology 101," as most technology-related investments were written off by REIT organizations in 2001. REIT managements should be given credit if new and profitable revenue streams can be created in this manner, but REIT executives are experts in owning, acquiring, managing, and sometimes developing commercial real estate and should be very careful about allocating substantial capital to new ventures in which they have had little experience. Most of these new investments will probably deliver the best rewards, certainly on a risk-adjusted basis, when they enable the REIT to leverage its existing development and property management expertise or to become more competitive in its basic real estate business by increasing tenant satisfaction, in other words, acting as a "gatekeeper" for other service providers, and offering cost-saving opportunities for their tenants. And, of course, some REITs will do a lot better with their TRS strategies than others.

SO MUCH MORE TO COME

"We're only in the top of the second inning in the equitization of real estate in the United States," says real estate investor Sam Zell, and, in the autumn 1996 issue of *REIT Report,* Peter Aldrich, founder and co-chair of the real estate advisory firm Aldrich Eastman Waltch, agreed, prophesying that "the industry's right on track now for a 25 percent compounded annual growth of market cap. Nothing should slow it now unless there's bad public policy."

REIT organizations and their investors remain very optimistic about the future of the REIT industry, although the volume of rhetoric has been turned down a notch or two as the industry has become wiser and more sophisticated. As noted in places throughout this book, a serious bear market began to claw the REIT industry beginning in early 1998. This was caused by an excessive amount of fund-raising by REIT organizations, high REIT stock valuations, errors in judgment by a few high-profile REIT managements, rising real estate prices (which made it more difficult for low-risk acquisitions to create value for REIT shareholders) and, most importantly, a flow of funds away from slower-growing, higher-yielding value stocks such as REITs and into tech stocks and other high-growth opportunities. However, the bear expired in 2000, and a new REIT bull market returned with a vengeance in early 2000 and danced in the meadows for several years thereafter. Interestingly enough, both REIT investors and REIT management teams refrained from engaging in "irrationally exuberant" strategies, and remained focused on old-fashioned blocking and tackling, as well as capital preservation, during some very difficult real estate markets. The REIT industry does indeed seem to have matured.

The ebbs and flows of investor sentiment will always influence price movements of individual stocks and entire equity sectors in the short term, but, over longer time periods, investors will base their buying and selling decisions on business prospects and investment merits. REIT organizations, led by some of the most innovative and creative management teams that have ever been assembled in the world of real estate, are truly capable of continuing to deliver outstanding returns for their investors, particularly when adjusted for their lower volatility and risk. This fact—more than any other—will insure a home for REITs in virtually all investors' portfolios. And the best, I firmly believe, is yet to come!

SUMMARY

◆ The rapid growth of the REIT industry is creating abundant opportunities for both real estate companies and their shareholders, as publicly traded REITs have greater access to capital and investors have many more investment choices.

◆ The REIT vehicle allows successful real estate organizations with vision increased access to needed capital and heretofore unfound flexibility in financing, enabling them more easily to grow their businesses and attract and motivate quality management.

◆ The availability of ever-larger and more capable REITs enables individual investors and large institutions alike to diversify their investment portfolios, while offering the prospects of competitive total returns.

◆ Should REITs increase the total value of their assets from their present size of $300–400 billion to as much as $2 trillion, that would still be just over half of the nation's institutionally owned real estate, and would still not exceed the percentage of securitized ownership that prevails in many other major world economies, such as that of the United Kingdom.

◆ The argument for the individual investor to invest in REITs is a compelling one: REITs provide high, stable, and growing dividend yields along with significant opportunities for capital appreciation, with only a modest amount of risk and low correlations with other asset classes.

◆ REIT investors have a wide choice, both in sector and REIT management strategy and objectives, and the choices are growing ever greater with the growth of the entire industry. For yield-oriented investors, REIT investing has provided outstanding rewards, but, based on the abundance of new opportunities available to participants in the REIT industry, the best is yet to be.

RESOURCES

APPENDIX A

DEATH AND TAXES

When they're not held in individual retirement accounts (IRAs) or other tax-advantaged accounts such as 401(k) plans, REITs have two significant disadvantages with respect to their common stock counterparts. More than 75 percent of the total returns expected by holders of most non-REIT common stocks consists of capital appreciation; today's dividend yields are skimpy, averaging approximately 2 percent for the average large-cap stock. If a stock is held for more than twelve months, the capital appreciation is taxed at a maximum tax rate of only 15 percent, or even 5 percent for low-bracket taxpayers. Furthermore, non-REIT dividends are now taxed at a rate not to exceed 15 percent. With REITs, however, as much as 50–65 percent of the expected total return will come from dividend income; not only does less of the return come from capital gains, but REITs' dividends are taxed at ordinary income rates.

Nevertheless, ownership of REIT shares does frequently provide the shareholder with some definite tax advantages—certainly vis-à-vis most preferred shares, all REIT preferreds, and all bonds. Very often a significant portion of the dividends received from a REIT is not fully taxable as ordinary income; some portion of the dividend may be treated as a long-term capital gain, and another portion may be treated as a "return of capital," which is not currently taxable to the shareholder. This return-of-capital portion of the dividend reduces the shareholder's cost basis in the shares, and defers the tax until the shares are ultimately sold (assuming the sale is made at a price that exceeds the cost basis). However, if held for at least twelve months, the gain is then taxed at long-term capital gain rates and the shareholder has, in effect, converted dividend income into a deferred, long-term capital gain. NAREIT data indicate that in 2004, for example, approximately 37 percent of REIT dividends were comprised of capital gains distributions and return of capital.

DIVIDEND DISTRIBUTIONS BY AMB PROPERTIES (2004)

	DIVIDEND PER SHARE	PERCENT OF TOTAL
Ordinary Income	$0.78	46%
ST Capital Gains	0.00	0%
Ordinary Dividends	0.78	46%
Qualified Dividends	0.00	0%
Unrecognized Sec 1250 Gain	0.15	9%
Other Capital Gains	0.37	22%
Capital Gain Distribution	0.52	31%
Nontaxable Distribution	0.39	23%
TOTAL DISTRIBUTION	**$1.69**	**100%**

How can this be? As we've seen in earlier chapters, REITs base their dividend payments on funds from operations (FFO) or adjusted funds from operations (AFFO), not net income; FFO, simply stated, is a REIT's net income but with real estate depreciation added back, while AFFO adjusts for straight-lining of rents and recurring expenditures that are capitalized and not immediately expensed. As a result, many REITs pay dividends to their shareholders in excess of net income as defined in the Internal Revenue Code (IRC), and a significant part or all of such excess is usually treated as a "return of capital" to the shareholder and not taxable as ordinary income. The return-of-capital component of a REIT's dividend has historically been 25 to 30 percent, but that percentage has been lower in recent years as REITs have been reducing their payout ratios during most periods.

For income tax purposes, dividend distributions paid to shareholders consist primarily of ordinary income, return of capital, and long-term capital gains. Therefore, if a REIT realizes long-term capital gain from a sale of some of its real estate, it may designate a portion of the dividend paid during the year of the sale as a "long-term capital gains distribution," upon which the shareholder will pay taxes, but normally at lower capital gain rates.

A good example of the type of dividend allocation that REIT investors might see between ordinary income, capital gain distributions, and return of capital in a typical year is provided by the

EXAMPLE

LET'S ASSUME AN INVESTOR purchased 100 shares of AMB Properties (AMB) at the end of 2003 at $31 per share, for a total cost of $3,100 (for simplicity, we'll ignore commissions). We will also assume a dividend rate of $1.69 per share. By the end of 2004, he or she will have received $169 in dividends. Based upon the components of the AMB dividend for 2004 set forth above, of the total of $169 in dividends, $78 will be taxed at ordinary income rates, $52 will be taxed at the more favorable capital gains tax rates, and $39 will be tax deferred as a return of capital. The investor must reduce his or her cost basis by the amount of the return of capital (in this case, $.39 per share), so that the new cost basis of the 100 shares of AMB would then be $3,061. Finally, let's also assume that the shares are sold in early 2005 for $35 per share, or a total of $3,500 (again ignoring commissions). The investor would then report a total long-term capital gain of $439 (the difference between $3,500 and $3,061) on Schedule D.

dividend distributions made by AMB Properties in 2004, shown in the chart above.

Shareholders cannot predict the amount of the dividend that will be tax deferred merely by looking at financially reported net income, as the tax-deferred portion is based on distributions in excess of the REIT's taxable income pursuant to the Internal Revenue Code. The differences between net income available to common shareholders for financial reporting purposes and "taxable" income for income tax purposes relate primarily to

◆ differences between taxable depreciation (usually accelerated) and "book" (usually straight-line) depreciation;
◆ accruals on preferred stock dividends; and
◆ deferral for tax purposes of certain capital gains on property sales (e.g., tax-deferred exchanges).

There is generally no publicly available information allowing us to determine, ahead of time, the portion of the dividend distribution from a REIT that will be taxed as ordinary income. The primary problem is that, as noted above, for tax purposes certain income and expense items are calculated differently from what appears in the current year's financial statements. This number must be generated by the company itself at the end of its tax year, and the shareholder will have to wait until early the following year to obtain the final figures.

Of course, all of the foregoing discussion is irrelevant if a REIT's shares are held in an IRA, 401(k) plan, or other tax-advantaged account. The dividends won't be taxable while held in such an account, but the distributions (when eventually taken out of the account) will normally be taxable as ordinary income.

What happens upon death of the shareholder? Under current tax law, the heirs get a "step-up in basis," and no income tax is *ever* payable with respect to that portion of the dividends classified as a return of capital (although estate taxes may have to be paid if the estate tax is not permanently repealed). In this scenario, it's therefore possible to escape entirely, by death, income tax on a significant portion of a REIT's dividends—though this is not a recommended tax-planning technique!

State tax laws, of course, may differ from federal law. Investors should confirm the status of their dividends under federal *and* state tax laws with their accountant or financial adviser.

None of the foregoing tax advantages will induce a nonbeliever to run out and buy REIT shares; furthermore, the lower tax rates on capital gains and non-REIT dividends would tend to give other common stocks an edge over REITs if tax savings were one's only investment criterion. Nevertheless, being able to defer a portion of the tax on REITs' dividends can have significant advantages over time and should not be overlooked.

APPENDIX B

STOCK SYMBOL	NAME	APPROXIMATE MARKET CAP ($ MILLIONS)
OFFICE		
EOP	Equity Office Properties	$12,156
BXP	Boston Properties	$6,472
TRZ	Trizec Properties	$2,727
CLI	Mack-Cali Realty	$2,676
RA	Reckson Associates Realty	$2,460
ARI	Arden Realty Group	$2,250
HRP	HRPT Properties Trust	$2,248
SLG	SL Green Realty	$2,185
CRE	Carr America Realty	$1,698
AFR	American Financial Realty	$1,617
BDN	Brandywine Realty	$1,585
PP	Prentiss Properties	$1,574
HIW	Highwoods Properties	$1,383
ARE	Alexandria Real Estate	$1,299
KRC	Kilroy Realty	$1,199
MPG	Maguire Properties	$1,115
OFC	Corporate Office Properties	$956
GLB	Glenborough Realty	$709
CRO	CRT Properties	$706
BMR	BioMed Realty	$689
PKY	Parkway Properties	$664
GPP	Government Properties	$198
PGE	Prime Group Realty	$167
AMV	AmeriVest Properties	$151
INDUSTRIAL		
PLD	ProLogis Trust	$7,229
AMB	AMB Property	$3,209
CDX	Catellus Development	$2,831

STOCK SYMBOL	NAME	APPROXIMATE MARKET CAP ($ MILLIONS)
CNT	CenterPoint Properties	$2,112
FR	First Industrial Realty	$1,715
EGP	EastGroup Properties	$815
FPO	First Potomac Realty	$300
MNRT.A	Monmouth Real Estate	$144
MIXED OFFICE/INDUSTRIAL		
DRE	Duke Realty	$4,505
LRY	Liberty Property	$3,511
PSB	PS Business Parks	$905
BED	Bedford Property Investors	$378
DLR	Digital Realty	$287
MSW	Mission West Properties	$196
GOOD	Gladstone Commercial	$127
RETAIL—STRIP CENTERS		
KIM	Kimco Realty	$5,907
DDR	Developers Diversified Realty	$4,278
WRI	Weingarten Realty	$3,153
REG	Regency Centers	$3,104
NXL	New Plan	$2,675
FRT	Federal Realty Investment	$2,599
PNP	Pan Pacific Retail Properties	$2,352
EQY	Equity One	$1,467
HTG	Heritage Property Investment	$1,432
IRC	Inland Real Estate	$1,074
SKT	Tanger Factory Outlet Centers	$653
KRT	Kramont Realty	$563
BFS	Saul Centers	$561
RPT	Ramco-Gershenson Properties	$476
AKR	Acadia Realty	$466
UBA	Urstadt Biddle Properties	$417
KRG	Kite Realty Group	$290
CDR	Cedar Shopping Centers	$235
AMY	AmREIT	$26
RETAIL—MALLS		
SPG	Simon Property Group	$13,696
GGP	General Growth Properties	$7,633
MAC	Macerich Company	$3,383

STOCK SYMBOL	NAME	APPROXIMATE MARKET CAP ($ MILLIONS)
MLS	Mills Corporation	$2,896
CBL	CBL & Associates Properties	$2,299
PEI	Pennsylvania Real Estate	$1,464
TCO	Taubman Centers	$1,431
GRT	Glimcher Realty	$913
FMP	Feldman Mall Properties	$140
RETAIL—NET LEASE		
O	Realty Income	$1,863
ALX	Alexander's Inc	$1,198
NNN	Commercial Net Lease Realty	$978
GTY	Getty Realty	$662
TSY	Truststreet Properties	$399
ADC	Agree Realty	$205
RESIDENTIAL—APARTMENTS		
EQR	Equity Residential	$9,193
ASN	Archstone-Smith	$6,620
AVB	Avalon Bay Communities	$5,001
AIV	Apartment Investment & Mgt	$3,621
UDR	United Dominion Realty	$2,929
CPT	Camden Property	$2,399
BRE	BRE Properties	$1,964
ESS	Essex Property	$1,653
HME	Home Properties	$1,345
PPS	Post Properties	$1,282
GBP	Gables Residential	$1,030
MAA	Mid-America Apartment Comm.	$766
AML	Amli Residential Properties	$701
TCR	Cornerstone Realty Income	$524
TCT	Town & Country Trust	$464
EDR	Education Realty	$324
ACC	American Campus Comm.	$255
AEC	Associated Estates Realty	$193
BNP	BNP Residential Properties	$137
RPI	Roberts Realty Investors	$42
PDL.B	Presidential Realty	$38
MRTI	Maxus Realty	$18

STOCK SYMBOL	NAME	APPROXIMATE MARKET CAP ($ MILLIONS)
RESIDENTIAL—MANUFACTURED-HOME COMMUNITIES		
ELS	Equity Lifestyle Communities	$767
SUI	Sun Communities	$665
ARC	Affordable Residential Comm.	$495
ANL	American Land Lease	$169
UMH	United Mobile Homes	$126
DIVERSIFIED		
VNO	Vornado Realty	$8,635
SFI	iStar Financial	$4,724
CEI	Crescent Real Estate Equities	$1,620
CUZ	Cousins Properties	$1,329
WRE	Washington Real Estate	$1,219
LXP	Lexington Corporate Properties	$1,064
CLP	Colonial Properties	$990
SFC	Spirit Finance	$747
IRET.S	Investors Real Estate	$418
OLP	One Liberty Properties	$187
BRT	BRT Realty Trust	$183
SIZ	Sizeler Property Investors	$159
FUR	First Union Real Estate	$133
HMG	HMG/Courtland Properties	$14
MPQ	Meredith Enterprises	$14
AZL	Arizona Land Income	$8
PRG	Paragon Real Estate Equity	$5
LODGING/RESORTS		
HMT	Host Marriott	$5,543
HPT	Hospitality Properties	$2,786
LHO	LaSalle Hotel Properties	$844
FCH	Felcor Lodging	$745
SHO	Sunstone Hotel Investors	$698
MHX	MeriStar Hospitality	$640
KPA	Innkeepers USA	$566
ENN	Equity Inns	$561
SLH	Strategic Hotel Capital	$493
HIH	Highland Hospitality	$406
AHT	Ashford Hospitality	$352

STOCK SYMBOL	NAME	APPROXIMATE MARKET CAP ($ MILLIONS)
WXH	Winston Hotels	$294
HTG	Hersha Hospitality	$238
BOY	Boykin Lodging	$167
PCC	PMC Commercial Trust	$163
EHP	Eagle Hospitality Properties	$143
MDH	MHI Hospitality	$58
HUMP	Humphrey Hospitality	$47
SELF-STORAGE		
PSA	Public Storage, Inc	$7,021
SHU	Shurgard Storage Centers	$1,826
SSS	Sovran Self Storage	$609
YSI	U-Store-It Trust	$552
EXR	Extra Space Storage	$433
HEALTH CARE		
HCP	Health Care Property Investors	$3,344
VTR	Ventas, Inc	$2,173
HCN	Health Care REIT	$1,771
HR	Healthcare Realty Trust	$1,732
NHP	Nationwide Health Properties	$1,376
SNH	Senior Housing Properties	$1,227
NHI	National Health Investors	$714
OHI	Omega Healthcare Investors	$536
LTC	LTC Properties	$354
UHT	Universal Health Realty Income	$353
NHR	National Health Realty	$175
WRS	Windrose Medical Properties	$161
SPECIALTY		
PCL	Plum Creek Timber	$6,884
RYN	Rayonier Inc	$2,383
GSL	Global Signal, Inc	$1,459
CARS	Capital Automotive	$1,445
EPR	Entertainment Properties	$1,007
GCT	GMH Communities	$344
CPV	Correctional Properties	$289
PW	Pittsburgh & West Virginia RR	$14

STOCK SYMBOL	NAME	APPROXIMATE MARKET CAP ($ MILLIONS)
MORTGAGE—HOME FINANCING		
NEW	New Century Financial	$2,413
TMA	Thornburg Mortgage	$2,380
NLY	Annaly Mortgage Mgt	$2,305
IMH	Impac Mortgage Holdings	$1,433
RWT	Redwood Trust	$1,309
AHM	American Home Mortgage	$1,250
NFI	Novastar Financial	$958
SAXN	Saxon Capital	$895
FICC	Fieldstone Investment	$650
MFA	MFA Mortgage Investments	$642
ECR	ECC Capital	$622
HMB	HomeBanc Corp	$532
AIC	Aames Investment	$507
ANH	Anworth Mortgage Asset	$443
MHL	MortgageIT Holdings	$335
BMM	Bimini Mortgage Mgt	$236
NTR	New York Mortgage Trust	$189
ORGN	Origen Financial	$183
CMO	Capstead Mortgage	$167
SFO	Sunset Financial Resources	$102
HCM	Hanover Capital Mortgage	$90
DX	Dynex Capital Inc	$80
CAA	Capital Alliance Income	$6
MORTGAGE—COMMERCIAL FINANCING		
FBR	Friedman, Billings, Ramsey	$2,648
NCT	Newcastle Investment	$1,229
RAS	RAIT Investment Trust	$677
AHR	Anthracite Capital	$635
GKK	Gramercy Capital Corp	$414
CT	Capital Trust	$404
ABR	Arbor Realty Trust	$392
LSE	Capital Lease Funding	$335
CMM	CRIIMI MAE Inc	$307
NRF	NorthStar Realty Finance	$207
AMC	American Mortgage Acceptance	$141
FLCN	Falcon Financial Investment	$120

APPENDIX C

The following example is an income statement derivation of adjusted funds from operations (AFFO) and funds or cash available for distribution (FAD or CAD), contained in a quarterly earnings report by Post Properties. Although the calculation below was published by the REIT a number of years ago, it is nevertheless typical of how AFFO, FAD, or CAD can be derived for most REITs.

POST PROPERTIES (PPS): THIRD QUARTER, 1996

(In thousands of dollars, except for per share.)

Revenue

Rental—owned property	$40,583
Property management	722
Landscape services	1,199
Interest	50
Other	1,661
Total Revenue	**$44,215**

Property Expenses

Property operating & maintenance	$15,115
Depreciation—real estate assets	5,877
Total Property Expenses	**$20,992**

Corporate and Other Expenses

Property management—third party	$558
Landscape management	1,013
Interest	5,970
Amortization of financing costs	293
Depreciation—non–real estate assets	197
General and administration	1,769
Minority interest	0
Total Corporate & other expenses	**$9,800**
Total Expenses	**$30,792**
Income before minority interests and extraordinary items	$13,423
Gain on sale of assets	$693

Minority interest in operating partnership	(2,535)
Net Income	$11,581
Plus	
Depreciation and amortization—real estate assets	$5,877
Minority interest	2,696
Less	
Net gain on sale	$(854)
Amortization of financing costs	(55)
Funds from Operations (FFO)	$19,245
FFO per share	$0.71
Less	
Recurring Capital Expenditures	$(692)
Adjusted funds from operations	$18,553
AFFO per share	$0.69
Less	
Nonrecurring capital expenditures	(687)
Funds or cash available for distribution	$17,866
FAD or CAD per share	$0.66
Weighted average number of shares/operating units	26,929

DISCUSSION

The following points should be noted by REIT investors when using cash flow measurements such as FFO, AFFO, FAD, or CAD to value REIT stocks:

1. Depreciation of real estate assets such as apartment buildings and other structures can be deceptive. The property (most notably the underlying land) could actually appreciate in value, particularly if well maintained; however, for accounting purposes, depreciation must be deducted in order to derive net income. Funds from operations (FFO) is calculated by adding back real estate depreciation and amortization to net income. However, property owners incur recurring capital expenditures that are certainly real and that need to be taken into account to provide a true picture of the owner's cash flow from the property. Examples include the necessary replacement from time to time of carpets, drapes, and roofs. In some cases, property owners may make tenant improvements (and/or provide tenant allowances) that are necessary to retain the property's competitive position with existing and potential tenants, and may pay leasing commissions to outside brokers. Since many of these expenditures are capitalized, they must be deducted from FFO in order

to determine adjusted funds from operations, or AFFO, which is the most accurate picture of economic cash flow.

Funds (or Cash) Available for Distribution (FAD or CAD) is sometimes calculated in a slightly different manner. Unlike AFFO, which deducts the amortization of real estate–related expenditures from FFO, FAD, or CAD is often derived by deducting nonrecurring (as well as normal and recurring) capital expenditures. FAD or CAD may also deduct repayments of principal on mortgage loans. Unfortunately, there is no widely accepted standard for making these adjustments.

2. When reviewing a REIT's revenues, it is a good idea to analyze lease expirations and existing lease rates and compare them to market rates within the REIT's property markets. This approach may help in determining whether rental revenues may increase or decrease when leases are renewed at market rates. This is often referred to as *embedded rent growth* or *loss to lease* (for lease rates that are below market rents) or *rental roll-down* (for lease rates that are above market rents).

3. Always distinguish revenues from services (whether from property management, a fee-development business, or consulting services) from revenues from rents. Rental revenue tends to be more stable and predictable, as fee-only clients can easily terminate the relationship (and the resulting service or fee revenue streams). Revenues from joint ventures, however, tend to have longer lives.

4. Always analyze the type of debt and debt maturities. REIT investors will normally prefer long-term debt to short term, and fixed-rate debt to variable rate.

5. Look for recurring capital expenditures that do not improve or prolong the life of the property, as well as unusual financing devices (e.g., "buydowns" of loan-interest coupons, forward equity transactions, etc.). These items will affect the quality of reported FFOs and help to calculate AFFOs.

APPENDIX D

COST OF EQUITY CAPITAL

Important as the concept is, there is no general agreement on how to calculate a REIT's "cost of equity capital." There are, however, several ways to approach this issue. One quick way to determine a REIT's *nominal* equity capital cost is to estimate the REIT's expected per-share FFO for the next twelve months. This per-share FFO should then be adjusted for any additional shares to be issued and the expected incremental FFO to be earned from the investment of the proceeds from such new share issuance (or the pay-down of debt). Finally, we would then divide such "pro forma" FFO per share by the price the REIT receives for each new share sold (after deducting underwriting commissions).[1]

Let's assume, for example, that Apartment REIT USA has 10 million shares outstanding and is expected to earn $10 million in FFO over the next twelve months. It intends to issue an additional 1 million shares and receive net proceeds of $9 per share (after underwriting commissions), which will be used to buy additional apartments providing an initial yield of 9 percent; this investment of $9 million will thus provide $810,000 of additional FFO (9 percent of $9 million). Therefore, on a pro forma basis, this REIT will have $10.81 million in FFO which, when divided by 11 million shares outstanding, will produce FFO of $.98 per share. Dividing this by the $9 net offering price results in a nominal cost of equity capital of 10.88 percent. Note that this is higher than the entry yield (9 percent) available on the new apartment investments, as a result of which this stock offering would be dilutive to FFO. Indeed, we can see that FFO drops from the projected $1 per share before

1. Some investors have simply looked at a REIT's dividend yield, which is quite misleading; FFO and AFFO, as well as other valuation metrics, are far more important than dividend payments in the context of determining REIT valuations, and thus the dilution from issuing additional shares.

the offering to $.98 per share afterwards. However, if we were to hypothesize that Apartment REIT USA were able to sell its new shares at a net price of $12, its nominal cost of equity capital would be 8.4 percent. Thus, the higher the price at which a REIT can sell new shares, the cheaper its nominal cost of capital will be, making it more likely that the offering and the investment of the offering proceeds will be accretive to FFO.

The above approach measures only a REIT's *nominal* cost of equity capital; its *true* cost of equity capital should be measured in a very different way. In the first approach, we divided pro forma expected FFO per share by the net sale proceeds per share, using expected FFO only for the next twelve months. But what about the FFO that will be generated by the REIT for many years into the future? This FFO will be forever diluted by the new shares being issued, and, for this reason, a misleading picture is presented when using expected FFO for just the next twelve months (e.g., why not twenty-four months? Thirty-six months?). How can longer time periods be taken into account?

One way that a REIT's true cost of equity capital may be better measured is to use the total return expected by investors on their investment in the REIT. For example, if investors price a REIT's shares in the trading market so that a 12 percent internal rate of return is demanded—and expected—well into the future (on the basis of existing and projected dividend yields, anticipated FFO or AFFO, and expected growth rates), why isn't the REIT's true cost of equity capital the same 12 percent? A few REITs may be so conservative (perhaps because of a very low-levered balance sheet and cautious business strategy) and well-regarded, and their FFO and dividend growth so predictable, that a more modest 8 or 10 percent annual return might satisfy investors; in such a case, the REIT's true cost of equity capital might very well be 8–10 percent. A difficulty with this approach is determining the total return that is demanded by investors; this isn't as easy as it might appear, as shareholders rarely tell their REIT what they expect. All of this discussion moves us into capital asset pricing models, "modern portfolio theory," and the like, which try to determine the amount investors demand in excess of a "risk-free" return such as 6-month T-bills or 10-year T-notes, based on various measurements of risk such as standard deviations and betas. But these are topics beyond the scope of this discussion.

Nevertheless, REIT investors who want to delve into this issue might want to try to determine the total returns expected by investors in particular REITs and use those figures to determine the REIT's true cost of equity capital. (See, for example, "The True Cost of Capital," *Institutional Real Estate Securities,* January 1998.) Keep in mind, however, that in view of REITs' historical total returns of 11 to 12 percent, few REITs should expect that their true cost of equity capital would be less than that, except perhaps during periods of unusually low interest rates, low real estate cap rates, or when returns from other investments are expected to be uncharacteristically modest. A significant portion of the cost of equity calculation depends on the extent to which the REIT uses debt leverage. Many REIT investors also calculate the cost of debt capital (which is more straightforward) and blend it with the cost of equity to determine a "weighted average cost of capital" (WACC) to help determine the wisdom of any new investment made by the REIT.

REITs' legal requirement to pay out 90 percent of net income to their shareholders each year in the form of dividends makes significant external growth in FFO or AFFO problematic (e.g., through acquisitions or new development) without either an aggressive capital recycling strategy or frequently coming back to the markets for more equity capital. Keeping payout ratios low certainly helps reduce the overall cost of equity capital, as does periodically selling off properties with less than exciting long-term potential. Well-executed joint venture strategies will also help. However, most innovative REIT managements who continue to find attractive opportunities will normally need to raise additional equity capital from time to time. It is, therefore, important for REIT investors to understand how to analyze a REIT's cost of equity capital, particularly its true longer-term cost of equity capital. The investment returns expected from external growth initiatives should be carefully compared with REITs' capital costs to make sure that shareholder value isn't destroyed when new equity is sold.

APPENDIX E

REIT PORTFOLIO MANAGEMENT

Following is a discussion, excerpted from the author's newsletter, *The Essential REIT,* of how one might go about managing his or her REIT stock portfolio.

Many, perhaps even most, people who own REIT stocks might own only two or three of them. After all, there are still lots of benighted investors out there who have allocated a puny 3–5 percent of their assets to REIT stocks (my apologies to those of you whom I've offended), and so a 2 percent position in each of three REITs gets them there. The following discussion, however, is addressed to the REIT diehards, that is, those who have a significant allocation to REITs, perhaps owning ten, twenty, or thirty REIT stocks, and have sometimes wondered about the strategies of REIT portfolio management.

First, a caveat. This is not a topic that one sees discussed regularly in *Money* magazine or the financial press; portfolio management tends to be the proprietary territory of the academic types, and most articles on the subject are apt to be filled with more arcane and incomprehensible formulae than what we might find on the blackboard at an MIT postgraduate seminar on string theory.[1] The *good* news is that I went to law school, not business school, so the following discussion will be notably devoid of higher mathematics (or even lower mathematics, for that matter). The *bad* news is that it offers no practical tips or five-step programs for immediate weight loss (oops! make that portfolio management).

All right, enough temporizing. First, let's clarify something. Not all REIT organizations are created equal, nor *are* they equal. They each own different assets in different locations, have very different business strategies, and the quality and depth of their manage-

---

1. Those who haven't heard of string theory—but who have masochistic tendencies—might want to check out http://superstringtheory.com/.

ment teams differ substantially. Some have strong and conservative balance sheets, while others don't mind "betting 'em high and (possibly) sleeping in the streets." Some are very clean and are good corporate citizens, while others are, well, not so clean. Perhaps all classical music sounds the same to the uninitiated, but connoisseurs certainly know the difference between Schubert and Shoenberg. Likewise, REITs can be quite different from one another.

These issues, as well as the relative valuations of REIT stocks, make the risk profile of one REIT stock quite different from that of another. So, to think of REITs as one might think of regional bank stocks—"who cares which one you own?"—is a big mistake. Risk profiles *do* count in REIT investing and, over time, will certainly affect performance and volatility. Think of it this way: If you want to invest in the "energy" sector, how do you stock your portfolio? The integrated majors, for example, Chevron, Exxon, et al.? Small E&P companies? Drillers? Natural gas pipelines? MLPs? Do you look for oil, or gas? Do you focus on big reserves in "exciting" places such as Algeria, or are you more comfortable in the Williston Basin? Your answers will, of course, affect your portfolio performance and risk profile.

It's the same with REITs. REIT portfolio management, I believe, should be driven by one's investment objective. Is it getting the best possible performance, risk be damned? To beat the benchmark by 100 basis points (bps) annually? To be a closet indexer? How important is risk—not just volatility, but the prospects of a permanent decline in portfolio values due to some REIT stepping into something very unpleasant, or a management team blowing it? Is volatility important? High dividend yields? Maximizing after-tax returns? We learned long ago that there is no free lunch in the wacky and wicked world of investing, and there's a price to be paid for everything, including safety. So let's take a closer look at some possible objectives.

a. Beating Benchmarks and Risk Management. We all want to beat the benchmarks, right? For those who get paid to manage portfolios, it's their raison d'être—and justifies their fees. For those managing portfolios on their own, superior performance gratifies the ol' ego. But we often don't focus too much on what's required to beat the benchmark—especially if we want to smash it to bits. Let's admit it: while the REIT industry has expanded by more than twenty times since the end of 1992 (and had an equity market cap of $307.9 billion at the end of 2004), it's still a somewhat small industry and our investment choices aren't unlimited, particularly if liquidity is an issue. And there are lots of new investors grazing in REITland, some of whom are surprisingly intelligent. Companies now regularly issue guidance, and most FFO/AFFO estimates out on the Street are very similar; beating, or failing to meet, consensus numbers by more than a few pennies is only a bit more common than seeing pigs fly.

So, it's very competitive out there. A select few may be able to beat the benchmark somewhat regularly by simply being skilled and conservative stock-pickers—but they won't beat the index by more than, say, 2 percent a year. On the other hand, trashing the benchmark by 3–4 percent requires one to embrace risk as one would embrace a cold lager after a ten-mile hike. So, let's assume that a portfolio manager wants to shoot the lights out; how should he or she manage an all-REIT portfolio?

There are lots of ways, including (a) active trading, seeking to scrape or claw an extra 2 percent here and 3 percent there, albeit at the cost of high portfolio turnover; (b) heavily overweighting or underweighting specific real estate sectors—REIT industry performance can vary widely by sector from year to year (even quarter to quarter), and finding oneself greatly overweighted in a strongly performing sector can do wonders for performance; (c) ditto for specific companies, particularly if they are not heavily represented in the benchmark, for example, taking 6 percent positions in, say, Cedar Shopping Centers, Feldman Mall Properties, and Mission West can put us well ahead of—or way behind—the benchmark; and (d) "cheating" a bit by owning non-REIT stocks such as Brookfield, St. Joe, and Starwood. Or perhaps IHOP?

Risk comes in various shapes and sizes, and can be increased or decreased in ways other than overweighting or underweighting sectors or stocks, or indulging in heavy trading. Some sectors are inherently more risky than others; the cash flows of hotel REITs, for example, are only slightly more predictable than the same-store performance of Wet Seal or Hot Topic. And, of course, risk differs substantially by company. While nobody can say whether there is more exposure to a short-term stock price decline in Crescent Real Estate or in Boston Properties, there is little doubt that the former is simply a riskier company to own—and not just because of stock price volatility.

Differences in company-specific risk are due to a number of factors, including management strategies (how risky is the strategy, and how much capital is being devoted to it?), stability and predictability of cash flow streams from real estate (and real estate–related businesses), and the extent of development risk and overseas investment risk. How reliable has management—and its forecasts—been in prior quarters? Are they likely to foul something up? And, of course, some balance sheets are simply riskier than others—due to high amounts of debt leverage, substantial variable-rate debt and/or near-term debt maturities. Liquidity in REIT shares can also become an issue, particularly if the company disappoints. The bottom line here is that one might generate better near-term performance from a portfolio chock full of Mission West, Crescent, and Meristar Hospitality, but it's going to be a riskier portfolio than one filled with Kimco, Equity Residential, and Boston Properties. So let's not kid ourselves: Performance is wonderful, but it comes at a price.

b. Reducing Volatility. If low volatility is our objective, there are some things we can do. One obvious approach is to focus heavily on low-beta stocks; beta figures are available from various sources, although I confess to paying little attention to them. Yesterday's high-beta equity may become tomorrow's sleeping dog, and vice versa. Several other tools can perhaps be more important and effective than beta in reducing portfolio volatility. Let's look at a few of them:

One obvious tactic is increasing cash levels. Nobody's going to call you a wimp for keeping cash at 5–8 percent, and doing so will certainly reduce volatility (though it will, of course, punish you in a bull market). Another is to make sure that positions aren't concentrated, in other words, don't put more than 3 percent of your assets into any single position. Again, this may entail a cost in performance if you are right about your stock picks, but volatility will be reduced. It will also be advisable to spread one's investments out over many sectors of real estate, as this will tend to even out daily and weekly performance.

I would be remiss if I didn't suggest that risk and volatility tend to be joined at the hip, and that riskier stocks will usually be more volatile. If this is so, focus on the *safer* companies in REITdom—from the perspectives of management quality, business strategies, development risk, cash flow predictability and stability, balance sheet strength, share liquidity, dividend coverage, and other issues that can affect a REIT's stock price level twelve months later. Shares of companies like Kimco, Simon, and—again—Boston Properties are likely to be less volatile due to their company characteristics and the ability of management to deliver on their forecasts and promises. So, if low volatility is your game, load up on the stalwarts.

c. Maximizing After-tax Returns. Many smart financial planners continue to remind us that what we keep, after tithing to Uncle Sam and our state government coffers, is what really counts. We may make $10,000 on a successful short-term trade, but in California and many other states we're lucky to keep $6,000 of that and we'll need to earn a very high return on any new substitute investment just to get back to where we were in terms of net worth. Of course, many investors own REITs in IRAs and 401(k) plans, so their mantra will be, "We don't need no stinkin' tax planning." Fine. But others do need to think about their taxes, perhaps even more in REIT investing than elsewhere.

Why? Think about it this way. Even long-term capital gains may be taxed at 30 percent (not 15 percent), when state taxes and AMT phase-outs are tossed into the equation. Can another REIT bought with the proceeds of a REIT we sell generate enough capital appreciation to make us whole within a year or two? Not likely—not when we should expect only 4–6 percent in capital appreciation annually on the typical REIT stock. So, those of us who invest in REIT stocks with personal funds need to think seriously about taxes and tax bills resulting from taking profits.

Fortunately, REITs are not as inclined to self-destruct as, say, a tech or Internet stock. It's highly unusual for a REIT to miss consensus estimates badly, and REIT assets seldom melt away like obsolete semiconductor inventory. Most REITs' cash flows are protected by long-term leases. So, it's not going to kill us to hold onto a REIT that has a big built-in capital gain that we would otherwise like to sell to take advantage of some other "screaming" bargain in

REITville. The best strategy, therefore, for those who want to keep capital gains taxes to a minimum, is to resist the temptation to sell or pare back every time a stock looks expensive or the risk profile increases modestly. Own only those REIT stocks you'd be happy to own three years from now. And watch your REIT mutual funds carefully; most of them are driven by performance pressures, and their portfolio managers care as much about taxes as my Golden Retriever, Sammy, cares about Brad Pitt's divorce.

d. Investing for Yield. Many believe that yield is the name of the game in REIT investing. And who can blame 'em? Historically, two-thirds of the total returns from REIT investing have come from the dividend yield alone (although this percentage has been drifting lower in recent years, and my own assumption is that about half of REITs' total returns will come from yield in the future). There are many REITsters who profess, "Hey, capital appreciation is nice, but I'll be perfectly content if my REITs provide me with a steady dividend, with occasional increases as circumstances warrant."

And let's be honest. Even if yield isn't one's *only* criterion in selecting REIT stocks, it remains an important consideration for most investors. *Should* a REIT investor focus *only* on yield? Of course not. But should he or she pay attention to yield? You betcha. Yield is certainly one of the distinguishing factors setting REIT stocks apart from their cousins in the broader world of equities, and a Chevron, clad in a 3 percent dividend yield taxed at lower rates, will be a formidable competitor to REITs with a similar yield.

But how should Mr. Yield Hog structure his portfolio? As I noted some time ago in a different context, "Here there be dragons." As many investors have learned, to their eternal sorrow, a yield that looks too good to be true usually isn't. But just as it's a truism that even though you may be paranoid doesn't mean that others *aren't* out to get you, even though you may have a jones for yield doesn't mean that you cannot invest in REITs successfully. Some of my best friends in REITdom bear higher than average dividend yields, and I cheerfully own them, for example, Nationwide Health and Prentiss Properties.

Of course, the "no free lunch" principle means that we must make certain sacrifices when we focus heavily on yield. Growth rates of higher-yielding REITs are apt to be lower; this is so for at least two reasons. First, a higher dividend yield resulting from a REIT paying out close to, or more than, 100 percent of free cash flow means that less retained earnings can be invested for future cash flow growth (and companies that pay more in dividends than provided by free cash flows are liquidating themselves unless they can continually sell assets at great prices and replace them with new developments at positive spreads). Second, generally a higher yield is an indication that "the market" is less than impressed with prospective future growth prospects and so demands that the current yield be high enough to offset this perceived sluggish growth.

Another trade-off is higher risk. If a particular REIT is perceived as an animal having sharp teeth and being unpredictable, investors will often price its shares to bear a higher current dividend yield so that they will be compensated for the heightened risk. Other examples include a number of mortgage REITs. Historically, some of the highest yields in REITdom have been attached to shares that you shouldn't take home to Mother.

The bottom line here is that there are good reasons why, at the present time, SL Green yields 3.9 percent and Crescent yields 8.6 percent. But those who work hard, study management teams and balance sheets, and have a firm handle on the risks presented by some higher-yielding REIT stocks can build a pretty good portfolio with them. And, of course, they will probably want to add a component consisting of fairly safe, higher-yielding REIT preferreds— although with these one normally gives up all opportunity for capital appreciation.

e. Personal REIT Investment Strategy. What's my personal REIT investment strategy? I try to blend several of the foregoing styles. However, my primary emphasis is risk avoidance; most investors, including your humble author, buy REIT stocks not for the purpose of shooting the lights out and bragging to their brother-in-law about their most recent coup but, rather, to preserve their capital, earn a good and predictable return on it, and to avoid disasters— and even potholes. As a result, I tend to focus on those companies in which I have a high level of comfort that they aren't going to do something that "seemed like a good idea at the time." They have superb management teams, own good-quality properties in good locations, strong balance sheets, and …. well, if you've read the book, you know the rest.

But here's a final thought. There is no "right way" to invest in REIT stocks; various strategies can work well if intelligently executed. That old saw claims that "bulls make money, bears make money, but pigs get slaughtered." Similarly, only those investors who flip-flop from one style to another, perhaps chasing "the hot REIT of the week," will get hurt owning REIT stocks.

The key, of course, is knowing one's financial objectives, performance criteria, risk and volatility tolerances, yield requirements, and willingness to pay capital gains taxes. But every active investment strategy requires knowing something about the REIT being bought or sold, including its management team, business strategy, assets and geographic locations, balance sheet and related considerations, as well as having a pretty good conception of relative valuations and risks. Those who don't want to play that game can always buy a REIT mutual fund or ETF, perhaps often with little loss of performance (but with the risk of being mailed big tax bills at the end of each year).

GLOSSARY

AFFO (Adjusted Funds from Operations). FFO (Funds from Operations), less normalized recurring expenditures that are capitalized by the REIT and amortized, and which are necessary to properly maintain and lease the property (e.g., new carpeting and draperies in apartment units, leasing expenses, and tenant improvement allowances); adjustments are also made to eliminate the straight-lining of rents.

Base Year. In a commercial lease, the year used as a reference against which revenues or expenses in subsequent years are measured to determine additional rent charges or the tenant's share of increased operating expenses of the building.

Basis Point. One one-hundredth of 1 percent (.01 percent). Thus, a one-basis-point increase in the yield of a 10-year bond would result in a yield increase from, for instance, 4.81 percent to 4.82 percent.

Beta. The extent to which a stock's price moves with an index of stocks, such as the S&P 500.

Bond Proxies. A slang term used to refer to the shares of a REIT that provide a high dividend yield to its shareholders but where FFO/AFFO and dividend growth are expected to be very low, for example, 1–3 percent annually.

Book Value. The net value of a company's assets less its liabilities, as reflected on its balance sheet pursuant to GAAP (see **GAAP**). Book value will reflect depreciation and amortization, which are expensed for accounting purposes, and may have little relationship to a company's net asset value if evaluated at real estate market prices or prevailing cap rates. See also **Net Asset Value**.

C Corporation. A C corporation is a typical corporation organized under the provisions of "Subchapter C" of the Internal Revenue Code, and may be publicly or privately held. It must pay taxes on its net taxable income, at the prescribed corporate tax rates in effect from time to time, and its shareholders must also pay income taxes on any dividends that they receive from such corporation.

Cap Rate. The unleveraged return expected by the buyer of a property, expressed as a percentage of an all-cash purchase price. It is normally determined by dividing the property's expected net operating income (before depreciation and taxes upon income) by the purchase price. Generally, high cap rates indicate greater perceived risk or, perhaps, lower than average NOI growth prospects. In determining the expected net operating income from a property, a "nominal" cap rate excludes such normal but often capitalized expenses as new carpeting or draperies (e.g., in apartment units), tenant improvements, or leasing commissions; an "effective" or "economic" cap rate includes the effects of such expenditures.

Cash Flow. With reference to a property (or group of properties), the owner's rental revenues from the property minus all property operating expenses. The term ignores depreciation and amortization expenses and income taxes, as well as interest on loans incurred to finance the property. Sometimes used interchangeably with **Net Operating Income** or **EBITDA**.

Collateralized Mortgage Obligations (CMOs). Real estate mortgages which are packaged together and sold in the form of participating interests.

Cost of Capital. The cost to a company, such as a REIT, of raising capital in the form of equity (common or preferred stock) or debt. The cost of *equity* capital should take into account the dilution of the interests of the existing equity holders in the company. The cost of *debt* capital is merely the interest expense on the debt incurred.

Debt Capital. The amount of debt (as opposed to equity) that a REIT carries on its balance sheet. This could be long-term fixed-rate mortgage debt, short-term variable-rate debt, secured or unsecured debt or debentures issued to public or private investors, borrowings under a bank credit line, or any other type of indebtedness. It does not include equity capital, such as common or preferred stock.

Discounting. In financial markets, the process by which expected future developments and events that will affect an investment are anticipated and taken into account by the price at which the investment currently trades in the market.

DownREIT. A DownREIT is structured much like an UPREIT (see **UPREIT**), but is usually formed *after* the REIT has become a public company and generally does not include members of management among the partners in the controlled partnership.

EBITDA. See **Cash Flow.**

Equity Capital. Permanent capital that has been raised through the sale and issuance of stock that has no right to repayment by the issuing company. This normally takes the form of common stock. Preferred stock is also generally regarded as equity capital, although some preferred stocks may create an obligation to redeem such shares at certain times or under certain conditions. Most REIT preferreds may be redeemed by the issuing company after a period of time, say, five years from issuance.

Equity Market Cap. The total value of all issued shares of a public company, such as a REIT, which is determined by multiplying the company's total common shares outstanding by the market price of the shares as of a particular date (see also **Market Cap**). Sometimes "equity market cap" includes OP units issued by an UPREIT or DownREIT that are convertible by the holder into common shares, and some investors include the stated value of outstanding preferred stock.

Equity REIT. A REIT that owns, or has an equity interest in, real estate (rather than one making loans secured by real estate collateral).

FFO (Funds From Operations). Net income (determined in accordance with GAAP), excluding gains or losses from debt restructuring and sales of property, plus depreciation of real property, and after adjustments for unconsolidated entities, such as partnerships and joint ventures, in which the REIT holds an interest.

GAAP. Generally accepted accounting principles, to which financial statements of public companies must conform.

GLA. Acronym for "gross leasable area," a measurement of the total amount of leasable space in a commercial property.

Hurdle Rate. The required rate of return in a discounted cash flow analysis, at or above which an investment makes sense and below which it does not.

Hybrid REIT. A REIT that both owns real estate and holds mortgages secured by real estate. Popular at one time, we rarely see hybrid REITs today.

Interest-Coverage Ratio. The ratio of a company's operating income (before amortization, depreciation, and interest expense) to total interest expense. This ratio measures the extent to which interest expense on existing debt is covered by existing cash flow.

Internal Rate of Return, or IRR. This concept allows the real estate investor to calculate his or her investment returns, including both returns on investment and returns *of* investment. It is used to express the percentage rate of return of all future cash receipts, balanced against all cash contributions, so that when each receipt and each contribution is discounted to net present value, the sum is equal to zero when added together. Many investors believe that IRR is the best way to measure their return on an investment.

Leverage. The process by which the owner of a property may expand both the economic benefits and the risks of property ownership by adding borrowed funds to his or her own funds that have been committed to the venture.

Market Cap. The total market value of a REIT's (or other company's) outstanding securities and indebtedness. For example, if 20 million shares of a REIT are trading at $20 each, 1 million shares of the REIT's preferred stock are trading at $25 each, and the REIT has on its books $100 million of debt, its market cap would be $525 million ($400 million in common stock, $25 million in preferred stock, and $100 million in indebtedness). See also **Equity Market Cap.**

Mortgage REIT. A REIT that owns mortgages secured by real estate collateral. This term also sometimes refers to REITs that lend money in real estate–related transactions though not always secured by real estate mortgages, for example, "mezzanine" loans.

NAREIT. The National Association of Real Estate Investment Trusts, the REIT industry's trade association.

Net Asset Value, or NAV. The estimated net market value of all a REIT's assets, including but not limited to its properties, after subtracting all its liabilities and obligations. Such net asset value, which is usually expressed on a per-share basis, must be estimated by analysts and investors since REITs don't obtain periodic property appraisals (although a few REITs prepare and disclose their own NAV estimates).

Net Income. An accounting term used to measure the profits earned by a business enterprise after all expenses are deducted from revenues. Under GAAP (see **GAAP**), depreciation of real estate owned is treated as an expense of the business.

Net Operating Income, or NOI. Recurring rental and other income from a property, less all operating expenses attributable to that property. Operating expenses will include, for example, real estate taxes, insurance, utility costs, property management, and reserves for replacement. They do *not* include items such as a REIT's corporate overhead, interest expense, capital expenditures, property depreciation expense, or taxes on income.

Overage. A provision in a retail or other lease that requires the payment of rent in addition to the base rental prescribed in the lease if the tenant's store sales or revenues exceed certain specified levels during the measurement period.

Overbuilding (or "Overdevelopment"). A situation in which so much new real estate has been recently completed and offered to tenants in a particular market that the supply of available space significantly exceeds the demand by renters and users, leading to falling occupancy rates, pressure on rental rates, and/or increasing tenant concessions.

Payout Ratio. The ratio of a REIT's annual dividend rate to its FFO or AFFO, on a per share basis. For example, if FFO is $1.00 per share and the current dividend rate is $.80 per share, the FFO payout ratio would be 80 percent.

Positive Spread Investing. The ability to raise funds (both equity and debt) at a nominal cost significantly less than the initial returns that can be obtained from real estate acquisitions.

Price-to-Earnings (P/E) Ratios. The relationship between a company's stock price and its per share earnings. It is calculated by dividing the stock price by the company's earnings per share, on either a trailing twelve-month basis or a forward-looking basis.

Real Estate Investment Trust Act of 1960. Legislation passed by Congress and signed into law authorizing the formation of REIT organizations, for the purpose of allowing individuals (and institutions) to pool their investments in real estate and receive benefits similar to those they would receive from direct ownership.

REIT or Real Estate Investment Trust. Either a corporation or, less often in recent times, a business trust, that has certain tax attributes prescribed by federal legislation, the most important of which is that the entity obtains a federal tax credit equal to dividends paid to its shareholders if certain requirements are satisfied (such as the requirement to pay out at least 90 percent of pretax net annual income to shareholders).

REOC, or Real Estate Operating Company. Refers generally to a public company that owns, manages, and/or develops real estate but which has not elected to qualify for REIT status under federal law. These companies are thus not required to make any specific dividend payments to their shareholders, nor are they subject to other requirements applicable to REIT organizations, which gives them more flexibility with respect to capital deployment. They pay income taxes at normal corporate rates and often use more debt leverage than do REITs, which creates interest deductions that can offset taxable income. Due to their very low (or nonexistent) dividend yields, their shares can be more volatile than REIT shares. Examples include Brookfield Properties, Forrest City Financial, and a number of hotel companies.

Resolution Trust Corporation, or RTC. A public corporation organized by Congress in response to the banking and savings and loan crisis of the early 1990s, to acquire and resell real estate and real estate loans from bankrupt and near-bankrupt lenders.

Retail REITs. Retail REITs include those specializing in neighborhood (or "strip") shopping centers, malls, factory outlet centers, "lifestyle" properties, and free-standing retail buildings.

Same-Store Sales. This term has been used in the analysis of retail companies, meaning sales from stores open for at least one year but excluding sales from stores that have been closed and from new stores, which often have unusually high sales growth. The "same-store" concept is applied to REITs' rental revenues, operating expenses, and net operating income from those of its properties that have been owned and operated in the same fiscal period of the prior year.

Securitization or Equitization. The process by which the economic benefits of ownership of a tangible asset, such as real estate, are divided among numerous investors and represented in the form of publicly traded securities.

Specialty REIT. A REIT that owns, or lends on the security of, a type of real estate other than the standard property types such as offices, industrial properties, apartments, or retail stores. Thus a timber REIT or a movie theater REIT would be a "specialty REIT."

Total Return. A stock's dividend income plus capital appreciation, before taxes and commissions. For example, if a stock rises 4 percent in price and provides a 5 percent dividend yield during the measurement period, the investor's total return would be 9 percent.

Triple Net. A type of lease that requires the tenant to pay its pro rata share of all recurring maintenance and operating costs of the property, such as utilities, property taxes, and insurance.

UPREIT. A REIT that does not own its properties directly, but owns a controlling interest in a limited partnership that owns the REIT's real estate. Other partners (besides the REIT itself) might include management and other private investors. See also **DownREIT**.

Volatility. The extent to which the market price of a stock tends to fluctuate from day to day, or even hour to hour.

CONTINUING-EDUCATION EXAM
for CFP Continuing Education Credit
and PACE Recertification Credit

Earn ten hours of credit toward your CFP Board CE requirement as well as PACE Recertification credit by passing the following exam online at www.bloomberg.com/ce, and entering code **157REIT6**.

All the material has been previewed by the CFP Board of Standards. If you wish to find out if this book and exam can be used to fulfill the CE requirement for a different organization, please contact its governing board directly.

ONE—REITS: WHAT THEY ARE AND HOW THEY WORK

1. Which of the following investment characteristics is generally applicable to stocks of property-owning REITs (equity REITs):

a. Low correlations with the S&P 500 and other asset classes

b. Predictability and stability of operations and cash flows

c. High dividend yields relative to other stocks

d. All of the above

2. Ibbotson Associates completed a study in 2001 demonstrating that, since 1972, by adding a 20 percent allocation of REITs to a portfolio consisting of 40 percent S&P stocks, 30 percent bonds, and 10 percent T-bills:

a. Risk increased but returns decreased

b. Risk decreased and returns decreased proportionally to match the decrease in risk

c. Risk increased and returns increased to match the additional increment of risk

d. Risk decreased, but returns increased

TWO— REITS VERSUS COMPETITIVE INVESTMENTS

3. REITs compete with which of the following investments, based in large part upon dividend or investment yield:

a. Electric utility stocks

b. Preferred stocks

c. Bonds and convertible bonds

d. All of the above

4. Shares of equity REITs, although providing relatively high yields, historically have not been as sensitive to changes in interest rates as fixed-income investments because:

a. Their dividend payments rise and fall with interest rates
b. They own real estate, and thus often benefit from increased demand for space from existing and potential tenants when interest rates rise in reflection of a stronger economy
c. Their cost of capital declines in high-interest-rate environments
d. All of the above

THREE—TODAY'S REITS

5. Which of the following statements applies to today's REIT industry:

a. REITs can have their properties managed only through an outside independent property manager
b. REITs must pay out to shareholders at least 90 percent of their net annual income (prior to calculation of income taxes, if any)
c. REITs can own both real estate and real estate mortgages, but the earnings of equity REITs are less predictable and their shares are more volatile
d. All of the above

6. How are REITs different from the real estate limited partnerships ("LPs") that were widely promoted to individual investors prior to 1986?

a. REITs, unlike the LPs, are not designed to shelter unrelated taxable income
b. The self-interest of REIT management is generally better aligned with the interests of their investors
c. REITs have greater capital raising capabilities, and are more like active businesses
d. REIT stocks are much more liquid than LP interests
e. All of the above

FOUR—PROPERTY SECTORS AND THEIR CYCLES

7. Real estate markets move in cycles, which can be influenced by excessive building of new properties, economic recessions, and/or manic investor psychology.

a. True
b. False

8. Industrial properties, like offices, provide space for businesses, but they are more cyclical and volatile than office properties.
a. True
b. False

9. Health care property owners normally enjoy robust prospects for percentage rent increases from their lessee-operators.
a. True
b. False

10. Mall owners can charge higher rents than neighborhood shopping center owners, but mall space must be able to generate higher dollar amounts of revenues per square foot to justify the tenants' higher rental rates.
a. True
b. False

FIVE—REITS: MYSTERIES AND MYTHS

11. Which of the following is *not* an effective method for reducing risk in real estate and REIT investments:
a. Using only modest amounts of debt when financing properties
b. Owning interests in a number of assets in different locations
c. Effective property and tenant management
d. Buying shares of private REITs that do not trade on a regular basis

12. Real estate owners, including REIT shareholders, invariably benefit from inflation—which is the primary driver of returns on real estate investments.
a. True
b. False

SIX—A HISTORY OF REITS AND REIT PERFORMANCE

13. The real estate buying frenzy of the latter part of the 1980s was bad for REITs because:
a. It generated excessive and unsustainable interest in REIT stocks
b. It touched off a huge wave of new property developments that substantially increased the supply of real estate

c. It led to an excessive amount of new REIT stock IPOs that flooded the market

d. All of the above

14. The 1993–94 REIT IPO boom ushered in a "modern REIT era," distinguishable from prior periods by which of the following:

a. An increase in the number of public REITs and sectors available to investors

b. Increased use of joint venture strategies, along with diminished development capabilities

c. An increase in the average percentage of cash flow paid out as dividends

d. All of the above

SEVEN—REITS: HOW THEY GROW

15. REIT investors like to use "funds from operations" (FFO), as well as "adjusted funds from operations" (AFFO), to measure a REIT's operating performance because:

a. These terms are less capable of being manipulated by management teams

b. These terms ignore real estate depreciation expense—as real estate tends to hold its value over time

c. FFO and AFFO are essential components of generally accepted accounting principles (GAAP)

d. All of the above

16. Which of the following growth avenues is _not_ considered part of a REIT's internal growth capabilities that are sustainable regardless of access to additional outside capital:

a. Upgrading the quality of the tenant base

b. Rental rate increases

c. Property developments

d. Increases in percentage rents

e. All of the above

17. Which of the following statements about development opportunities is _false:_

a. Development is a low-risk enterprise that has always been part of REITs' arsenal

b. "Pre-leasing" of certain development projects, such as office buildings, can help to reduce tenancy risk
c. Successful developments often result in double-digit returns on invested capital
d. Development returns are normally higher than the returns available on the acquisition of stable income-producing properties

EIGHT—SPOTTING THE BLUE CHIPS

18. Some REITs, at certain times, are capable of generating double-digit rates of growth either because of a boom phase in a real estate cycle or because REIT management is able to implement a very aggressive acquisition or development strategy.
a. True
b. False

19. Which of the following factors is *not* a hallmark of a "blue-chip" REIT, that is, a REIT that delivers consistent, rising, long-term growth in cash flows and dividends:
a. Outstanding management with a strong long-term track record
b. Wide diversification among real estate property types
c. Access to capital to fund growth opportunities
d. Minimal conflicts of interest
e. A strong balance sheet

20. A low dividend payout ratio is advantageous because:
a. It makes the dividend more sustainable in the face of unexpectedly weak real estate markets
b. It demonstrates the quality of the investment portfolio
c. It provides a source of retained earnings that allows the REIT to take advantage of new opportunities
d. Both a and b
e. Both a and c

NINE—THE QUEST FOR INVESTMENT VALUE

21. A REIT's net asset value (NAV) can be easily calculated on the basis of:
a. The REIT's public disclosure documents
b. Readily available outside independent appraisals of the REIT's properties, less debt as disclosed on the financial statements

c. The REIT share price, multiplied by shares outstanding, less the amount of debt and liquidation preferences on the outstanding preferred stock

d. None of the above

22. Which of the following methods are frequently used to estimate the fair market value of an equity REIT's stock:

a. Net asset value (NAV) analysis

b. Discounted dividend and cash flow growth models

c. Analysis of P/FFO and/or P/AFFO ratios and multiples

d. Both a and c

e. a, b, and c

TEN—BUILDING A REIT PORTFOLIO

23. Which of the following statements regarding the building of a REIT investment portfolio is true:

a. Because so many of today's REITs own properties in widely diversified locations, it is not necessary to own more than two or three high-quality REIT stocks

b. Because the REIT industry is still relatively small, REIT stocks are very volatile

c. Because REIT stocks have shown historically low correlations with other asset classes, their inclusion in a diversified portfolio can reduce portfolio volatility

d. All of the above

e. None of the above

24. Given the increased size and scope of today's REIT industry, investors can diversify in the REIT industry by real estate property types, geographic locations, and even by investment characteristics.

a. True

b. False

25. As the "modern REIT era" is still fairly new, we can invest in actively managed REIT mutual funds, but thus far there is no REIT index fund available to investors.

a. True

b. False

ELEVEN—WHAT CAN GO WRONG

26. Which of the following is *not* a significant risk to which REIT investors may be exposed generally or with respect to specific REIT organizations:
a. Rising interest rates
b. Excess supply of real estate, through excessive development or a shortfall in tenant demand for space
c. Legislation rescinding REITs' tax deduction for dividends paid to shareholders
d. The cut-off of REITs' access to equity capital with which to expand or pay maturing debt
e. A balance sheet with substantial variable-rate debt and short-term maturities

27. Management mistakes that may lead to poor returns for investors in a particular REIT include:
a. Overpaying for real estate acquisitions
b. Generating poor returns on development projects
c. Repurchasing stock at discounts to estimated NAV
d. Both a and b
e. Both b and c

TWELVE—TEA LEAVES: WHERE WILL REITS GO FROM HERE?

28. Which of the following factors is *not* a reason for more private real estate companies to go public as REITs:
a. To increase liquidity and facilitate estate planning for existing private owners
b. To access the mortgage debt markets
c. To access large amounts of equity capital to fuel expansion and cash flow growth
d. To provide more flexible incentives to motivate management
e. None of the above

29. Pension funds and other institutions are likely to increase their investments in REIT stocks because:
a. REIT executives are increasingly being asked to serve as trustees of large pension funds
b. REIT stocks are increasingly liquid and can be bought and sold in size

c. REITs have been able to expand in size, increase operating efficiency, and otherwise become key players in certain markets and real estate property types

d. Both a and b

e. Both b and c

30. A landmark event for the REIT industry was Standard & Poor's decision to include REITs in the S&P 500 index on the basis, among other factors, that most of today's REITs are now operating companies rather than passive collections of assets.

a. True

b. False

INDEX

ABOUT BLOOMBERG

Bloomberg L.P., founded in 1981, is a global information services, news, and media company. Headquartered in New York, the company has sales and news operations worldwide.

Serving customers on six continents, Bloomberg, through its wholly-owned subsidiary Bloomberg Finance L.P., holds a unique position within the financial services industry by providing an unparalleled range of features in a single package known as the Bloomberg Professional® service. By addressing the demand for investment performance and efficiency through an exceptional combination of information, analytic, electronic trading, and straight-through-processing tools, Bloomberg has built a worldwide customer base of corporations, issuers, financial intermediaries, and institutional investors.

Bloomberg News, founded in 1990, provides stories and columns on business, general news, politics, and sports to leading newspapers and magazines throughout the world. Bloomberg Television, a 24-hour business and financial news network, is produced and distributed globally in seven languages. Bloomberg Radio is an international radio network anchored by flagship station Bloomberg 1130 (WBBR-AM) in New York.

In addition to the Bloomberg Press line of books, Bloomberg publishes *Bloomberg Markets* magazine. To learn more about Bloomberg, call a sales representative at:

London:	+44-20-7330-7500
New York:	+1-212-318-2000
Tokyo:	+81-3-3201-8900

ABOUT THE AUTHOR

Ralph L. Block has been a participant in the REIT industry in various professional investment and advisory capacities since 1993, and has been investing in REIT stocks since 1975. He is presently a principal and senior REIT portfolio manager for Phocas Financial Corp., a registered investment advisory firm, and is the owner and proprietor of Essential REIT Publishing Co., an independent adviser to, and publisher of information for, the REIT industry. From 1993 through August 2003, he was chief REIT portfolio manager with Bay Isle Financial LLC, a Bay Area investment advisory firm. From 1998 through 2003, Ralph was co-portfolio manager, with William Schaff, for Undiscovered Managers REIT Fund.

Ralph is also the author of *The Essential REIT* (formerly *REIT-WEEK*), a newsletter dedicated to REITs and REIT investing, and has written regular columns for REIT Portfolio and *REITStreet* magazines. He has been quoted in numerous media articles, has spoken at various investment forums and, in recognition of his books, articles, and newsletters, received the NAREIT Industry Achievement Award in 2004. Ralph is a member of the Hoyt Fellows, an organization that interfaces the needs of professional real estate investors with the academic community.

Prior to becoming a REIT professional, Mr. Block practiced corporate and securities law in Los Angeles, California for twenty-seven years, and served as a director of various private and public companies. He is a graduate of UCLA and the UCLA School of Law, where he was on the Board of Editors of the *UCLA Law Review* and member of the Order of the COIF. He lives in Westlake Village, California, with his wife Paula, her mother Evelyn, and their irrationally exuberant golden retriever, Sammy.